The
Wrong
Mr. Right

The Wrong Mr. Right

Stephanie Archer

ORION

Stephanie Archer writes spicy laugh-out-loud romance. She believes in the power of best friends, stubborn women, a fresh haircut, and love. She lives in Vancouver with a man and a dog.

For spicy bonus scenes, news about upcoming books, and book recs, sign up for her newsletter at:
https://www.stephaniearcherauthor.com/newsletter

Instagram: @stephaniearcherauthor
Tiktok: @stephaniearcherbooks

To check content warnings for any of Stephanie's books, visit www.stephaniearcherauthor.com/content-warnings

This one was for me.

An Orion paperback

This edition first published in Great Britain in 2024 by Orion Fiction
an imprint of The Orion Publishing Group Ltd
Carmelite House, 50 Victoria Embankment
London EC4Y 0DZ

An Hachette UK company

The authorised representative in the EEA is Hachette Ireland,
8 Castlecourt Centre, Dublin 15, D15 XTP3, Ireland (email: info@hbgi.ie)

5 7 9 10 8 6

A CIP catalogue record for this book is
available from the British Library.

ISBN (Mass Market Paperback) 9781398724440
eBook ISBN 9781398724457

Printed in UK Clays Ltd, Elcograf, S.p.A.

www.orionbooks.co.uk

Hannah

ONLY IN MY worst nightmares would I make eye contact with Wyatt Rhodes while a customer read orc erotica to me.

"This is the part where I knew something was up," Don, our town photographer and news blogger, said. He adjusted his reading glasses and ran his finger down the page of the book. *"Yeuk gave an almighty roar and the surrounding forest shuddered. His gargantuan shaft sprayed semen all over Lady Nicoletta, so much semen. Buckets of—"*

"Okay." I held a hand up. "I get it, Don. Please stop."

"I saw the cover and I thought it was like *The Lord of the Rings.*" He swallowed and stared out the front window of the shop, lost in thought and shaking his head a little. "It's not," he whispered. "It's really not." He flipped the page. Movement over his shoulder caught my eye.

Wyatt Rhodes stood shirtless in my bookstore, leaning on a bookshelf and watching us with amused curiosity. My stomach dropped through the floor.

Wyatt Rhodes was in my bookstore.

My gaze snagged on his abs. There were so many of them, stacked on top of each other like books on the shelf beside him. Abs for days.

Wyatt Rhodes owned a surf shop in town but spent most of his time on the water, training to go pro. He was over six feet, and the sun had lightened his dark blond hair. He always needed a haircut. He wore swim shorts and sneakers. He'd never been in Pemberley Books before and his gaze swept around the small space, taking in the worn carpet, the bookshelves in need of repair, and the stacks of books on the floor. Outside, the mural my mother commissioned twenty years ago was faded and crumbling.

Embarrassment twinged in my stomach, and my face warmed.

Why was he here? He didn't even know my name.

I tucked my hands further into the sleeves of my oversized sweater.

"Listen to this part." Don cleared his throat. *"Lady Nicoletta shoved the great orc down on the bed with all her might. 'Give me your seed, orc,'"* he read in a higher-pitched voice, and Wyatt's eyebrows shot up.

I was going to die, right here in the bookstore.

Don lowered his timbre to read the orc's part. *"'Tiny human, my enormous pleasure wand is far too large for your tiny lady cavern. You will be destroyed by my enormous penis—'"*

"Thank you, Don." I snatched the book from him, opened the cash register, and pulled out a twenty-dollar bill the store couldn't afford to lose.

Don's eyes widened when I slapped the money on the counter. "I don't want a refund."

A noise that sounded a lot like a snort came from Wyatt, but he covered his mouth with his hand. My gaze stayed glued to Don.

Don gestured at the shelves in the corner. "I just want you to move the others from the fantasy section. It should be in erotica."

We didn't have an erotica section because we were a small-town bookstore, but I nodded vehemently. Anything to end this interaction. "I will, right away. Thank you."

Don gave me a sidelong look before taking his book back, tucking it safely under his arm and leaving the store.

Ignoring Wyatt still leaning on the bookshelf, looking like a Greek god, I shuffled over to the shelf where the orc books sat and gathered them into my arms. There were six books in the series, and Liya, the other employee here, must have purchased them thinking they were fantasy. I carried them back to the desk and deposited them. I'd find a spot for them in the sprawling romance section later.

Wyatt still stood there. What did he want? I couldn't ignore him forever.

The universe must have heard my wish because the bell on the front door tinkled and Thérèse swept into the store in all her elegance, charisma, and style.

"My darling Hannah," she sang, gliding over.

Thérèse Beauchamp was the most elegant woman I'd ever met. She was French, so she said my name like 'annah. She was Black and wore her natural hair in a short, stylish cut, and often painted her mouth in blood-red lipstick that looked lovely against her deep skin tone. Thérèse always dressed as if she were about to step into a photoshoot. She was a social media influencer, so brands paid her to travel around the world, be gorgeous, and live a beautiful life.

Today, she wore faded, wide-leg blue jeans which fell above her ankles, a white silk button-up knotted at the waist, and black sandals. She clutched a black velvet bag under one arm and carried a paper shopping bag in the other. Her signature lipstick glowed with life in my shabby little store.

See? Simple, elegant, timeless. Sometimes, I didn't know why she was even friends with me. We were so far apart in social status.

Thérèse breezed right past Wyatt and straight toward me. "Bonjour, Wyatt."

He nodded to her. "Thérèse." He didn't move from his spot, still waiting for me.

I could escape out the back. Liya had left early but maybe if I went home too, he'd get the message and leave.

It wasn't that I didn't like Wyatt. Everyone liked Wyatt. He was impossible not to like.

It was that I had had a crush on Wyatt for as long as I could remember, and I had no freaking clue how to talk to him. I could barely look him in the eye. The only men I could talk to were the fictional ones from the books I sold.

"Come." Thérèse gestured for me to follow her, and I shot a glance at Wyatt, still waiting and watching. "I have something for you."

"For me?" I followed her to the back of the store, where two overstuffed blue chairs sat. These chairs were older than I was, and my friend Avery and I often hung out back here after hours, drinking wine while I played Spice Girls or showed her hilarious Scandinavian music videos. I lived with my dad in a tiny house a few blocks away, and until last year, Avery lived in a crappy old apartment that smelled like feet, so the back of the store was our hangout zone.

Thérèse took a seat and handed the bag to me. "My love, I will be flying back to Paris for the summer, and I'm not sure I'll be home in time for your birthday."

Cold dread trickled through me, and my throat constricted.

My thirtieth birthday was two months away, in September.

"Chanel has invited me for a residency at their fashion house." Thérèse paused and tapped her chin with narrowed eyes. "Or perhaps it was Yves St. Laurent." She tilted her head. "Gaultier? *Mon dieu.* I cannot remember." She laughed at herself. "So many haute couture designers call my agent, I can't keep them all straight." She gestured at the bag. "Open it."

I slid a white box from the bag and placed it on my lap. "What's a residency?"

She waved a manicured hand with a sigh. "I sit around and they create couture dresses for the next season."

I blinked. "You're their muse?"

She shrugged in that casual French way of hers. "Something like that. Hannah, open the box."

I flipped it open and my mouth fell open.

She made a noise of disappointment. "You hate it."

"No," I was quick to tell her. "It's just…" The gold sequins sparkled even in the dim light as I lifted the dress, pinching the fabric of the sleeves like it would burn me.

It was a hot girl dress. The hem would fall around mid-thigh. Short sleeves. Deep V in the front. This dress was for a woman who wanted to be seen and adored. The dress was gorgeous, no doubt about that. Fun and flirty and wild and glamorous. Unfortunately, I was none of those things.

This was a Thérèse dress. This was *not* the right dress for me. I was shy, quiet Hannah Nielsen, the girl with her nose in a book.

Thérèse nodded with understanding. "You already have one like it."

I snorted. "No. Definitely not." I shot her a curious glance. "Thérèse. I'm grateful for the gift, but why did you choose a sparkly gold dress for—" I gestured at my oversized wool sweater, black jeans and white sneakers, the same outfit I wore every day. "—me?"

Thérèse smiled to herself and shot me an appraising expression. "I was in Sydney a few weeks ago, and when I saw this, I thought of you." She propped an elbow on the chair arm and watched me. "I knew it was perfect for you."

"If I wear this dress, everyone will look at me." My skin crawled at the thought.

She lifted one shoulder in a shrug. "So let them look. Make their view worth it."

Thérèse had clearly hit her head and thought I was someone else. "I've always wanted to visit Sydney. I've heard the food is incredible."

"It's like Vancouver but warmer, and the people are much friendlier. I fell in love several times while I was there."

"In love with people?"

She nodded with a serene, dreamy smile. "Oui." She sighed. "I love falling in love. I've been in love many, many times."

"Oh. Wow. I've never been in love." I'd read about it hundreds of times in books. My mom had read me *Pride and Prejudice* when I was a kid, and the store was named after Darcy's estate in the book. I loved reading about love.

But I'd never been in love. My heart twisted in longing at the reminder. When I returned to Queen's Cove after university, I took over the daily running of the store so my dad could retire. For seven years, I'd been hiding in this dim little bookstore with shabby carpets, broken shelves, and peeling paint.

Thérèse tapped her chin again. "Oui, I do not think there are many eligible suitors waltzing into your store." She gestured in the direction of the front door. "Hannah, you must go outside and find someone to fall in love with."

I laughed. "Okay." I flipped the box closed and tucked it back in the paper bag. "Thank you for the gift, Thérèse. It's lovely."

She lifted one eyebrow. "Will you wear it?"

I nodded. "Sure." Alone in my bedroom, maybe.

This seemed to satisfy her, so she stood and squeezed me tight in a hug. "Au revoir, Hannah. I'll be back at the end of September."

"Bye. Enjoy being a muse."

"I always do." She flashed me an effortless smile over her shoulder.

I followed her around the corner and my stomach dropped through the floor.

Wyatt Rhodes leaned on the front desk, reading the orc erotica with a small smile. Panic shot through me.

Thérèse disappeared out the door with the bell chiming, and I raced over to Wyatt and tried to snatch the book from his hand, but he held it out of my reach.

"May I please have that back?" I asked, trying to keep my voice polite. The panic rose through, though.

"So you do see me." He shot me an amused look before reading from the book. *"Yeuk and Gragol thrust their thick, monstrous members into Lady Nicoletta in tandem. Her cries of pleasure and delight echoed throughout the mountains—"*

Oh my god.

"Wyatt." I reached again for the book, but he turned away from me.

His eyebrows shot up and I was close enough to see how gray his eyes were. "You even know my name."

I rolled my eyes. "Of course I know your name. Now, give me the book."

"Lady Nicoletta's feminine cavern began to quake with the force of her pleasure—"

I grabbed for the book again, brushing his arm and practically hugging him from behind. My fingers made contact with the book, and I snatched it away before straightening up. My face was on fire once again.

I cleared my throat and set the book back on the pile. "Something I can help you with?"

"I'm here for the orc erotica."

I gave him a flat look and he returned it with a lazy, amused grin. No doubt, he could see how red my face was.

"My mom asked me to pick her book up for her. She's in Victoria until this evening and wanted to start it tonight. She said you told her it was in this morning."

Victoria was the nearest city, a three-hour drive away. Wyatt's mother, Elizabeth, a warm and funny woman, had ordered in a historical romance I recommended the month before. It had been on back-order from the publisher for a few weeks.

I located the book on the shelf behind me where we kept the special orders and handed it to him. "She's already paid."

"Great." His gaze skimmed me, and I felt naked.

This was the difference between hot people like Thérèse and Wyatt, and myself. I peeked at people around book-shelves, shot quick glances when they weren't looking. Wyatt and Thérèse stared openly, with zero shame or embarrassment.

One side of Wyatt's mouth hitched. "Thanks, Hannah."

It was the first time I'd ever heard him say my name. We'd gone to the same elementary school and the same high school, and now we both lived in our tiny coastal town of Queen's Cove as adults, and not once had he said my name. The guy didn't notice me most of the time because he was out surfing and I was here, in this musty old bookstore my mom opened when I was a baby.

The memory of his hand on my lower back was seared into my mind. Wyatt and I had been at Avery's wedding last year. She married Wyatt's brother, Emmett. When we signed the marriage certificate, Wyatt's hand came to my lower back and he nudged me forward with a wink.

I still shivered, thinking about how warm his hand had been on my back, even through the fabric of my dress. The quick, roguish grin he had flashed me while I stood, mouth hanging open.

And now he was here in my old bookstore, standing shirt-less with all his muscles and damp hair.

"You can't be shirtless in here," I blurted out. "It's a health hazard."

He raised an amused eyebrow. "A health hazard."

My face heated and I said the first thing that came to mind. "You could get hair in the books."

What?

8

"I could get hair… in the books," he repeated, rolling his lips to hide a smile.

"Yep. Chest hair."

He snorted and I wanted to sink into this ugly carpet from the nineties.

"Well, in that case, I'll be going." He turned and headed to the door, his network of back muscles moving as he walked. "Let me know if you find any chest hairs, I'll come get them."

He disappeared out the door and I could breathe again.

I spent the next few minutes clearing space in the romance section for the orc erotica. The romance section was growing and took up more shelves than crime and thrillers. That thought made me smug. Last year, the romance and erotica industry made double what crime and thrillers had made. Romance novels accounted for half our measly sales.

I wished we could only sell romance novels, but my dad wouldn't like that. He didn't have anything against romance novels themselves, he just didn't want to change anything about the store. The store was my mom's, and if we changed it, well, that was practically spitting on her grave.

A notification pinged on the store email, and I woke the computer up to check it.

My heart stopped.

Liya's paycheck had bounced. There hadn't been enough money in the account last night. My stomach knotted itself over and over as I rushed to transfer money from my savings back into the store account. She didn't say anything today so maybe she hadn't noticed yet. I transferred the amount to her manually and prayed she wouldn't notice the first failed payment.

I guess I wouldn't be taking a salary for the foreseeable future.

Disappointment bled into my stomach and I pressed my mouth into a tight line, scrolling through the accounts. My dad owned the building so there was no mortgage to pay, and we could thank the low property prices in Queen's Cove in the nineties for that because there was no way we could have afforded it today. Utilities, Liya's salary, taxes, fees for our credit card system, they added up to a total which exceeded our sales.

This was my mom's store, and I was running it into the ground. My dad trusted me to carry on her dream, and whatever I was doing, it wasn't enough.

Rocks churned in my stomach as I thought about how much she loved this store. She passed when I was sixteen from an aneurysm. She was folding laundry. I was at a friend's house working on a school project, and my dad found her.

I shot a glance over to the blue squashy chairs where I would sit as a kid, reading and listening while she raced around the store, thrusting books into customers' hands and talking as fast as she could. She loved books, she loved people, and she was lit from within with charisma, light, energy, and fun.

My mom was the life of the party. She used to throw them all the time here in the store, just for fun. Just because she could.

I smiled to myself at the memory.

One day, you'll find your true love, just like Mr. Darcy, she would tell me, excitement lighting up her eyes.

My gaze flicked to the white shopping bag, still sitting on the blue chair. There were no customers left in the store, so I strolled over, brought it to the desk, slid the box out, and lifted the dress up once again.

It was dazzling.

My mom would totally wear a dress like this.

And if she saw me now, hiding in the bookstore, letting it fail, wasting my life? She'd be so disappointed.

I let out a long sigh, toying with this painful idea.

What would she do in this situation? She'd do everything

she could to make the store successful again. And she'd go out and find someone to fall in love with.

When my mom was thirty, she had it all—a partner, me, a business she loved, and a great life. The store was hers, and my dad trusted me to run it.

I couldn't let them both down, even if she was gone. I had to find a way to turn the store around.

2

Hannah

"I'M HOME," I called when I stepped in the front door of the little house I shared with my dad.

"Hi, honey." My dad was in his favorite chair in the front room, reading John Grisham's latest. "Good day at the store?"

I shot him a tight smile as I kicked my shoes off. "Thérèse stopped by to say hello."

He didn't notice me dodging the question. "That's nice."

"I'm going to finish up some paperwork."

When I got to my bedroom, I slid the white shopping bag Thérèse had given me under my bed as far as it would go.

Then, I took a seat at my desk, opened my laptop, and tallied the sales for the day.

Four sales.

We hadn't even covered Liya's salary today. I sighed and stared out the window at the trees behind our house. Another month in the red. That was eleven. Eleven months in a row, we had been losing money. I thought about the shop the way Wyatt must have seen it today—worn, ugly carpet, faded wall-paper, books stacked everywhere.

The store couldn't survive in our tiny town any longer. Panic clawed at me. It was only a matter of time before I ran out of savings and my dad found out how the store was *really* doing.

This is the way she wanted it, he said whenever I hinted we'd see more sales if we made a few changes. *Your mother put everything into that store.*

His tone always made it clear: if we changed the store, we were erasing her memory.

We hadn't made any changes to the store since the day she passed. The same artwork hung on the walls. The same dusty maroon carpet lay on the floor. Bookshelves stood where they were installed years ago. Even our website was from the nineties. It was a joke of my mom's, when I was a teenager, that we had such an old website. No one used it back then, anyway.

But that was fourteen years ago. Now, people used websites all the time.

On my laptop, I opened a browser and typed in the website address. It loaded and a tinny, tinkly music played, a Victorian tune that sounded like something from the 1800s. *Pemberley Books* appeared above a picture of my mom at the front desk, surrounded by books, smiling from ear to ear.

I let out a long sigh. She was beautiful, and when she smiled like that, it was so obvious that owning her own bookstore was her dream.

And now I was running it into the ground.

I snapped the laptop closed and shoved the image from my mind.

Half an hour later, the timer on the oven dinged and I pulled a pan of roast veggies and chickpeas out.

"Something smells good." My dad walked into the kitchen. It was what we had most nights before we both picked up our books and read in the living room.

"Hey, Dad?" I set the pan on the stove and pulled a couple plates down.

"Mmm?" He opened the cutlery drawer and pulled out forks and knives.

"I was thinking." I kept my gaze on the food as I transferred it between two plates. "There are some great bookstore social media accounts. They take nice photos, they make book recommendations, and they're a free way to advertise." He was quiet and I spared him a glance. "All the bookstores have them," I continued, setting the plates down on the table.

He sighed and took a seat across from me. He gave me a sad, tentative smile. "Honey."

With that word, I knew. My stomach sank. "I think it would help boost sales."

His expression strained. "We've had this conversation before. Pemberley's charm is that we don't do things like everyone else." He waved his fork. "These big box stores with their fluorescent lights and escalators? You know what they sell?"

I tried not to roll my eyes. "Scarves."

"*Scarves.*" His eyes widened. "Candles. And you know what else I've heard they sell?"

I waited.

My dad glanced around the kitchen as if there were people in here who would overhear him. "*Personal items.*"

I frowned. "What kind of personal items?"

His face was going red. He cleared his throat. "Miri Yang told me she saw a *vibrator.*" He barely whispered the word.

I pressed my lips together so I wouldn't laugh. "Why was Miri Yang telling you about vibrators?"

He shook his head. "We don't want to be like those big box stores, Hannah. Pemberley has family-business charm. That's how your mother wanted it."

Well, there it was. Couldn't argue with that, could I? Anytime I wanted to improve the store, this was his final playing card. *That's how your mother wanted it.* I could practically hear the door slamming shut. It wasn't my store, it was my

14

dad's and my mom's, and I just worked there. It wasn't my place.

I opened my mouth to say something to my dad about how we should try something new, but my throat knotted and my mouth snapped shut. I wasn't good at this part, the arguing part.

"You haven't been inside in a while."

His gaze zeroed in on his plate and a crease formed on his forehead. He shook his head. "I've been busy these days." He took a bite of broccoli and waved his fork at me. "I know you have it covered."

I bit back another retort. Busy? He hadn't been inside the store in a while because my mom's ghost lurked in every corner.

Unease moved through my stomach, and I stabbed a cube of roast yam. Every night, I came home and ate dinner with my dad at the table. After, we'd read our books on the couches in the living room with our mugs of tea. He'd drink Earl Grey and I'd drink peppermint. At ten o'clock, he'd yawn, give me a kiss on the forehead and go to bed, and at eleven o'clock, I'd get into my pajamas before going to bed myself.

It was the same every night, and it would be the same every night for the rest of my life. For the last seven years since I came home from university, I'd worn the same clothes, eaten the same food, woken up and gone to the bookstore most days. I had the same long, straight blonde hair, often tied up into a ponytail. When my glasses broke a couple years ago, I bought the same ones again.

Nothing had changed, not in the store and not with me. My chest hollowed at the thought. Was this how the rest of my life would go?

No, it wouldn't, I realized, because the bookstore wouldn't be around much longer if things continued the way they were going. Panic streaked through my mind again.

"I forgot to tell you," my dad said, standing and taking

our empty plates to the dishwasher. "Your uncle Rick needs a house sitter for the summer, so I'm going to stay there for a bit. His neighbor fell through because they sold their house."

My uncle lived on Salt Spring Island, a small island off the coast of Vancouver. Every summer, he sailed up and down the coast of British Columbia while his neighbor took care of his house. He had a couple goats and cats who needed daily feeding.

"You're going to be gone the whole summer?" I blinked behind my glasses. "That's a long time." He'd never been away this long. I'd be home alone the entire summer.

A worried expression came over his face. "Are you going to be okay here by yourself?"

I forced a laugh. "Of course. I'm an adult."

Later, in my room, I flopped face-down on my bed. I could sense the dress's presence, even tucked into the dark corner beneath the bed.

Two minutes later, I was reaching over my shoulder to zip it up before turning to gawk at myself in the mirror. Thérèse had guessed the size correctly and it fit me in all the right places.

Wearing this dress felt like a joke, though. Like when people put adult sunglasses on a baby and everyone laughs.

Here I was, nearly thirty years old, and I had nothing to show for it. I still lived with my dad, I had accomplished nothing, and I'd never been in love. I'd never had a boyfriend. I'd never been to Europe or Australia or New York, like the characters in the books I read.

One day, Hannah Banana, you're going to find your true love, my mom would always tell me, right in this very room, usually with a book in her hand. I remembered her soft smile as she tucked me in. *You're going to find someone who makes you feel incredible, and you'll wonder where he had been hiding this whole time.*

I was the one who was hiding. The love of my life would

never find me behind the stacks of books in my dusty old store.

A picture of Avery and me at her wedding sat on my dresser. We were smiling at each other, and she radiated happiness. Last year, Emmett convinced Avery to be his fake fiancée while he ran for mayor. He had come into my bookstore and asked me to help him pick out a ring. The care and attention he put into finding the perfect ring? It was never fake for Emmett. On their wedding day, Avery and Emmett couldn't take their eyes off each other. They still couldn't. I had watched her fall in love with him, watched as they became the most important thing to each other.

I wanted that, too.

A rock landed in my stomach.

My mom would be so disappointed in me. I crossed my arms over my chest, remembering how driven she was, how passionate and excited about the shop she was. She'd see my sad little life and wince with disappointment, or worse, embarrassment.

I studied the dress and ran my fingers over the coarse sequins. I wanted to be worthy of this dress. I wanted to make the shop profitable again. I wanted to find someone to fall in love with.

I stared at my reflection for one more moment before opening a drawer and pulling out a piece of paper and a pen.

Before 30:

1. Save my failing bookstore.

Since my dad was stuck on keeping the store in the nineties, I would have to get creative.

2. Find my true love.

I cringed at how cheesy that sounded. No one would ever see this list.

I glanced at my reflection again. The sequins reflected pinpricks of light on my bedroom walls.

3. Become a hot girl.

The sparkly dress was a hot girl dress. If I wanted true love, I had to go out and get him. I couldn't sit in my bookstore with my boring sweaters and wait for him to show up.

This was so stupid.

A thought struck me, and I raised an eyebrow.

Wyatt knew hot girls. Wyatt didn't really date, but I had seen him with women a few times, and they were always drop-dead gorgeous. Shiny hair, perfect makeup, stylish outfits out of a magazine. Hot girls.

The image of him in my bookstore earlier that day flashed into my head. Hot people attracted other hot people. That was a fact of life. And Wyatt? He had girls falling all over him.

The funny thing was, he didn't seem to care. He only cared about surfing.

Which made women want him even more. I frowned and narrowed my eyes. I was on to something here.

I chewed my lip before writing the last one.

4. Make Mom proud.

A rock formed in my throat, and I blinked tears out of my eyes. There. I said it. I knew she'd look at my life now and wish I had done more.

Alright, enough moping. Once I was in my pajamas, I reached for my laptop on my desk and flipped it open, pulling up a Scandinavian music video.

After a few videos, the tension in my stomach unraveled and I settled into bed. I grinned, watching a video by one of my favorite Europop artists, Tula. She was a tiny woman with a lot of hair and enormous eyes. In this video, she dressed as a mermaid, perched on a rock with a scaly tail, and twisted her fingers in her long green wig while she sang in Finnish. Behind her, muscular mermen stood in the ocean, dancing and thrusting to the music. Some held trident spears, some wore fishing nets as capes.

God, I loved Europop.

The video cut to a close-up of one of the mermen, and I nearly fell off my bed.

My mouth hung open as Wyatt Rhodes thrust against the air behind Tula.

My eyes were saucers as I scanned over the same muscles I had seen this afternoon in the store. Except these muscles moved under silver body paint, with decorative scales glued on.

Oh my god.

That merman was Wyatt. I was positive. It was his shaggy blond hair slicked back and painted silver, his lean muscle, his lazy, confident, panty-melting grin.

I watched the video six times to be sure, alternating between cringing and snickering.

There was no way Avery knew about this. She knew I loved Europop, and she hadn't mentioned this to me, which meant she didn't know. Which meant Emmett didn't know.

Which meant no one knew.

Huh.

My eyes narrowed at the screen. Wyatt twirled his trident around in the air, and I snorted.

It was no secret in town that surfing was Wyatt's whole life, his whole existence. He was out on his board almost every day, no matter how cold or choppy the water was. Everyone knew about his dreams of going pro, and Avery had mentioned he was trying to get a sponsorship deal with one of the big surf brands.

My skin prickled with anticipation and danger. Wyatt had all the hot girl knowledge I wanted, and now I had dirt on him.

I could ask Avery to help me become a hot girl, but she wasn't like me. She was confident. She wouldn't understand. She had never wanted to fall in love before Emmett. She'd actively avoided it. Besides, she would tell me to be myself.

Being myself had wasted a decade of my life and got me nowhere. No, I wasn't going to ask Avery for help.

Wyatt, though, he was perfect. He had all the qualities I needed. I had a little crush on him, but he was the last guy in the world I would *ever* fall for. The guy of my dreams was sweet, chivalrous, friendly, and above all, loved books and Queen's Cove. Wyatt was leaving town as soon as he got a sponsorship.

Most importantly, I had something in my back pocket that Wyatt didn't want getting out.

Making the store profitable, I could figure out on my own. The true love thing would fall into place once I became a hot girl like Thérèse. She had said it herself in the store, *I've been in love many, many times.*

My pulse beat in my ears and I sucked in a breath, chewing my lip. I didn't want to stop him from getting a sponsorship, so I'd never show a soul the video, I'd just use it to convince him to help me.

Wyatt Rhodes was going to teach me to be a hot girl.

3

Wyatt

JUST AFTER DAWN, I stepped out onto the sand, carrying my surfboard, and stared up at the indigo sky. The sun rose and the sky was washed with more blue by the minute.

Fuck yeah.

A light breeze pushed my hair back, and I waded into the water. Like every morning, the water's cold bite woke me up and reminded me I was alive.

I waded further out, dropped my board onto the surface and began to paddle. Water made its way into my wetsuit as my arms moved. Something inside me clicked into place. The sky was still brightening, splashing colors across it, and once I was deep enough, I sat on my board with my legs on either side, staring up, floating along with the water. Emerald forests rose out of the ocean, towering trees which had seen thousands of sunrises like this one. I took a deep breath.

Every day, I got out here as fast as I could, waking at dawn and hustling out the door of my tiny bungalow on the beach. Every day, I marveled at the fucking beauty of this place, this tiny town I had grown up in.

Queen's Cove was popular around the world for surfing. We were one of the only places in Canada to catch waves, and despite the cold water, we attracted world-class surfers every summer, as well as a million tourists. Ocean, mountains, forests—what else could someone want?

Every day, the ocean reminded me how insignificant I was. If I let it, the ocean would eat me up and spit me out.

Sitting on the board for a few minutes every morning before surfing was my salutation to Mother Nature.

Thank you for letting me experience this. Thank you for not eating me.

A grin hitched at my mouth, and I rolled off my board into the water and paddled further out behind the break, where the good waves would be. Like usual, I was the only person out on the ocean at this time. You know that feeling of running through fresh, untouched snow? That satisfaction of crunching into the smooth white surface before anyone else? That's how I felt every morning. The ocean was mine for a couple hours.

During these morning hours, it was like I was the only person on the planet.

I spotted a wave as I swam into the cove, propped myself up on my board, and paddled hard, aligning myself with it. The wave approached and as I crested it, I hopped up on my board, using every muscle in my body to stay upright as the fluid power beneath my feet propelled me forward.

A rush of adrenaline hit my bloodstream.

This surfing thing never got old. If I worked hard enough, if I stayed focused, I would qualify to go pro and I could do this for the rest of my life.

After a few hours, I headed back to shore for breakfast and to open up the surf shop I owned. It was prime-time tourist season and the shop needed all hands on deck, but I had hired a couple extra people this summer. The shop could afford it, and it meant I could spend extra time out here.

I arrived at the surf shop half an hour later with a coffee in one hand and a breakfast bagel in the other. I unlocked the door, flipped the lights on, and woke the computer up to check for any important emails.

"Hey, bud," Carter, one of the summer workers, called from the door. Carter was in his early twenties, had shoulder-length shaggy hair, and moved to Queen's Cove to surf and party. He was a pretty good surfer, actually, and taught the beginner lessons.

"Hey," I called back, clicking through emails, deleting junk mail, flagging a few to deal with later. My gaze snagged on one, though, and my gut twisted hard.

Pacific Rim Worlds caught my eye.

The Pacific Rim World Competition was a surf competition held yearly in Queen's Cove. It was a qualifier level, which meant if surfers placed high, they could move on to pro-level competitions and be considered professionals. They would get attention of the big surf brands, and many signed sponsorship deals at that level.

Not just anyone could compete at Pacific Rim. You had to apply. Year after year, they rejected me. Finally, last year, I got in.

And then I fucking bombed.

Last year was my shot, and I choked. I still remember the way the water ripped the board out from beneath me. The bruising crash of water on my face and chest. My stomach burned with the memory.

I hadn't told a soul the truth of what happened.

All year, in the back of my mind, I had been sure they'd reject me again. Maybe they figured one shot was enough.

Pack your bags, because you've been accepted to the Queen's Cove Pacific Rim Worlds Competition in September, the email read.

A grin spread across my face and I exhaled. Going pro was still possible. Surfing was as much mental as physical, and there was no point to worrying over last year. I had two months to get my head on straight.

"Bro," Carter drawled over my shoulder, peering at the

screen. "You got in? Congrats." He held his fist out and I snorted but knocked my knuckles against his.

"Thanks, man."

"You need a guy to take over your shop when you go pro?"

I laughed and closed the email. "Let's not get ahead of ourselves." Between running the shop and the mortgage payments on the little house I had bought from my aunt, I was doing fine for money, but I wasn't flush with cash. Going pro meant flying all over the world for competitions and festivals, and that was going to add up fast.

Pacific Rim wasn't just my chance to go pro, it was an opportunity to get a sponsorship deal. That was how all the pros did it. Competitions paid a bit of money, but the sponsorships were where it was at. All I had to do was wear their gear, surf on their boards, and pose for a couple photos once in a while.

If I didn't get a sponsorship, I'd have to do more music videos like the one I did last winter for that popstar. I laughed to myself and rubbed my face, remembering how the body paint clung to my skin. The video had paid well, but I didn't want to do more of them. I hadn't told anyone in town because I'd never hear the end of it, especially from my brothers.

The door opened and a family with three teenagers entered the surf shop.

"We're here for our surf lesson," the mom told me, beaming with excitement, and I grinned back at her.

"Cool. Welcome." I gestured at Carter beside me. "Carter's going to help you out. Have fun, it's a great day out there."

Carter strolled out and clapped his hands. "Alright, Hathaway family! Are you ready to hang loose?"

I snorted and headed to the back to change out of my swim shorts. I had already hung my wetsuit out to dry on the railing behind the shop. The family would be struggling into their wetsuits in the change rooms for at least twenty minutes so I opened the back door and changed out of my suit there. No one ever came back behind the shop except employees, and this morning, it was just Carter and me.

I tossed my shorts over the railing beside my wetsuit. I was buck naked as I reached for my bag.

I heard a soft gasp behind me.

Hannah Nielsen stood with wide eyes and an open mouth, staring at my bare ass. She blinked three times before her face turned bright pink and she whirled around.

I bit back a laugh. Poor Hannah looked like she had seen a ghost. A naked ghost. Amusement pulled at my mouth.

Hannah was my sister-in-law Avery's best friend. Emmett's wedding last year was a fun party, and the guy seemed happy. The whole marriage and long-term commitment thing wasn't for me. Everything in the universe was temporary, including relationships and love, but if Emmett wanted to dive in head-first, it was his life.

Hannah was a witness at their wedding, and we had gone to the same schools growing up here, but yesterday in her bookstore was the longest exchange we'd ever had. Not for lack of trying on my part, though. Hannah was afraid of her own shadow and something about me seemed to make her nervous.

Her mortified expression yesterday as I read the orc erotica flashed into my head and my grin widened.

I unzipped my bag at a leisurely pace. "Something I can help you with?"

"Why are you naked?" Her voice was a squeak.

"I was taking off my swimsuit. Why were you staring at me naked?" I grinned and pulled a pair of boxer briefs on. I could see the blush on the back of her neck from ten feet away.

"I didn't mean to see you naked. Carter said you were back here."

"You can turn around, I'm not naked anymore."

She tilted her head first, shooting a quick glance over her shoulder to make sure I wasn't lying, before she relaxed. Her gaze lingered on my chest, though, like yesterday in her shop.

I bit back a laugh. Avery's shy, quiet little friend, checking me out. Who would have thought?

Something stirred in me and I had the urge to push her buttons further. She kept to herself. I never saw her at parties or in the bar, never at the beach on a nice summer day like everyone else. She just stayed in her bookstore.

She didn't realize it, but she was cute. At my brother's wedding, she had worn a light blue dress that brought out the color of her eyes. I'd never seen her wear something like that dress, and throughout the night, my gaze kept returning to her, watching how it moved over her skin, how it hugged her ass. Her body was gorgeous, with slight curves and smooth skin.

I'd never thought of her in that way before.

Today, she wore a baggy sweater with sleeves too long for her, jean shorts, and sneakers. Her legs were long and pale, and again I noticed how soft her skin looked.

I shook the thought out of my head. Hannah wasn't a hookup girl. Hannah was shy and terrified of everything.

Her throat worked and her gaze lingered on my boxers before she blushed again.

"What's up? Did you get a new shipment of erotica you wanted to show me?"

She shot me a quick, annoyed glance and I rolled my mouth to keep from grinning. She shifted in place. "Do you have an office we can talk in?"

That piqued my curiosity. "My office is winter wetsuit storage right now."

"Oh." She swallowed. She was cute, wringing her hands like this. "Never mind, then." She whirled around.

I admired the curve of her ass as she walked away. I was about to turn to go back inside the shop when she stopped walking, took a deep breath, and stalked back to me, chin in the air and a determined expression on her face.

"I have a proposition for you."

My mind went to a dirty place. "Well, knock me over with a feather." A lazy grin tugged at my mouth and my gaze raked over Hannah as I pulled a pair of shorts on over my boxers. Her muscles were so tense and tight. "Quiet little Hannah is going around town asking for sex."

She choked and her face was so red, it could burst into flames. "I am *not* going around town asking for sex. I need your help with something."

I nodded. "Sex."

Her head whipped around in frustration. "No! Nothing to do with sex. Or, not sex with you." She shook her head. "Forget the sex part. I need your help with…" She bit her lip, and I raised an eyebrow. "I need your help with becoming—"

"A surfer."

"No—"

"A homeowner." This game was fun.

"No—"

"You want to travel more."

She hesitated. "Yes, but no."

"You want to enjoy your life, take it one day at a time, fully accept we're insignificant compared to the power of the universe, and that we should enjoy every second of our lives without guilt or attachment."

Something shifted in her gaze and she chewed her lip. Her eyes met mine. I had always thought her eyes were blue but there were shades of green in them, too. "Sort of."

Now she could *really* knock me over with a feather. What was going on in this bookworm's head?

"I want you to teach me how to be a hot girl."

I stared at her, confused and speechless and uncertain.

She waved her hands to clarify. "You know a lot of hot girls. You sleep around a lot."

I reared back with an amused grin. "That sounded a little sex-shamey to me."

She shook her head adamantly, eyes wide behind her glasses. "I didn't mean it like that. I mean, you know what all those women have in common. You only sleep with hot girls."

My expression was a mixture of surprise and amusement. Was this what people thought of me? She was right that I didn't care what people thought. That seemed to help in the hookup department.

She took a deep breath and nodded. "I want you to teach me how to be like that."

"Like me?"

She nodded again. "Like you."

My eyes narrowed. "Why?"

Her mouth hitched to the side. "It isn't any of your business."

I snorted. "I'll make my own assumptions, then. You're sick of hiding in that dark bookstore all day and want to meet someone."

Her eyes widened. Bingo.

"I'm turning thirty soon." She twisted her fingers together. "It's time to make some changes."

My eyebrows pinched together. She didn't need to change a thing. She was adorable, with her pretty eyes and sweet little mouth. Even her glasses were cute in that dorky-girl way. The collar of her sweater was pulled to the side and a pale pink bra strap peeked out, and my gaze raked down her form. At Emmett's wedding, I was going to ask her to dance but every time I tried, she had disappeared.

A pang of regret hit me in the chest. I should have tried harder to ask her to dance at the wedding.

Her wanting to change bummed me out. Lots of guys in town would jump at the chance to be with her, but she didn't realize that. She just needed to leave her store once in a while.

There was no way to tell her this without sounding condescending, though. I stood there, crossing my arms over my chest, studying her while she looked like she was about to bolt if I spoke too loud or made any sudden movements.

A tiny, tiny part of me wanted to do this. Something about her had me curious. The quiet determination under her meek little exterior. I wanted to poke at her, scratch the surface and see what was underneath.

Maybe something interesting.

Surfing had taught me to trust my instincts, and my instincts pointed me straight toward her.

Pacific Rim lingered in the forefront of my mind, though. I had two months to catch as many waves as I could. Two months to get my head in the game. I didn't have time for distractions.

"I don't have time to show you how to flirt. Sorry, bookworm." I shrugged and leaned on the doorway. Her gaze dropped to my bare stomach again and satisfaction flickered in me.

Poor little horndog Hannah. She just wanted to get laid.

"If you want to get guys," I said, "go to the bar, wear that dress from the wedding last year, sit by yourself at the counter, and within ten minutes, someone will come up and talk to you."

An image of her dancing at the wedding with Avery popped in my head. They were laughing, being silly, enjoying themselves. With Avery, she smiled openly and let something shine through. She had a spark of fun in her, but she kept it locked away.

She wasn't this shy little shrimp deep down.

I shook it out of my head. Not my problem.

She crossed her arms over her chest, mirroring my stance,

and set her jaw. "You want to get a sponsor, right? Avery told me. I'll help you run your social media. All the other surfers have social media, even before they get sponsors. People need to notice you."

I paused and frowned at her. She made a good point. I hated dealing with social media, staring at a screen all day. I didn't care enough to be good at it. I'd rather stare at the ocean, the mountains, or the sky.

"Surfing is how I'll get a sponsor," I told her. I wasn't sure if I believed that. "I need to focus on surfing."

She swallowed and her chest rose as she took another deep breath. "I didn't want to do this, but you left me no choice." Her gaze met mine. "I know about the Tula video."

My eyebrows lifted with surprise, but I snorted. "Okay."

Her mouth dropped in shock.

I laughed again. "What, you want me to get on my knees? Please, Hannah, don't tell anyone about the video?"

She sputtered. "I don't... I don't know."

"Look, I don't care if people know about the video. I don't care what people think. Sorry, bookworm." I opened the back door to the surf shop.

"No cool surf brand would sponsor a silver mermaid!"

I paused in the doorway and cocked my head at her. "Mer*man*."

She raised her eyebrows in a challenge, struggling to hold eye contact. She wanted to crumble. I could feel it.

The corner of my mouth tugged up. "Are you black-mailing me?"

Her eyes were so wide. She crossed her arms and set her chin. "Yep."

This was a side of Hannah I had never seen before. Ballsy. She stared me down, forcing me to help her.

I weighed my options. I didn't care that much if everyone found out about the video. It had paid my way to a surf festival in Australia, and I didn't regret doing it.

She shifted again. Her resolve waned. I could see the cracks in whatever tough front she had put on today. She was about to fold, walk away, and never mention this again.

For some reason, this version of her intrigued me, and I wanted to see more.

Handing my social media over to someone would be a relief. All I had to do was give her a few gentle shoves out of her comfort zone.

"Alright, bookworm." I took a few slow steps toward her, watching her closely. Her expression changed from defiant to shocked.

"Alright?" She blinked. "Really?"

I nodded, stepping even closer. "Mhm. On one condition."

She bit her lip and her gaze rose to mine. "What's that?"

"You have to do everything I say." My voice was low.

She swallowed. "Everything?"

"Everything." I shot her a lazy smile. "You'll always be safe, but you're not allowed to be a chicken anymore."

"Not allowed to be a chicken anymore," she repeated to herself. She nodded again. An internal battle warred in her head. "Yes. Yes. Okay." She stuck her hand out and met my gaze, chin set again in that determined way.

A handshake? Adorable. I took her soft hand in mine and shook. My chest felt funny. Excited, filled with anticipation.

"Meet me here tomorrow at five thirty."

Her mouth made an O. "The bookstore doesn't close until six."

I headed back to the shop. "Five thirty in the morning," I called over my shoulder. "Bring your swimsuit."

Her eyes flared with alarm, and she opened her mouth to protest but I stepped inside before she could say anything.

My day just got a lot more interesting.

4

Hannah

MY FEET CRUNCHED on the gravel beside the surf shop, and I glanced over my shoulder at the trees. The sky was a dim gray, and nervous anticipation bubbled in my stomach.

My eyes were dry. I had barely slept. I hadn't been up this early since high school, when our history class took a day trip to Victoria to visit a Titanic exhibit at the museum. I often stayed up late reading, rolled out of bed, and headed straight to the bookshop for the nine o'clock open. I still stayed up late reading last night. I couldn't help myself.

What was I doing here? Alarm whistled through my veins. I had replayed yesterday's conversation with Wyatt a thousand times. I couldn't believe I actually went through with it.

I couldn't believe he said yes. Half of me expected him to laugh in my face.

Excitement shivered through me. If anyone was going to make me into a hot girl, it would be him. I'd get the bookstore finances in order, I'd find my true love, and in six months I'd be out for dinner, sitting across from the guy I'd spend the rest of my life with. He'd be leaning on the table, watching me the way Emmett watched Avery. When Thérèse returned, she wouldn't recognize me.

I bit my lip. I couldn't wait.

Wyatt waited for me at the back of the shop. The top half of his wetsuit dangled at his waist, his arms crossed over his bare chest, and he leaned against the railing. Upon seeing me, he straightened up.

"What took you so long, bookworm?" He didn't sound mad, though. He tossed me a wetsuit that had been hanging over the railing. "This will be your size. Suit up and let's go."

I froze. "Um. Go where?"

A lazy smile grew on his face. "Where do you think? We're surfing."

Oh, how I wished someone would take a picture of my incredulous expression in that moment. "I can't... surf, Wyatt. I read and sell books. That's all I do."

He let out a short laugh. "I know you can't surf." He shot me a quick wink and my stomach flipped. "I happen to be a surf instructor."

He waited while I stared at the limp wetsuit with horror.

"But it'll be cold."

He nodded. "Yep. Really cold. That's why I'm wearing a suit too."

The thought of the frigid ocean hitting my toes made me want to turn around and go home. I didn't do outdoor things. I used to camp with my parents, but we hadn't gone since my mom passed. I didn't swim in the ocean because it was too cold most of the year. Sometimes I'd put my feet in and walk along the shore.

Maybe this wasn't such a good idea anymore.

"I won't let anything bad happen to you," Wyatt said, tilting his head to watch me, and I wondered how many of my thoughts he could see.

He glanced at the sky, a couple shades lighter than when I arrived, and blew out an impatient breath. "Look, bookworm, I'm itching to get out there so it's now or never. My rules, remember?"

I nodded. "Your rules. Okay." I reached for the wetsuit. "How do I…?" I looked up at him, unsure of the next step.

He pointed to the back door and placed a hand on my shoulder, guiding me inside. His warmth zinged me through my sweater. "You can change inside, there's no one in there. Put your swimsuit on and step into the wetsuit, I'll help you zip it up out here."

I nodded. Right. Okay. One step at a time. Right now, I was putting on the wetsuit. I wasn't surfing or getting thrown face first into the ocean or getting eaten by a whale. I wasn't coughing up seawater or heaving for breath. I was just putting on a wetsuit.

I turned at the door. "I don't see what surfing has to do with being a hot girl—"

"My. Rules."

"Okay, okay." I spun around again and stepped into the little building. It was dark without the lights on, and I found a small room that looked like it was for changing. I pulled on my swimsuit, a navy-blue one-piece with a front that dipped too low for my taste and cut-outs along the side. Avery made me buy it last year and I'd never worn it. I wished I had something more practical but this was the only suit I owned, and it wasn't like I had a lot of time to prepare.

With some effort, I pulled the bottom half of the wetsuit on. The fabric was thick, spongy, and I wondered how many people had peed in this suit. How often did they clean them?

Nope, not worrying, I told myself. Just going to go outside. That was the next step.

"Well, look at you." Wyatt gave me a lopsided grin and straightened up. His gaze flicked down to the low neckline of my suit and my face heated immediately. He spun his finger in the air. "Turn."

I gave him my back and slid my arms into the suit. He pulled it closed at the back, not roughly or forcefully but with authority. Like he'd done this a hundred times. Like he didn't want to wait for me. Like he was in charge.

My skin tingled with awareness, but I ignored it.

He pulled the zipper up quickly and I wondered what it would be like in reverse, Wyatt yanking the zipper down as fast as he could, impatient to get it off me.

My face burned. I couldn't turn around now, blushing like this.

I swallowed and thought about the frigid water around the corner that I would soon be stepping into. There. That was helping.

I hoped these fantasies about Wyatt would go away. Maybe the more I got to know him, the more my body would realize what my brain already knew, that Wyatt was all wrong for me.

"Leave your glasses here." Wyatt hopped down the steps and strode across the gravel the same way I'd arrived before disappearing around the corner of the surf shop. I watched his tall, lean form, hypnotized with the fluid way he moved, before I set my glasses on the side of the step and hurried after him. I couldn't see very well without them, but I could still make out his form in front of me, moving across the sand with enthusiasm and long strides.

Two boards lay on the sand near the shore. I automatically stood near the smaller, sleeker board. The other one was huge and all banged up with marks and scratches.

"No way." He shook his head and gestured for me to stand near the bigger board. "You get the crappy starter board today, bookworm." He crouched near the bigger board, pointed at a strap of velcro tethered to the bottom and gestured for me to come forward. "This is your leash," he told me, and he undid the velcro before fastening it around my ankle. One of his hands encircled my ankle and the warm contact of his skin shocked me.

If he ran that warm, no wonder the guy was always shirtless.

The contact ended before my thought did and he strode over to fasten his own leash before he lay down on his front on the board, head up and watching the ocean.

"This is the ready position." He tilted his chin at me, gesturing for me to do the same. "Come on."

I matched his position on my own board.

He braced his palms on the board beside his shoulders. "If you see a wave coming that you want to take a bite out of, you're going to hop up on your board like this." He sprung up so he stood in a balanced crouch before he glanced over his shoulder at me. "Your turn."

I copied his actions, but there was no way I made it look as easy as he did. I looked like a drunk baby deer, stumbling around and trying to find my balance.

He glanced at my legs. "Bend your knees more." He nodded when I did. "Good. Okay." He shrugged. "And then you try to stay on your board and ride the wave."

I blinked at him. "It's that easy?"

That lazy grin returned. "It's not, but it's something you learn by doing." He stepped off the board and picked it up, tucking it under his arm. "Let's go." He began to jog to the ocean.

Alarm shot through me. "Wait!" I called after him. "I'm not ready."

"You'll never be ready, bookworm," he called back before wading into the water. "Come on."

He started paddling, and I watched his blurry form cut through the water. It was like the ocean drew him forward.

The board was lighter than I expected, but the water was as cold as I anticipated. I winced and inhaled sharply. Gentle waves rolled in, and I followed Wyatt deeper and deeper until he paused and waited for me, lying on his board—no, *lounging* on his board. It was like he was lying on the couch.

He watched with amusement as I made a few failed attempts to lie on the board. It was trickier on the water, and the board kept moving under me. My face flushed with embarrassment. Finally, I managed to lie on the board. When I started to float away from him, he reached out and held my board, anchoring me to him.

"We're going to paddle. Do what I do, okay?"

I nodded, swallowing, and he let go of my board before he paddled further out against the waves, muscular arms dipping into the water to propel him forward.

Just like that, I told myself. Just paddling. Easy peasy.

It was *not* easy peasy. My arms burned, but my pride wouldn't let me call it quits. The water grew darker as I swam further out, and I tried not to think about what lurked underneath and how my feet wouldn't touch the bottom if I fell off my board. I worked harder to stay close to Wyatt. Every few strokes he glanced over his shoulder to make sure I was near. Even without my glasses, I could see the guy was hardly breaking a sweat. Me, on the other hand, I breathed hard and my muscles burned, even the ones in my legs that I didn't think were working. My abs hurt already.

The area we paddled to wasn't as calm as where we started. The waves were bigger out here, picking me up and dropping me as they passed. I swallowed and my pulse beat in my ears from the exercise and nerves. My board tipped with a passing wave and I nearly fell off, wobbling and clinging to it hard.

I had to work hard to keep my balance lying down. What would standing up be like?

As if he read my thoughts, Wyatt stopped paddling, reached out for my board and steered it so we both had our backs to the wave.

I looked over my shoulder with alarm at the approaching wave. "What are you doing?"

He shot me a challenging grin. "Here you go, bookworm. Your first wave."

I shook my head vehemently. "No. I'm not ready."

He nodded. "Sure you are. Get in the ready position."

My hands came to the board at my hips without my permission. It was like his words had authority over my body. Traitorous hands. Wyatt did the same over on his board. I drifted away from him. My heart beat in my ears. I shook my head at him, fear pounding in my ears, and he nodded back at me with bright eyes.

The wave was right behind us.

"Start paddling," he said, and began to propel himself forward.

"What?" I called after him. "You didn't tell me this part!" I tried to follow him but he was too fast.

The water crested around me. Was this the part where I was supposed to assume the ready position or get up? I placed my hands on either side of my hips, about to pop up on my board but before I could, the wave knocked me off, face first into the water.

My nose burned as my head submerged, and my eyes stung. I hated getting water in my eyes. My chest heaved with a cough and I inhaled a mouthful of water. My leash tugged on my ankle and a moment later, the board bonked me on the back of the head—a stark reminder that I didn't know what the hell was I was doing.

I wrenched my burning eyes open above the surface and took a breath as another wave crashed into my face, sending even more water up my nose.

A firm hand wrapped around my upper arm, hauled me up onto my board with ease, and I crumpled onto it, coughing and sputtering.

"Nice work," Wyatt crowed. He paddled us single-handed into a nearby cove, where it was calmer, while gripping my board.

I blinked at him with a frown. "Are you making fun of me?"

He laughed. "Of course not. You're doing great."

I spat more salty water back into the ocean and coughed again. My eyes watered. "Wyatt, I hate to be rude, but you're a terrible surf instructor."

He laughed and continued paddling. "You're on an accelerated curriculum."

My mouth fell open and I tried to sit up on my board. It rocked with my teetering weight and I slipped back under the water.

When I re-emerged, I shot him a glare. "What *lesson* did I just learn?"

His teeth flashed with a grin. "That was your first bail. Not so bad, right?"

Unbelievable. "Are you kidding me? *Yes*, it was so bad. You dragged me out here in the middle of the night to humiliate me."

He shook his head. "When we come back out next time, you won't be as afraid of falling off your board." He took in the sky, a clear, light blue, dotted with a few clouds over the forest. "And now that you've worked for it, you can enjoy the view."

We floated on our boards, listening to the sound of the waves behind us on the shore. Two seagulls bobbed in the water nearby, ignoring us. My feet were frozen solid, and I wiggled them to get my circulation moving.

Beside me, Wyatt studied the sky with a wistful expression. That playful smirk of his was gone, replaced with a calm, thoughtful look.

"Do you come out here every day?"

"Yes."

"Wow. One with the ocean, and all that."

He smiled to himself. "I wouldn't say I'm one with it. The

ocean is like this huge, unpredictable monster that could kill us at any time."

"What?" My eyes widened, and I glanced down at the water around us. I couldn't see further than a couple feet beneath the surface. Panic hit my bloodstream. "What do you mean, kill us? Like, sharks?" I pictured the scene from *Jaws* where the shark hoisted himself into the boat.

Wyatt nodded. "Yep, there are sharks out here. Sometimes when we're paddling, the silhouette of us on our boards looks like a seal to them." He wiggled his eyebrows. "Dinner."

"Dinner?" My voice squeaked and that mischievous grin returned to Wyatt's face.

"I'm teasing you, bookworm." His teeth flashed. "There have been sightings of great whites but only a few. If you see a shark, it's likely a salmon shark, not a great white."

"Do those bite?"

"Everything bites if it's in the right situation." He must have seen the terror on my face. "It's rare. Sharks don't go around looking for a fight like a drunk gym bro at a bar. They mind their own business. Like you and I."

In the small cove, the water was so calm and still. I swallowed and studied the surface of the water.

"This is so dangerous." I shook my head at him before tilting my head at the waves. "Some of those waves are huge. You could get hurt. You could drown."

He laughed easily and shrugged. "You could get hit by a car tomorrow. One of the bookcases in your shop could fall over and crush you to death. The Big One could wipe out the entire town." The Big One was the earthquake the West Coast was due for. Our side of Vancouver Island was unprotected, hence the surfing. Every year, the entire town did a drill when the sirens went off. In the event of a big earthquake, every resident knew to get to higher ground before the massive tidal wave hit.

Wyatt was right. Death was around every corner. My mom

had thought she had her whole life in front of her. My throat was tight as I swallowed, staring at the board in front of me. I traced the scratches with my fingernail.

"Why not enjoy what we have while it's here," Wyatt said, quieter this time. "Here for a good time, not for a long time."

We floated on the water for a few more minutes until Wyatt noticed my teeth chattering and suggested we paddle back in.

"I'll bring the wetsuit booties for you next time," he called over his shoulder. "They'll keep your feet warm but they make it harder to grip the board."

We were halfway to shore when something grabbed my ankle. My head whipped around and all I could see without my glasses was dark movement in the water.

"Shark!" I shrieked and jerked my ankle, flailing and splashing in the water. "It's a shark!"

I slipped off my board and my head dunked under the surface. Water rushed up my nose and I coughed and swallowed a mouthful.

Wyatt was suddenly next to me. His arm wrapped around my waist and he yanked me towards him. "It's seaweed, Hannah." He held me against his chest as I thrashed, and with his other hand, he tried to pull whatever it was off me.

"Seaweed?" I gasped, still coughing and heaving breaths. My pulse pounded in my ears.

He lifted the slimy green bundle out of the water and tossed it a few feet away. My pulse slowed a few notches. He was still holding me against his hard chest.

This was nice.

"Just seaweed. Relax." His voice was calm and low. I nodded, and my pulse returned to normal. "That's one way to wake the sharks up." He flashed me a roguish grin and I made a weird sound in my throat, like a growl. He laughed and let me go, holding my board so I could hoist myself back up.

Back on shore, we walked our boards across the sand, back

to the shop. He had undone the top half of his wetsuit before we even left the water and it hung from his waist. His back muscles were on full display, and I tried not to ogle.

"If I wasn't here, how long would you stay out?" I was out of breath from paddling.

He smiled to himself. "A couple hours. Until I got hungry." He set his board down in front of the shop and pointed beside it. "You can leave the board here."

Once my board was on the ground, something tugged on the back of my wetsuit and I heard the *zzzzt* of the zipper. Cold air rushed in.

"Thanks." Wyatt was basically undressing me. I had a swimsuit on underneath; it wasn't like he was unzipping my dress or something.

With a quick flash of the look he had given me at Avery's wedding, his heated gaze skimmed down my form. My cheeks flushed.

"You can leave the suit to dry on the back patio," he told me over his shoulder, walking down the beach. He lived in a small house in that direction. "Good work today, bookworm."

Without my glasses, I could only see his form move as he walked with athletic ease, in control of his entire body.

That was it? "Wait. Aren't you supposed to give me homework or something?"

All I had done today was paddle and get water up my nose. I wasn't any closer to being a hot girl.

He turned, walking backwards. "Homework? Not really my style, but okay. Um." He rubbed his jaw. "Ask ten guys out."

Another shot of panic through my stomach. "What?!" My voice sounded like I had inhaled helium. "I can't do that. That's like half of Queen's Cove."

"Sure, you can. It's way less dangerous than surfing." He waved and turned. "Same time Friday."

Ten guys? No. No, no, no. I didn't ask guys out. I had

never asked a guy out. I hadn't even flirted with a guy. I didn't know how to. That was why I was here in the first place, so Wyatt could teach me all those things.

He clearly didn't understand what my goals were.

"You're supposed to help me get a haircut and pick out better clothes!" I called back in desperation. "Not make me look like a fool."

"My rules," he called back.

I made a noise of anguish and headed to the back of the shop, where I yanked off my suit and hung it on the railing. Inside, I crept into the bathroom to change out of my wet swimsuit, and nearly gasped when I put my glasses back on and peered into the mirror.

I looked feral. My waterproof mascara? Not waterproof. My eyes were ringed in black smudges. My hair was a knotted mess, half wet, half dry. The salty ocean water had made it frizzy and poofy. My face was still flushed from talking to a member of the opposite sex for so long.

Wyatt must have thought this was hilarious, me wanting to be a hot girl. I swallowed and wiped off the mascara smudges with toilet paper. I didn't want to think about it too hard, because if I did, I would come to the conclusion that I was the joke. A meek little bookworm, wanting to be someone else. I couldn't even stand up on my board. I'd seen tourists surfing small waves within an hour of their first lesson and all I could do was scream and inhale a face full of water.

I blew a breath out. Maybe this whole thing was a mistake.

On my way home, my body replayed Wyatt pulling me against his chest. My stomach rolled. He was so warm and solid.

So I fell off my board. I got water in my brain and thought a piece of seaweed was a great white shark. I tried something new today. That's what hot girls did. Thérèse wouldn't let one bad day get her down.

I was one step closer.

5

Wyatt

A COUPLE DAYS LATER, I stood in front of Pemberley Books, studying the exterior. The paint on the front of the shop peeled. I glanced at the mural on the side of the building, in the alley next to the shop. As a kid, I remembered it clear and freshly painted, classic books from every genre in a grid.

Now, it looked kind of sad. The paint had faded from the sun and time, and most of the titles were difficult to read.

"Hey, buddy. I heard you got into Pacific Rim. Congrats."

I turned to see Beck Kingston, one of my oldest friends, walking up the street toward me. "Thanks, Dr. Beck."

He laughed. After we graduated high school, Beck had gone to university in Vancouver and then medical school with the intention of taking over his parents' practice one day here in Queen's Cove.

"How were the waves this morning?" Beck sometimes joined me out on the water but always in the evenings. He wasn't a morning person.

"Perfect. Nice and clean."

"Ready for Pacific Rim?"

I crossed my arms over my chest and ignored the twinge of panic in my gut. I didn't panic. That wasn't my style. I shrugged. "Ready as I'll ever be. Still going to get out there every morning, though."

Beck grinned. "Wouldn't expect anything less of you." He tilted his chin at the store. "I have a book to pick up, I'll talk to you later."

"I'll join you. I need to talk to Hannah about something."

The bell on the door rang when he opened the door and held it for me. It took a moment for my eyes to adjust to the dim lighting, but I spotted Hannah chatting with a customer. Beck headed off in search of a book with a wave to me.

I wandered over to the squashy chairs I had seen her and Thérèse sitting in and took a seat while I waited for her to finish up. I eased back into the chair, studying the store.

Every shelf burst with books. Stacks sat on the floor beside shelves and between the big chairs. There were empty spaces where it looked like a shelf used to be but had given out. I could only see half of the front desk from where I sat, but even from here I could see the weathered desk and old, outdated register. The carpet was thin and the place smelled musty. Not unpleasant, just old.

They hadn't updated this place in a long time.

Her murmur traveled through the stacks of books.

The front door bell rang again as the customer left and Hannah's footsteps approached. She stopped short when she came around the corner and saw me.

She reared back. "What are you doing here?"

I snorted. "Now *that's* customer service. '*Welcome to Pemberley Books. What are you doing here?*'"

She crossed her arms and gestured at the chair. "You can't sit there."

"I'm wearing a shirt this time."

A hint of pink bloomed on her cheeks. "I noticed. Thank you for doing the bare minimum." She blinked. "Again, what are you doing here? Do you need me to teach you how to read?"

I burst out laughing. "You're kind of mean for a shy girl."

Her eyes widened. "I'm so sorry. I don't know why I said that. I know you can read."

The grin stayed glued on my face. I liked this side of her. "It's okay, bookworm. I know you jest. I'm here to check up on you and see if you've done your homework."

She froze. "My homework."

"Yep. Since you get off on having homework, I thought I better make sure you did it." I winked and her eyes widened.

"I don't *get off* on having homework," she hissed. "And no, I haven't done it." I noticed her cheeks redden further, even in the dim light at the back of the bookstore.

I rubbed my jaw and narrowed my eyes, pretending to think. "What was that we agreed on again? My way, my rules, something like that?"

She rolled her eyes. "Don't think too hard, you might hurt something."

Another laugh burst out of me. "You're cranky today."

"I'm not cranky."

I stood. "Well, I don't have all day, so let's get to it."

Panic flared in her gaze, and she took a step back into a bookshelf. "Get to what?" It was the same squeaky voice as a couple days ago when we were on the water, when I was teasing her about sharks.

"You're going to ask ten guys out, like we agreed."

Her eyes darted around, and she chewed her lip. She didn't want to do this, I could tell, but I didn't care. A sick part of me liked pushing her boundaries.

A couple days ago, she didn't want to get on the board. Fuck, she didn't even want to get into her wetsuit, but she showed up. A part of her wanted to do something new, push herself out of the safe little box she hid in most of the time. And *that* was how she would become this hot girl she wanted to be. The look she gave me when I pulled her back on her board, sputtering and coughing? She was furious.

I thought about the way she had melted against me when I hauled her to my chest in the water. Something about it sent a thrill through my veins.

She crossed her arms over her chest, frowning at me.

"Bookworm, you want to be a hot girl? Hot girls don't care what people think of them. They don't worry if they fuck up because failure is part of life. Do you trust me?"

She snorted. "No."

I grinned.

"I do trust that you know what you're talking about," she admitted.

I wasn't going to give her a chance to bail on this. "Come on." I moved past her and noticed another employee behind the desk, a Black woman with bright blue earrings.

"Hi." I nodded to her. "Liya, right?"

She beamed at me. "Yeah, and you're Wyatt?"

"You know it." I gestured at Hannah. "I'm going to steal Hannah for a few minutes. Is that okay?"

Liya glanced between me and Hannah, who shrank like she wanted to disappear into the floor. "Sure."

"Cool. Come on, bookworm." I put a hand on her back and guided her out of the store.

"Where are we going?"

"We're going to stand right here," I said, holding the door open, "and you're going to ask out the next ten guys you see."

Her hands twisted in front of her. Her throat worked as she swallowed. "This is not how I pictured finding a boyfriend."

"Hey." I leaned down to meet her eyes, waiting until she raised her gaze to mine. "Remember when you fell off your board and got a face full of water?"

Irritation replaced her worry. "Yes."

"You were fine after, right?"

A tiny nod. She inhaled. "Okay. Fine. Let's get this over with."

"Excellent." I scanned the street. It was just after ten in the morning on a Thursday, so no weekend summer crowds yet. A few people moving in and out of stores, chatting with neighbors and friends on the sidewalk, enjoying their morning. Don, the retired guy who ran the local news blog, the Queen's Cove Daily, walked up the street carrying a couple bags of groceries.

"Don." I waved. "How you doing, buddy?"

Hannah froze. "He's married," she hissed at me under her breath.

I kept the grin on my face but lowered my voice. "Doesn't matter, not the point."

Don nodded and smiled at us. "Good morning. Not too bad. Canned kidney beans are on sale at the grocery store and there's only a couple left, you two should get over there. Ninety-nine cents."

"Wow, nice." I grinned before turning to Hannah with an expression that said *go on*.

She swallowed and shook her head. I nodded with raised eyebrows.

"Hi, Don." Her voice wobbled.

"Hi, Hannah."

Hannah's mouth snapped shut and she glanced at the door of her bookshop, like she wanted to run inside and hide.

I crossed my arms over my chest and leaned against the brick wall. "Hannah has something she wants to ask you."

Don's eyebrows lifted. "Oh? Well, go on." He shifted the bags in his hands.

"Wouldyouliketogetdinnerorsomethingsometime?" She said the words in a rush and I nearly burst out laughing there, but held back. She was doing the scary thing, and I wanted to see how she'd handle this. I didn't want to push her so far that she'd bail on this whole thing. It was just getting interesting.

Don blinked at her. "I'm sorry, I didn't catch that."

"Dinner. Would you like to get it sometime?" She stared at her sneakers, face burning.

Don's mouth made an O. "Oh, Hannah. I'm married."

"Right," she managed. "Married."

Her face burned, and the red flush crept down her neck to her collarbone.

Don shook his head at her with pity. "Oh, honey. You'll find someone." He reached into his bag. "Take a can of beans."

She put her hands up. "No, that's okay—"

"Please, I insist." He pushed the can into her hands and shot her another wince. "I'm so sorry if I ever gave you the wrong impression about us."

Hannah made a strangled noise in her throat.

I tilted my chin at him, still smiling. "See you later, Don."

"Later, Don." Hannah's voice warbled. When Don was far enough away, she whirled at me and slapped my arm.

I burst out laughing.

"That was so embarrassing."

"I know. You did great. One down, nine to go." I peered over her shoulder as Max approached. "Round two, let's go, before you have time to think about it."

Max was in his mid-twenties and managed Avery's restaurant, The Arbutus. He gave us a wave. "Hey."

"Max, will you go on a date with me?" Again, she rushed the words out, like she couldn't get rid of them fast enough.

One of his eyebrows rose in disbelief. "You know I'm gay, right?"

Hannah's throat worked and she nodded.

Max glanced between us with interested suspicion. "What's going on here?"

I shrugged. "Don't worry about it."

His gaze narrowed. "I'm not going to go on a date with you, Hannah, but you can come over and watch *The Bachelor* with Div and me tomorrow night. We eat a lot of pizza and make fun of everyone." He raised an eyebrow at her. "This is purely platonic, on account of me still being gay."

Hannah gave a quick nod. "Sure. Tomorrow night. I'll bring spinach dip."

He pointed at her. "Now, you're thinking." He glanced between us again and gestured between her and me. "I'm intrigued. Goodbye."

Hannah shifted on her feet, twisting her hands. "Bye."

Max walked away, casting curious glances over his shoulder at us as I grinned and waved at him.

"Great. Now he's going to tell Avery what a weirdo I'm being. Standing outside my own bookstore, harassing innocent men."

"Bookworm, that was amazing. Two rejections, one after the other? When this is over, you're going to be bulletproof."

Her nostrils flared and another spike of happiness rose in my chest. If only she could be this feisty with others.

We'd get there.

We kept waiting on the sidewalk for people to pass. The next three guys were in relationships but flattered someone as cute as Hannah was paying attention to them. I had gone easy on her and let her skip the ones that were walking with another woman. I didn't want to completely mortify her. Just a little.

Div walked by, in a full suit like always. Div worked for my brother Emmett, first at the construction company Emmett and my other brother Holden owned, and now at town hall, where Emmett was mayor.

"Hey, Div," I called as he passed. "Hannah wants to ask you something."

Div raised an eyebrow. "Are you going to ask me out, too?"

Hannah nodded, shoulders sinking. "Max told you."

"And Don." He studied her before gesturing. "Well, go on."

"Div, will you go on a date with me?" Her tone was so

dreary and dejected that I had to hide my grin behind my hand.

He shook his head, studying her. "No, but I'm going to ask you questions tomorrow night when you come over."

"That's reasonable." She nodded, pressing her lips together.

Div's phone rang and he read the name on the screen. "I have to take this." He answered the call and walked away.

"Four to go, bookworm." I shot her a wink.

She huffed and chewed her lip. At least she wasn't mortified anymore. Just irritated.

"Wyatt, my dude!" Carter, the twenty-three-year-old who worked at my surf shop, raised his hand for a high five. He shot Hannah a lazy smile. "Who's the lady friend?"

"This is Hannah."

Carter's dopey smile lingered. It was after eight in the morning so he was probably stoned. I didn't care if he was high working at the surf shop, as long as he didn't get stoned before teaching any lessons. "Hey, Hannah. What's your story?"

"Um. I work at a bookstore." She gestured behind us. "This one."

"Wow, cool." He made an explosion noise in his mouth. "Books, ya know?"

"Yep, books." She sighed. "Do you want to go on a date with me?"

Carter's mouth fell open. "For serious? Hell yeah!"

Hannah snapped to attention and blinked a few times. "Oh. Okay, then."

"I'm going to the bar tomorrow night. You want to come with? They have darts," he told her. There were a few bars in Queen's Cove but only one that the locals frequented, a dingy old bar that had been standing since the sixties.

She glanced at me before nodding at him. "Okay. Sunday night at the bar."

Carter fist-pumped the air. "Right on. See you then, chica. Later, boss." He made finger-guns at her before backing away. I heard him whoop as he bobbed down the street.

"Nice one, *chica*."

"Shut up." Her mouth twitched. "This was your stupid idea."

From the way she was trying not to laugh, instead of trying to blend in with the wall outside the bookstore like before, my idea didn't seem stupid at all.

She winced. "He's way too young for me. What will people think?"

I shrugged. "Who cares? They'll probably think, 'wow, Hannah can get it.'"

"Oh my god." She buried her face in her hands and I grinned.

The bell on the door jingled and Liya stuck her head out. "Han, do we have any copies of *Pride and Prejudice*?"

Her fingers came to her hair, playing as she thought with a little frown on her face. "Second stack from the supply room. On the right."

"Great." Liya grinned at us. "Thanks."

We turned back to the street to see my brother Holden staring at us with a frown on his face. "What are you doing here?"

"Good morning, sunshine."

He frowned deeper. "You're wearing a shirt and you're standing outside a bookstore."

Hannah crossed her arms over her chest. "We're doing a thing. Holden, do you want to go on a date with me?"

Under the brim of his baseball hat, his eyes widened with alarm. He hadn't dated anyone in years. His frown deepened and he cleared his throat. "There's an art exhibit at the gallery next weekend I was going to go to."

I tilted my head, studying him. Didn't expect that.

"Oh." Hannah's eyebrows rose in surprise. "The Emily Carr one."

He grunted in acknowledgement and shot me a warning glance. My mouth quirked.

Hannah nodded with a small smile. "Okay."

"Saturday at two. I'll buy you food after. Don't be late." He turned and walked away, leaving Hannah and I standing on the sidewalks, me shaking with laughter and her with her mouth hanging open.

She stared after Holden before giving me a hesitant glance. "I don't like Holden like that. What if he gets the wrong idea?"

"I'll talk to him."

She groaned. "No, that's worse. I'll think of something."

The bell behind us jangled again and Beck stepped out.

"Hey, Hannah." He gave her a warm smile and held up a stack of books. "I got lucky today. I got that book you ordered in for me about medical research."

Hannah gave him a shy smile. "It's *so* funny. Mary Roach is so sharp and witty."

"And I'm going to read this *Pride and Prejudice* you won't stop talking about."

I turned to study Hannah. She hadn't mentioned this book to me.

She chewed her lip, biting back a smile. "I'm so happy you've decided to take your life in the right direction."

I frowned, watching her smile up at him. Her eyes glowed. She was lit from within, talking about this book. Where was the shy, terrified Hannah? She seemed to melt away in Beck's presence.

"You love this book, huh?" He beamed at her, and there was a spark in his gaze.

She nodded. "It's my favorite. It's so... It's the ultimate romantic comedy." She gestured at the weathered store sign above us. "There's a reason the bookstore is named this." She beamed again. "You'll see."

I crossed my arms over my chest. My shoulders tightened.

Beck gave us a quick nod. "I look forward to it. See you later, you two."

Hannah shot me a side-long glance but I held my hand up to Beck. "Hannah wants to ask you something."

Her face went red. That made my shoulders even tighter. She didn't blush with Holden.

"Um…" she started.

"Go on." I tilted my chin at her, keeping my arms crossed.

Beck glanced between us with narrowed eyes. "What is it?"

Hannah winced at him. "I'm trying a thing. Do you want to go out with me?"

Beck's gaze flared with interest. "Yes, I do. Is this because I'm reading your favorite book?"

She laughed and there was a weird stab in my stomach. "No, no. Wyatt's making me ask people out to embarrass me."

Beck looked impressed. "Good for you." He glanced at me and did a double take before shooting a quick smile at Hannah. "I have to get back to the clinic, but I'll come chat with you tomorrow."

She nodded. "Okay. Bye, Beck."

He waved. "Bye."

I watched him walk down the street. Beck was tall like me, with a good head of dark hair, nice teeth, and he was always in a good mood. He was a regular at the gym. He was pleasant to everyone, well-liked around town, and single.

Hannah hummed to herself, glancing up and down the street and rocking on the heels of her sneakers. "One left."

A weird feeling hit my stomach. I couldn't explain it, but my mood had soured.

"You've done enough. Good job today, bookworm."

"Oh. Okay." She shrugged. "That wasn't so bad, I guess."

She remembered the can of beans in her hand and winced. "Actually, yes, it was." She tilted her head, passing the can back and forth between her hands. "I do want to see that exhibit at the gallery, though. And Beck is cute." Her gaze followed him down the street. "Super cute."

I stepped in the way of her line of sight. "We have another surf lesson tomorrow. Dawn."

She groaned. "So early."

I pictured her with messy hair, rolling out of bed and turning off her alarm. "We have to catch those clean waves, bookworm. They're the easiest to learn on."

"I'm going to fall off my board again." Her mouth twisted to the side.

"Undoubtedly."

"It's going to suck."

"Hey." I nudged her. "You got rejected by half the town today, and you're still standing."

Despite the embarrassed flush on her face, she laughed. "Ugh. Please let me forget." She glanced at the store. "I should go back in. Oh." She paused. "I've been reading about social media marketing. What's your brand?"

One eyebrow lifted. "My brand?"

"Like, your vibe."

I shrugged. "I don't know. That everything is temporary?"

"Uh, no, that's depressing." She shook her head. "It's fine, I'll come up with something. Can I take a few videos of you tomorrow morning after we surf? Do you have time?"

Oh, right. That social media thing. Knowing someone was thinking about it and that I wouldn't have to do anything was a relief. "Sure. Whatever you want."

She flashed me a smile, a real one like she showed Avery, and my chest squeezed. I smiled back at her.

"See you tomorrow, Wyatt."

"See you tomorrow, bookworm."

———

WHEN I RETURNED HOME from surfing that evening, I had a missed call from Avery.

"Why do you want my copy of *Pride and Prejudice*?" she answered as soon as I called her back.

"I want to read it."

She snorted. "Why?"

"I'm curious about it." I pictured Hannah's eyes lighting up, talking about it. There must be something good in that book.

"I left it on your front porch."

I opened the front door and saw it sitting there on the welcome mat. "Here it is. Thanks, Av."

"What's this I hear about Hannah asking out half the guys in town?"

Even though Avery was Hannah's best friend, I held back from elaborating. "She was doing her homework."

We said our goodbyes and I settled onto the couch before cracking the book open. There was a stamp inside the front cover.

Sold with love by Pemberley Books

6

Hannah

ANOTHER WAVE ROLLED in and he caught it, shooting forward on his board, riding it toward the shore. He was so at ease, like he was more comfortable on water than on land. Above us, blue skies stretched over the mountains, trees, and ocean. A few other early bird surfers dotted the ocean around us, but Wyatt had the big waves to himself.

I took another video of him on Liya's nice camera I had borrowed.

He paddled his board back out before the break and waited for the next one. I unzipped the top half of my wetsuit and let it hang off my waist. My muscles ached from my disastrous surf lesson the other day. The day was warm already and my hair was almost dry from me falling off my board again this morning. I saw why Wyatt preferred to surf first thing in the morning, even if the water was ice-cold.

On the shore, I recorded more video as he caught another wave. He carved the water so gracefully, gliding over the surface like it was made of ice. Through the zoom lens, I watched the muscles on his torso ripple as he balanced. He made it look so easy, when I had inhaled face-full after face-full of water this morning. My nasal cavity still burned and my hair hung around my shoulders in frizzy tendrils. I knew better than to wear mascara this morning, though. I didn't care if I looked tired and my eyes disappeared behind my pale eyelashes, it was better than wiping the smears off around my eyes afterward.

Wyatt rode a wave closer to shore and paddled in, grinning from ear to ear. I took a sneaky picture of him as he shook the water off his hair, carrying his board in, and I laughed to myself. *We'll make a social media star of you yet, Wyatt.*

Up close, he was gorgeous like this, all muscle and dripping water and bright eyes. A smile from ear to ear. I blinked, taken aback. My pulse picked up.

I shook myself. Wyatt wasn't my type.

Someone like Beck, *he* was my type. A handsome, kind man who read books and took an interest in things I liked. If things worked out with us, Beck and I could read books together every evening.

I nearly snorted. If things worked out? He was a hot doctor, and every single girl in town was interested in him. He probably only agreed to the date because he felt bad for me.

"Bookworm?" Wyatt was right in front of me.

I jolted to attention. "Hi. Yes."

His mouth twitched with amusement at my daydreaming. "Didn't realize you were still out here."

I held up the camera. "I was getting some footage."

He shrugged. "Okay. Let's get breakfast."

"Breakfast?"

He nodded and kept walking.

I checked the time before jogging to keep up with him. "I have to be at the bookstore by ten."

"We'll get you there in time."

I picked up my board again, letting my camera hang from the strap on my shoulder, and we walked along the sand towards the surf shop.

"So, did you figure out what my brand is?"

A big smile lifted on my face. In the evenings, I had been reading about marketing and social media engagement, and the thing that resonated most with me was that a brand should be authentic to the person or business, and unique.

"I did," I told him, pulling my too-eager smile back as we walked over the sand. "It's this." I gestured out at the water behind us.

His eyebrows rose in amusement. "Surfing?"

I laughed. "No. I mean, partially surfing, but being out in nature and being in Queen's Cove. It's part of you. Queen's Cove is one of the most beautiful places on earth, and you surfing with the mountains in the background…" I sighed and shook my head. "Gorgeous."

"You think I'm gorgeous?" The side of his mouth hitched further in a roguish grin.

I stumbled on the sand and huffed an embarrassed laugh. Of course, I did. "I meant the mountains. The mountains are gorgeous."

"Mhm. You like this social media thing."

Warmth filled my chest and I nodded. "I do. It's fun."

"Glad someone enjoys it. How are your dates going?"

My stomach tied itself into a knot. "I think I'm going to cancel."

Every time I remembered asking all those guys out, I shuddered with embarrassment. Now I had to go out and make conversation with men in a public place, when I'd rather be in my pajamas at home under a blanket with a glass of wine and the latest Talia Hibbert book.

But I'd been doing that for years and it got me nowhere.

"What? No." He shook his head. "You can't cancel, book-worm. The hard part is over."

"The hard part is *not* over; the hard part is me having to spend time around people and convince them to like me."

He frowned. "You don't need to convince anyone to like you. People either like you, or they don't know you well

59

enough, or they don't matter. You can leave your board there." He gestured to the sand in front of the shop. "Carter's teaching a beginner class this morning."

I set the board down on the sand and dusted my hands off. "I'm meeting him at the bar tonight."

Amusement grew on his features. "Better get your dart game ready."

I groaned. "I don't want to go."

He nudged my arm. "Come on, bookworm. This is how you figure out what you like."

"By dating half the town?"

"Yep."

"Are you only saying that because that's your method?"

Another flash of teeth, wolfish this time. "Except we don't really date, if you know what I mean."

A quick stab hit me in the gut. I made a grumbly noise and rolled my eyes. Why did I care if Wyatt had hooked up with every girl in town? I didn't. In fact, that was why I was here. Because Wyatt was so good at dating and meeting people. Wyatt knew hot girls. I should be getting tips from him instead of making it weird.

He tilted his chin across the street. "Leave your suit on, we can sit outside the food truck. I'm going to put my board away."

He disappeared into the shop with his board and returned a minute later. We wandered barefoot across the street to the small patio with picnic tables. Music played and greasy food smells wafted out of the truck. Something sizzled inside.

We studied the small menu and I shot him a side-long glance. "So, say I wanted to hook up with Carter, what would I do?"

He crowed with laughter. "You don't."

No, I didn't, but I wanted to know what I would do in case it ever came up with anyone else. "Maybe I do."

The look he gave me made me feel like he could see inside

my brain. He shook his head, still laughing. "Your body language with him told me you don't."

I thought about getting naked with Carter and my face automatically pulled into a grimace.

Wyatt laughed again and pointed at my face. "You'd rather go back out on the water and bail off your board all morning than go anywhere near Carter's bed."

I wrinkled my nose at him. "You're right. But what about someone like Beck? If I wanted to hook up with him, how would I make that known?"

The grin dropped off Wyatt's face. "We should order." He turned to the person running the truck and ordered a breakfast sandwich before turning to me. "Do you want the same?"

"Uh, sure." I blinked. "Thanks. Wait." I glanced between us, still in our wetsuits. "I don't have any money on me. Neither do you."

"He has a tab," the woman in the truck called out.

"Oh. Thanks, Wyatt."

He winked. "Don't mention it."

We took a seat at a picnic table and within a few minutes, our food arrived.

My foot tapped a rhythm on the ground while we ate. What if Carter tried to kiss me tonight? I cringed. I really didn't want to kiss him. Was it unethical if I went on a date with the guy and I didn't even like him, not as more than a friend? I didn't want to lead him on. Maybe Wyatt was right in that I needed the practice to figure out what I wanted.

I didn't want Carter, though.

"You're still thinking about the date with Carter tonight?"

I swallowed a bite of food and nodded at Wyatt.

He studied me for a moment. A piece of hair had fallen into his eyes, and he pushed it back. "Would it make you feel better if I was there?"

I snorted. "Like, on our date?"

There was that lazy grin again. "No, at the bar. If you get

uncomfortable or something, you can give me a signal and I'll jump in to help."

I straightened up. "Yes. That would be amazing." I tilted my head at him. "You'd do that for me?"

He rolled his eyes. "Relax, bookworm. I'm going to a bar to have a beer. It's not a big deal."

My face warmed. "Right. I know. I just appreciate it."

"Don't mention it."

"How about I touch my ear?" I asked, brushing my fingers over my earlobe. "Like this. If I need help."

He nodded, the corner of his mouth hitched in amusement. "Sure. I doubt you're going to need my help, but I'll be there in case you do."

There was a flutter in my stomach. Nerves about the date that night, probably. "Thanks, Wyatt."

———

"HANNAH! HANNAH! WATCH! WATCH ME!"

I shot Carter a tight smile and nodded. "I'm watching."

His friends crouched down, grabbed his legs, and flipped him upside down. He chugged the beer but choked, coughing and spraying it everywhere. The group of his friends gathering nearby—six other guys—all groaned and laughed.

"Almost got that one." He wiped his mouth and dropped into the seat across from me. Beer splattered the collar of his shirt.

"Almost," I agreed, playing with the condensation on my glass.

Across the bar, Wyatt sat back in his seat, watching with amusement in his eyes. His gaze rested on me but I refused to meet it. I didn't know whether it was because I was embarrassed or because I'd start laughing and never stop.

I took another sip of my beer and shuddered. Gross. I didn't like beer, but Carter had bought a pitcher and placed a glass in front of me when I arrived, and I didn't want to be that girl. You know. The one who made a big fuss.

"I bet you've read like, lots of books." Carter suppressed a burp against his fist.

I played with the paper coaster under my glass. "I mostly like romance, but I was reading this book by a sleep researcher that I couldn't put down. It's amazing how sleep is tied to almost every aspect of our health." His foot bumped mine and I shifted, tucking my feet further under my bar stool.

He smiled at me. His eyes were glassy. "Wow. That's cool."

I didn't know what to say so I shrugged. "You moved here from Calgary?"

He nodded and put his arms in the air. "C-TOWN, BABY!" His friends all turned from where they stood at the dart board and cheered. He shrugged at me. "No surfing there, though."

I shook my head. "Nope."

"You ever been?"

Another shake of my head. "Nope."

He nodded. "That's cool, that's cool." He slugged back half his beer.

I squirmed in my seat and glanced around, again avoiding Wyatt. This whole thing was a huge mistake, and I was totally failing on my date. I couldn't even hold a conversation. My chest was tight at the awkwardness.

The silence stretched between us and embarrassment burned in my stomach. He clearly regretted saying yes.

Carter slapped the table and I jumped. "You know what we need to do? A beer bong."

His friends in the corner raised their arms and cheered. "Beer bong! Beer bong!" They surrounded our table, chanting, and one of them produced a long tube with a funnel.

"You guys brought a beer bong to the bar?" I asked Carter.

He nodded. "I bring it everywhere. You never know when

you're going to need it." He moved to a kneeling position and his friends cheered again.

The entire bar was staring at us.

Oh my god. My face heated and I glanced around for Wyatt, already tugging on my ear. He wasn't in his spot. He sat there a second ago and now he wasn't there. His beer was still there, though.

Carter held the bong up and one friend poured his beer into the funnel. Carter's throat worked as he chugged.

"CHUG! CHUG! CHUG! CHUG!" His friends cheered as the rest of the bar patrons watched with open mouths.

I wanted to die. My gaze darted around the bar again. My earlobe was about to come off, I was pulling it so hard.

Beer trickled from the corners of Carter's mouth, down his neck, soaking the collar of his t-shirt. Male cheers boomed around me as he finished, stood up, and raised his arms in the air with victory. He pointed straight at me and panic streaked through me.

"You're up!"

I shook my head and opened my mouth to protest but a warm hand landed on my shoulder.

"Why don't you join me at my table for a bit?" Wyatt said in my ear. His breath tickled my skin and made me shiver.

Olivia, the bartender, was right behind him, and she was pissed. Her hot pink hair was tied up into a messy bun on top of her head. She glared at the group of Carter's friends. She was half the size of some of them but they recoiled from her in fear.

"Out." She pointed at the door. "No frat boy bullshit in here. Bars are where people come to be depressed. No chanting."

"Come on, bookworm." Wyatt's hand came to the small of my back and he gave me a gentle push away from Carter and his friends.

We approached his table and I glanced over my shoulder

at Carter disappearing through the door. He didn't even look back to see where I went. My face heated more. I could feel it crawling down my neck.

I took a seat across from Wyatt's spot. "I think that was me falling off my board." Face first into the water, nose burning and choking on seawater.

He shook his head, that familiar amused expression back on his face. "You're doing great. Carter fucked up this date, not you." He tilted his head again.

Olivia appeared at the table and placed two champagne flutes between Wyatt and me.

"Hey, Hannah." She shot me a wink. Olivia had grown up in Queen's Cove too, but she was a year younger than me. She lived in Vancouver during the year, working on her PhD, and returned home every summer to help with her dad's bar during the busy tourist season. "I haven't seen you in ages. Are you going to sing?"

"Sing?" My eyes went wide, and I glanced between her and Wyatt with alarm. "Why would I sing?"

Olivia nodded at the corner of the bar, where a mic stand stood. "It's karaoke night."

I burst out laughing. "God, no. I can't sing at all." I shook my head. "No. No. I would never."

Wyatt grinned across the table and I rolled my eyes at him. "How's school?" I asked Olivia.

She tilted a shoulder. "It's good. I submit my thesis next year." Someone leaned against the bar, waiting to place their order. "I should go. Drop in again and say hey sometime."

She left and I turned back to Wyatt, pointing at the champagne flutes. "What's this for?"

"You had your first bad date, and we're celebrating." He lifted his glass and when I lifted mine, he clinked it.

"Champagne?" It sparkled on my tongue, and I made a pleased humming noise. "Didn't think you were a champagne drinker."

He shrugged. "You don't like beer."

I winced. "Was it that noticeable?"

"You gagged every time you took a sip."

I shook with laughter. "I'll do better next time."

"Don't bother. Don't drink something you don't like. Order the good stuff next time, Hannah. Order what you like. You deserve it."

He was watching me in an intense way that made my stomach flutter. "There isn't going to be a next time. Look how awkward I was with Carter. I'm terrible at conversation."

"You weren't terrible talking with Olivia."

"That's different. I'm not attracted to Olivia."

"And you *are* attracted to Carter?" His voice was wry.

I rolled my eyes. "Of course not."

He leaned back in his chair, arm resting on the table, easy gaze on me. "Sometimes people don't click, but that doesn't mean you did anything wrong." He shrugged and spread out, taking up all the room. "Just move on."

"Just move on. Like that."

"Mhm. You're going to the gallery with Holden soon?"

I nodded and took another sip. "Saturday. I hope I'm not awkward around him."

"It's impossible for you to out-awkward Holden."

We grinned at each other.

"Hello, Queen's Cove!" Joe, the bar owner and Olivia's dad, crowed into the mic in the corner and cheers rose up around the bar. "Are you ready for some karaoke?" More cheers.

I glanced at Wyatt with excitement, and he grinned back at me.

"First up is our favorite photographer and blogger, Don, singing 'Total Eclipse of the Heart.'"

I remembered a couple days ago when Don shoved the can of beans into my hands, feeling sorry for me, and when

Wyatt's gaze met mine, I knew he was thinking of the same thing. We both burst into laughter.

"He felt so sorry for me," I whispered as Don warbled through the song.

Wyatt shrugged. "It's okay to make an ass of yourself once in a while. Are you still embarrassed about it?"

I took another sip of champagne. The sharp stab of embarrassment had turned into more of an annoying flicker. "A little." I snorted again. "It's more funny now." I glanced at my almost-empty glass. It must have been the champagne making me care less.

Wyatt slid his full glass over to me and took another sip of his beer.

We watched Don finish his karaoke song and cheered for him and all the others who sang. The energy in the bar was so fun, supportive, and silly. Everyone knew each other. It didn't matter if people were bad at singing, everyone got big cheers and applause.

Community, I realized with a sweet, happy hum in my heart. This was my community. I loved this little town.

"What would you sing up there?" Wyatt asked as Olivia brought another glass of champagne for me and a beer for Wyatt.

"Oh, another? I'm going to get silly."

"So get silly." Wyatt's gaze flicked over me. "I'll walk you home." He glanced over to the empty corner with the dart boards.

I snorted. The champagne had loosened the laughs from me. "I can't do worse than Carter." I pictured the beer running down his chin and cringed.

"You're doing great, bookworm." Our eyes met and his gaze warmed me all the way to my toes in my sneakers. "Just great." He tilted his head and narrowed his eyes. "Tell me more about why you want to be a hot girl."

"Who wouldn't want to be?"

He raised an eyebrow, pinning me with his gaze.

I squirmed. My skin prickled like he could see through my clothes. "I'm never going to meet someone hiding in my bookstore."

He considered this but didn't say anything.

"I'm turning thirty in a few months." I played with the stem of my glass, spinning it in a slow circle on the table. "There are a lot of things I haven't done yet." I shrugged, staring at the bubbles in the glass, rising to the surface. "By the time she was thirty, my mom had done so much. She had traveled all over the world, gotten married, had me, started her own business."

He watched me, listening closely, and my mouth snapped shut. He sipped his beer, waiting for me to go on. My face heated.

"I wish you wouldn't do that."

He blanched and laughed. "Do what? Listen while you talk?"

A noise of frustration came out of my throat, but I laughed. "That watching thing you do."

"You don't like it when I watch you?" His tone dripped with innuendo and my face warmed further.

I rolled my eyes. "You know what I'm talking about. You're trying to make me uncomfortable so I'll say more."

He shot me a roguish grin.

"You like to push my boundaries."

His eyes were warm but mischievous. "Mhm." He took another sip of his beer, regarding me over the rim. "You're so locked up, bookworm, but sometimes you let out another person who I think might be the real you." He snorted. "Like when you asked if you needed to teach me to read."

I buried my face in my hands and he laughed. "That was so mean. I'm sorry."

"I liked it."

I lifted my gaze to his and laughter bubbled out of me.

Something occurred to me and I straightened up. "I forgot to tell you." I pulled my phone out. "Your social media is doing so well. A bunch of the other surfers recognized you from events." I showed him the main account pages where I had posted footage from the other morning. On the photo app, there was a shot of him at the food truck, shirtless with the top of his wetsuit hanging from his waist. On the video app, I had posted footage of him gliding through the water.

At least half the comments on every video were about how hot Wyatt was. I had smiled as I read them, but at the same time, something pinched under my ribs.

He glanced at the videos and read through some comments before he set my phone back down on the table. "Thanks for doing that."

"Of course. You're helping me with, um…" I shrugged, suddenly embarrassed to say it out loud. "It's fine. I like doing social media stuff."

"Why don't you do it for the store? You like it and it would be good for business."

"Oh. Um." My mouth twisted to the side and my stomach tightened. My dad had phoned from Salt Spring the other morning and I was *this close* to asking him about social media for the store, but I had chickened out. "You know, it's not really our thing."

Wyatt narrowed his eyes at me.

"I mean," I sucked a breath in and shifted in my seat. "My dad likes to keep the store the way my mom had it."

His eyebrows pulled together and his eyes narrowed further.

One of my shoulders lifted in a shrug and I shook my head. "It's fine."

He was doing that watching thing again. I avoided his gaze and focused on sipping my drink.

"He doesn't want you to make any changes?"

I sighed. It was hard to explain. "He says we have a small-

69

town charm, and anytime I bring up the website or ripping out that ugly carpet, he gets uncomfortable. It was my mom's store and he still misses her." My heart twisted. "I do, too."

Wyatt nodded slowly. "So, say your dad changed his mind and was on board for whatever changes you wanted to make, and you had enough money to make it happen. What would you do?"

I bit my lip, a smile growing on my face. "First, I'd get rid of that ugly maroon carpet. I hate that fucking carpet."

Wyatt burst out laughing. "Whoa, bookworm, language."

I laughed with him. "Sorry. It's like something out of a prison or a high school. I'd paint the inside a lighter color to brighten the place up, and add a pretty wallpaper. Something floral." I leaned in, gaze locked with Wyatt. "Something bold, frivolous, fun, and wild. I'd have a ton of plants inside if I could get them to grow. I'd take photos every day around the store and post them to social media so people around the world could picture themselves there." I tilted my head, thinking. "We could have a cool chair near the window that people could sit in and take pictures in. We'd have to get a better website so people could place orders online."

I remembered something I had seen online. "Oh, and the lighting. I'd get new lighting, something pretty, some antique chandeliers or something fluffy and silly."

"Fluffy lighting," Wyatt repeated with a grin.

"You heard me. Fluffy. Books are all about fantasy, getting immersed in a story and characters. People read as an escape, and I want stepping into the store to be like that, too. Plus," I shrugged, playing with the end of my ponytail, "why fit in? Why not do something memorable and cool?"

His gaze traveled over my face and he nodded.

"I think if we had *endless* funds, I'd have the mural repainted. Right now it's faded and crumbling, and it could be spectacular. And the books on the mural?" My nose wrinkled. "They're outdated. Sure, some of them are classics, but those books leave out a lot of people." I chewed my lip, thinking about Liya, Max, and Div.

He nodded. "They're for straight white people."

"Exactly. And I know my mom didn't mean to leave anyone out, but I know better. I sell lots of books for lots of people. I don't want anyone to feel excluded." A memory passed through my mind and I smiled. "My mom used to say, there's a story for every soul." I leaned my chin on my palm. Something happy fizzed in my chest, talking Wyatt's ear off like this about silly dreams. "I believe it. I believe the right book is out there for everyone. I love that part of my job."

He sipped his beer and watched me with a warm gaze. "Updating the mural is a great idea."

I clasped my hands together. "I don't know. My dad would never go for it. All my ideas are kind of out there."

He raised an amused eyebrow. "Even more out there than feathery lighting?"

My chest shook with laughter. "I said *fluffy* lighting. And yes, even more out there than that." I hesitated. "I'd make the store into a romance-only bookstore."

I waited for him to tell me this was a terrible idea, but he only crossed his arms over his chest and tilted his head at me. "Because you like romance books?"

I shook my head, sucking in a breath and gathering my thoughts. "It's more than that. Yes, I love romance books, but so do so many others. Romance is the number-one selling genre. Every year, romance sells *double* the next highest genre, crime and thriller. Most bookstores have a couple shelves dedicated to romance, and you're lucky if the staff read romance and can recommend books. People buy a lot of romance online because they either can't get the books in stores, or they're embarrassed."

I leaned forward. "One time, Avery and I were in Victoria, and I went into a bookstore to see if they had a certain romance book, and the guy *laughed* at me."

Wyatt's eyebrows shot up in surprise.

My nostrils flared and I swallowed. My stomach boiled at the memory. "He laughed at me, Wyatt, for wanting to read a book with a happy ending." My eyes narrowed. "That guy was a dick." I shrugged. "I want to create a space where people aren't embarrassed to read books that make them happy. No women are killed in romance books the way they always seem to be in crime novels." The champagne fizzed on my tongue again as I sipped it. "There are tons of regular bookstores on the island where people can buy other genres, not to mention overnight delivery services. If it were up to me, I'd create something special, unlike any other store around here. Besides, my store is kind of small. It would be so easy to fill it up with romance. I can always special-order other books for people who want them and don't want to go to Port Alberni." That was a larger town on the island that had a big bookstore.

I tipped the remainder of my drink back and realized that Wyatt and most of the people sitting near us watched me, listening. I froze and my face flushed.

"And that's enough from me," I said with a laugh. I cleared my throat. "That's what I'd do with the store if I could."

Wyatt rubbed his jaw. "You've thought a lot about it."

A long sigh escaped me. "Well, the store has been kind of struggling, and my mind wanders sometimes."

"Do you agree that your mom would want you to keep the store the same as she had it?"

My stomach clenched. My mom was like the store I wanted to create—bold, fun, silly, and wild.

"No," I whispered. My throat was tight. "She'd love my ideas." I lifted my gaze to his.

Wyatt shrugged and rubbed his thumb up and down the condensation on his beer. "Look, bookworm, for what it's worth, if the store isn't doing well, you need to change something."

I wanted to, but in order to do that, I had to go against what my dad wanted. Panic and guilt clawed at me, so I changed the subject. "Are you nervous about Pacific Rim?"

He wrinkled his nose and shook his head. "I'm not really thinking about it."

"Why not?"

He sighed and hesitated, like he was organizing the thoughts in his head. "It won't change anything, worrying about it. I'll still go surfing every day. I'll still give my A-game out there." That lazy smile hitched. "You've got my sponsorship covered with social media." He tilted his chin to my phone and I smiled in return.

"Say you did well, what would happen then?"

"I'd get a sponsorship and start traveling more. There are surf events all over the world, in Australia, Indonesia, Hawaii…" A crease formed between his eyebrows and he lost that lazy, amused smile. "I'd have to leave Queen's Cove."

"You'd miss it."

The corner of his mouth hitched, but the smile didn't reach his eyes. He'd miss it but he didn't want to admit it. "No point in discussing what hasn't happened yet."

"Well, if you left Queen's Cove, the town would miss you," I told him.

He sat forward and pulled his phone out of his pocket. The screen lit up with an incoming call. *Josie.*

My stomach sank and I frowned. Of course Wyatt had girls calling him.

"You can answer that if you want," I told him. My voice sounded tight.

He declined the call and slipped his phone back in his pocket. "Not important." He gestured to the stage. "What would you sing?"

"Spice Girls." I answered before I even thought about it. I put both hands flat on the table and leaned forward. "I *love* Spice Girls, Wyatt. You have no idea."

He leaned on his elbows towards me, our gazes locked. "Which Spice Girl are you?"

"I mean, I look like Baby Spice." I pointed at my pale hair. "But I think deep down, I want to be Ginger. I mean," I rolled my eyes. "Everybody wants to be Ginger. You could never find the Ginger Spice Barbie. She was the coolest, the bravest, and she didn't care what people thought. She was so badass." I sighed.

He listened with a smile on his face, like I was talking about the most interesting thing in the world.

"She wore this one dress, it was a Union Jack and it was so short that her black underwear was visible." I said the last words in a whisper, holding eye contact with him. I shook my head. "I was just a kid but I couldn't believe it. It was the sexiest thing I'd ever seen at the time."

The gold sequinned dress popped into my head. I had slipped the box under my bed and it had sat there untouched for a couple weeks.

Wyatt's eyes were bright, like he wanted to burst out laughing.

"You can laugh," I told him. "It's okay. I can take it."

His grin reached from ear to ear. "I won't laugh at you. *Now* what's the sexiest thing you've ever seen?"

"Huh?"

"You said at the time. That was twenty years ago. What's the sexiest thing you've ever seen now?"

"Um." My tongue twisted. All I could picture was Wyatt on the surfboard a couple days ago, and then walking on the sand toward me, shaking the water out of his hair. Water running down his bare skin. Lean muscle with a dusting of hair across his chest. I swallowed. "Um. I don't know. Oh!" A laugh burst out of my mouth. "I saw some merman in a Eurovision music video a couple weeks ago. That was pretty sexy."

That made him laugh. Nice save on my part. "That would

be my karaoke song, only because I heard it so many times on set that day. I dreamed the lyrics for a week."

I laughed and tipped back the rest of my drink before inspecting the empty glass.

"I forgot how much I like champagne."

"You look cute tonight," Wyatt said, and my mouth parted in surprise.

When I stood in front of my closet earlier tonight, I forced myself to pick an outfit that a hot girl would wear. I wore a light pink top that had hung in my closet for two years. It had tiny bees embroidered on it, barely visible except up close. I bought it on a whim a couple years ago, but it was too dressy to wear to the store. Although I wanted to wear my typical jeans tonight, I forced myself to wear a tan suede skirt.

I still wore my sneakers, though. Something stubborn in me wouldn't let them go.

"Oh." I blinked about six times in a row. "Thanks."

"Mhm." He nodded and kept watching me with that half-amused, half-thoughtful expression.

We watched the rest of the karaoke night without talking, just cheering and laughing and enjoying the music and vibrancy of our little community pub, but I held his attention the entire time. Little shivers ran down my neck every time our eyes met.

Later that night, as I brushed my teeth, I replayed the evening. Why didn't Avery and I go out to the bar more often? Even though the date with Carter had been awkward, the rest of the evening was so fun. Wyatt was so easy to talk to, I didn't know why I had been so shy around him for so long.

I mean, I guess I knew a little. *You look cute tonight.* I kept hearing it in my head, and each time I did, my stomach fluttered and I bit my lip. I gave myself a shy grin in the mirror.

He probably said that to all the women in his life. He probably said that to his mom, to Avery. To women he felt platonic towards. Or worse. Maybe he felt bad for me and wanted to give me a confidence boost. I winced. I really, really hoped he didn't feel bad for me.

I'd have to do a better job on my date with Holden on Saturday. I was going to show Wyatt that I could do this.

The conversation with Wyatt about the bookstore popped back into my head, how I rambled on about all the changes I would make, and the fluttery warmth in my stomach as I pictured what the store would look like. What it could be.

Before my guilt could get in the way, I opened a social media account for the store and posted a picture I had taken of Liya the other day surrounded by a new shipment of books.

My dad didn't want the store to change, but my dad also wasn't involved in the store and had no idea how bad the finances had gotten.

I had a business to run, and we couldn't keep my mom's memory alive if the store went under.

7

Hannah

THE CUPCAKES GLOWED behind the glass and I tapped my chin as I stared at them. "I should get a few of those as well."

Veena grinned and placed them into the box with all the other baked goods I couldn't say no to.

I straightened up. "And four pop tarts, please."

Veena's was a tiny bakery in town, named after the owner and head baker. She was a petite woman in her forties with very shiny black hair and bright eyes. I often stopped in at lunch to pick up some treats for Liya and myself, and always enjoyed my chats with the friendly Veena.

"How many people are you watching *The Bachelor* with?"

"Just four of us."

She laughed. "You have enough for a hockey team here."

"It's your baking. It's like crack."

"You say the sweetest things. I should put that on the window." She sealed the box up and cleared her throat. "How's your dad?"

"He's good. He's house sitting for his brother over on Salt Spring for a couple months."

She nodded, turning her back to me to place the box in a

carrying bag. "Right. He mentioned that. He has a farm, right?"

"Yep. Does my dad come in a lot?" My dad didn't like sweets.

When she turned, her smile strained. "Sometimes."

"Next time, you should remind him that I like cupcakes and that he should bring me some at the store."

The warmth returned to her eyes. "I'll do that."

I left the bakery with the treats and walked over to Div's apartment.

Max opened the door when I knocked, and I held out the bag. "Treats."

His eye lit up. "We like you. You're forever welcome on *Bachelor* night." He stepped back and gestured for me to come in.

"Is that Hannah?" Div called from the kitchen.

I slipped my shoes off and placed them in the closet. "Yes."

"Does she want a glass of wine?"

"She does," I replied, following Max into a pristinely clean kitchen.

Avery sat at the counter, pouring red wine into four glasses, while Div arranged gummy bears on a plate. He caught sight of the bakery bag and gave me a flat look.

"Veena's?"

"Where else?"

He approached the bag like there was a wild animal inside and peeked in before closing his eyes and inhaling. The moan he let out made all of us uncomfortable.

"Div, are you okay?" Avery asked, laughing.

Div frowned at the bag like he didn't trust it. "Hannah, why are you tempting me like this? Do you hate me?"

My mouth fell open. "Of course I don't hate you. Everyone should experience Veena's cupcakes." I nudged the bag closer to him. "Taste one."

He patted his stomach. "I like having abs."

"Oh my god." Max shook his head. "No one needs to hear about your abs anymore. We get it."

We collected plates, glasses, and the bag, and moved into the living room.

"Why don't you start surfing?" I asked Div, placing my glass on a coaster on the coffee table. There wasn't an object out of place in Div's living room and I didn't dare get rings on the table. "Wyatt eats whatever he wants and you could shred cheese on his abs."

Avery clapped, delighted. "Well, since you brought it up—"

"You shouldn't have brought it up," Div sang.

Avery settled next to me on the floor, staring hard at me with a huge grin. "Hannah."

I cut a glance between the three of them. "I feel like I'm being set up."

Max put his hands up. "I'm just here to make fun of people on TV."

Avery rested her chin on her palm, watching me with bright eyes. "What's going on with you and Wyatt?"

I made a face. "Nothing."

"You're hanging out." She narrowed her eyes. "A lot. He doesn't really do that."

"Hang out with people?"

She nodded. "He surfs. That's it. Sometimes he goes for a drink with Emmett or Holden, or Finn if he's in town, or a friend, but mostly he just surfs."

Max raised an eyebrow. "Yeah, and what was the deal with you asking people out while he supervised?"

"*What*???" Avery's pitch was so high, it could have cracked the TV screen.

I did my best to skewer Max with my eyes. He fought a grin, staring at the TV. "I thought you were just here to watch TV."

"I'm shutting up now." He stuffed half a cupcake in his mouth.

Avery stuck her face very close to mine and I started laughing. Her eyes bored into mine. "Tell. Me. Everything."

I shrugged and wiggled away from her. "It's nothing. Wyatt's teaching me to surf."

Avery narrowed her eyes. "By making you ask guys out?"

My face was hot and I was blushing again.

Div cleared his throat. "There was a blog post."

Avery and I whipped our heads at him in unison. "What?"

Div handed his phone to us. We read the title of the post on the Queen's Cove Daily blog. My stomach dropped through the floor and Avery fell back, laughing. I took the phone and read with an expression of total fucking mortification.

"*Are millennials desperate?*" I read. "*Hannah Nielsen of Pemberley Books aggressively pursued all men in the vicinity on Thursday.*"

Avery wiped tears from her eyes as her chest shook. Max covered his mouth with his hand, chest also shaking. Div winced.

"Don wrote about this on the blog? This is so embarrassing!"

"Hannah." Avery stopped laughing so hard and sat up. "What were you doing?"

"Wyatt is teaching me how to be a hot girl."

"What?" The three of them repeated it in unison, staring at me like I'd grown another head.

Div studied me. "I can see it."

"Hot girl?" Avery reared back. "What?"

I sighed. "I'm turning thirty in one month and three weeks and I'm sick of being boring little Hannah who's shy and scared of everything." *And I want to find true love*, I didn't say.

Avery blinked in surprise. "Hannah." Her tone was soft.

"I didn't say anything to you because I know what you're

going to say. You're going to tell me to be myself or some crap like that."

"That's exactly what I would say. You're already a hot girl."

I gave her a flat look.

"What? You are!"

"Div." I knew he'd tell me the truth.

He glanced up from his phone. "You should cut your hair. Something shoulder-length and choppy. And stop wearing sweaters two sizes too big."

Avery threw a gummy bear at him and it fell down his shirt. She turned back to me. "Hannah. You're gorgeous and funny and smart and—"

"I know, I know." I shrugged. "I just want to try something different."

Avery rolled her lips. I knew what she was thinking, but she'd never say it. She was wondering what a guy like Wyatt was doing hanging out with a girl like me.

"I'm doing his social media stuff," I explained. "He's trying to get a sponsorship. See?" I stood to retrieve my phone from my bag by the door, and by the time I returned to the living room, I had pulled up Wyatt's page.

Div's gaze skimmed over the stats on my page. "Wow. You did this?"

I nodded with a smile. "Yeah. I started last week."

"Last *week*?" Max's eyes bulged and he grabbed the phone from Div. "You have a lot of content already and your account is doing great. This video has two million views."

It was the video of Wyatt walking out of the sparkling water the other morning with his board tucked under his arm, shaking his hair out. He'd probably hate that this video existed, but it had catapulted his social media to a new level.

Avery watched the video over Max's shoulder before giving me a funny smile. "Hannah. This is amazing."

I shrugged but a smile broke through on my face. "It's nothing."

"It's not nothing." She shook her head, watching me and thinking. "It's cool. Not a lot of people could do this."

"Thérèse commented," Max said, showing me the phone.

theresebeauchampofficial: *mon dieu, the man should be on billboards*

The comment had ten thousand likes and several hundred comments in a thread below it. My heart squeezed and I grinned big at my phone.

Max unwrapped his second cupcake. "Who else did you ask out?"

My gaze snapped from my phone up to him. "Hmm? Oh. Let's see. You two, Don," I counted, starting to laugh at the memory of Don's pitying expression. "A couple tourists, Holden, Carter, and Beck."

"Carter?" Avery winced. "Oh no."

"We went to the bar last night." I took a bite of one of Veena's pop tarts. "He did a beer bong and got kicked out."

Div cringed. "Good god."

"Holden's a babe," Max added.

Avery made a face. "He's my brother-in-law, dude."

He shrugged. "I don't care. He's hot."

I reached for my water on the coffee table. "Holden's nice, but I'm not into him. He's a practice date."

"Okay, but Beck?" Avery raised an eyebrow. "Beck is cute. Paging Dr. Gorgeous, am I right?"

Max nodded and fake coughed. "Doctor, I think I'm sick."

A giggle ripped out of me, and Avery snorted. This was fun, even if we were covering all the topics I didn't want to talk about tonight. I spent a bit of time with Max and Div leading up to Avery's wedding last year, but we had never all hung out like this. Maybe I'd have them over next time, now that I had the house to myself for the rest of the summer.

"Beck is cute," I agreed, but when I thought about asking

him out, Wyatt's face popped into my head, sitting across the table at the bar last night. Any time I glanced at him during karaoke, he was watching me with a little smile. Even the memory sent zings through my chest.

If only all my dates could be as fun as hanging out at the bar with Wyatt.

Max turned up the volume. "Everyone shut up right now, it's starting."

8

Wyatt

"IT'S a beautiful day to ride some waves, bookworm."

"I wouldn't know anything about that. I'll probably swallow a bunch of saltwater today, though."

I leaned against the railing behind the surf shop as she approached, pretty hair swinging in a ponytail and eyes bright. She looked different today. I narrowed my eyes at her.

"I'm wearing contacts," she explained off my expression. "I'm sick of not being able to see anything out there."

My eyebrows quirked. "Uh oh."

"What?"

"You're catching it."

"Catching what?" She frowned.

"You're starting to like surfing." I wiggled my eyebrows at her.

"I haven't even surfed yet." She laughed and pulled her shirt over her head.

My cock reacted immediately.

It shouldn't have. I didn't know why today was different. I saw Hannah in her swimsuit all the time. She was changing into her wetsuit like we had done a few times already. It wasn't a big deal.

Today, her swimsuit was a two-piece meant for swimming laps at the pool. Functional. No bells and whistles, no strings holding it together.

But today, something about the slight swell of cleavage over the neckline caught my attention. And the way she whipped her shirt off, I pictured her doing that in my bedroom.

She unzipped her denim shorts and tossed them over the railing.

Her ass. It was so cute. Two handfuls. Slappable. I stiffened further in my wetsuit.

Jesus Christ, Rhodes.

I turned around and stared into the forest behind the surf shop, eyes wide open and seeing nothing. It wasn't like that with Hannah. I wasn't her type. She wanted someone charming, polished, and stable. Hannah was a true love type of girl, not… whatever I could offer. She wanted forever, and I was all about temporary.

She wanted someone like Beck.

Irritation prickled on the back of my neck.

"Wyatt?"

I snapped to attention. She was right beside me. "Hmm?"

"Can you zip me up?" She offered me her back.

Even in the wetsuit, her ass was so cute. This must be what people were talking about when they referenced intrusive thoughts. I shoved them out of my head and zipped up her wetsuit before we grabbed our boards and headed to the water without another word.

She yelped when the cold water hit her feet.

"Oh, shit, I forgot the booties." I set my board down on the sand. "I'll go grab them."

She shook her head and put a hand on my arm to stop me. "I'm going to try without them today. Is that okay?"

"Of course." Her feet were going to get cold, though. "Tell me when you're ready to go in."

She nodded and smiled at me before wading into the water.

We paddled out into the white-water area, where Hannah had been learning.

I glanced over at her, paddling beside me. "You're getting stronger."

She shot me a pleased smile. The sun's reflection off the water lit up her skin and danced across her face. She moved through the water with more ease and confidence than before. Something warm and proud hit me in the middle of the chest.

We paddled to a spot behind the break and positioned our boards to face the shore. Hannah watched a wave approach, and without needing encouragement from me, she began paddling to catch it.

I sprawled across my board, watching her arms dip in and out of the water. It rose and fell around me as the wave passed me but my gaze stayed on her. The wave approached her, and I had the urge to call over to her when to jump up on her board. I held back though, pressing my hand to my mouth, watching and grinning against my fist.

At the perfect second, she flattened her hands on the board and snapped up—

The board slipped from under her and she fell face first into the water.

Damn it.

I smiled big at her when she paddled back.

"Wipeout," she called over to me, water dripping off her ponytail.

"You got up at the exact right time." I winked at her and she nodded. Another small wave approached and I gestured at it. "Okay, bookworm, get back on the horse."

She took a deep breath, nodded, and her tenacity made me smile. This was the third time we had been out on the water, and she still hadn't gotten up on the board to ride a wave. Most people would have given up by now.

Not her, though.

I had been thinking more and more about our deal, how Hannah wanted to be a 'hot girl'. How she had compared herself to her mom.

I'm never going to meet someone hiding in my bookstore, she had said the other night at the bar. And now here she was, bright and early in the morning, perched on her board, watching over her shoulder for approaching waves.

Huh. She must really want to find someone.

Something weird twisted in my stomach but I focused on Hannah paddling as the wave rolled past me and caught up with her.

"Come on," I muttered to myself, leaning on my board, gaze glued to her.

She glanced over her shoulder, saw the wave, paddled harder, and as the water rose under her, she hopped up.

"You got it, bookworm, stay up." I bit my fist as if I was watching a hockey game in shootout. My heart beat in my ears.

She wobbled once, twice, but caught her balance, hands out, knees bent, board skimming the surface as the wave carried her forward. My heart was in my throat.

She turned her head to shoot me a wide, elated grin and I beamed back at her.

"Yeah, Hannah!" I called over. "You're doing it."

She lost her balance, bailed off her board, and a laugh burst out of my chest. That big grin stretched over her face, even as she paddled back to me.

"You did it, bookworm."

"I did it." The clear sunlight made her eyes brighter.

Something warm and tight expanded in my chest, seeing her with her hair soaking wet, the sun on her face, and the biggest, proudest smile.

"You want to go again?"

She nodded eagerly.

Again and again, she paddled hard as the waves approached. She bailed a few more times but caught three more waves. She was getting the hang of it. I watched the whole time, hanging out on my board and enjoying the morning sun on my back.

Half an hour later, her arms moved slower in the water and her jumps up on the board didn't have the same snap as before.

"Bookworm, I do believe you've earned your moment of solace in nature this morning." I jerked my chin in the direction of the quiet cove. "Let's go chill out for a bit."

She nodded and we paddled out of the surf to where the water was calm.

"Hand me your leash, would you?" I held my hand out and she undid the velcro around her ankle before tossing it to me. I fastened it around my ankle. Now she wouldn't float away from me. "How are your feet?"

She hoisted herself up on her board and wobbled into a seated position, cross-legged, before wiggling her toes. "Pretty cold but they'll warm up out of the water." She closed her eyes and tilted her face up to the sun. She sighed. My throat felt tight.

She opened her eyes, taking in the blue sky dotted with wisps of clouds, the forest beside us, the seagulls gliding through the air. "It's nice here."

We floated there for a few minutes, listening to the sound of the waves lapping the shore and the seagulls calling out to each other. The thought of leaving this place one day if I went pro broke my heart.

Going pro had been all I wanted since that summer I stayed with my aunts when I was sixteen. Aunt Rebecca had been diagnosed with early onset Alzheimer's, and her wife, my Aunt Bea, struggled to take care of her alone, so I moved in to help out with things. In the mornings, I surfed, and in the afternoons, I picked up groceries, cleaned the kitchen, took the garbage out, or mowed the lawn. I had surfed since I was a kid but that summer, it became everything to me.

I couldn't stay in Queen's Cove *and* go pro. I wanted to compete, and I wanted to win.

Last night, I watched footage of my competitors, surfers who had been competing since they were kids. They were used to the pressure. They were used to everyone knowing their name.

"What's wrong?" Her hands rested flat behind her, holding her up.

I shook my head. "Nothing."

"You don't have your usual stoned surfer look today."

That made me smile. "I'm never stoned while surfing."

"You know what I mean."

I inhaled a long breath and let it out. "You know when we were at the bar and I said I wasn't worrying about Pacific Rim?"

She nodded.

I didn't answer. The words were stuck in my throat.

"You've been worrying?"

I gave her a quick nod. "Not so chill, huh?"

She tilted her head and gave me a soft smile. "You don't have to be 'so chill' all the time. You're human, Wyatt." She regarded me, thinking. "What do you worry about?"

"That I'll get out there and choke." Again. "That I'll do well, place in the competition, and have to leave Queen's Cove."

She gazed out across the water. "Damned if you do and damned if you don't."

I huffed a laugh. "Yeah. Something like that."

Ripples radiated from her fingertips as she skimmed them through the water. She pulled her lip into her mouth between her teeth. "Can't you come back to Queen's Cove in between competitions?"

"Sure, but it won't be the same."

"No. It won't." Her gaze flicked up to me. "What do you think about out there when you're surfing?"

"Nothing. My mind goes blank. My body knows what to do, my instincts tell me when to paddle and hop up and when to stay put."

"Why do you think you'll choke?"

Because it happened before. At last year's competition, I panicked.

I cleared my throat. "I have a good life. I surf, I have the shop, and I love living here. I shouldn't mess with a good thing."

The summer with my aunts taught me everything was temporary—relationships, jobs, even love. The idea of going pro and surfing around the world was both electrifying and terrifying.

Once I had it, I could lose it.

My chest was tight with anxiety, so I cleared my throat again. "What about you, bookworm, would you ever leave Queen's Cove?"

She chewed her lip before answering. "I can't leave. I have the store." She let out a long sigh and stared up at the sky. "I'd love to travel, though. I've never been anywhere except to university in Victoria. I read about all these places in books and it's like I'm there but…" Her mouth twisted in a rueful smile. "It's not real. I want to go there for real."

"Could your dad run the store for a bit? Or Liya?"

She shifted her weight on the board, wobbling but maintaining balance. "Um. I guess. I don't know, it's a lot of responsibility and I don't think Liya wants that. And my dad hasn't worked at the store in a while so he doesn't know where anything is." She lifted a shoulder in a half-shrug. "I'd have to close the store for a couple weeks and then the customers would be all grouchy because they couldn't get their books."

I pinned her with my gaze. "Have you talked to Liya about running the shop when you're away?"

She shifted again. "No, but she's busy and I don't want to make her uncomfortable by asking too much of her."

"So you're trapped."

She sat up and shook her head. "I love the store. I wish—" Her throat worked and she frowned. "My dad's stuck."

The guy had been handed a rough deal, losing his wife like that. But it wasn't fair to Hannah to have to run the business like a monument to her mother. Hannah was in charge now. She had all these incredible ideas to change the store and they sat idle in her head.

"What was your mom like?"

A smile grew on her face. "She loved books."

"Runs in the family."

Her smile lifted all the way up to her eyes. "She had a degree in English lit, like me. She loved it when people found a book they couldn't put down and came back to tell her about it. She was always recommending books to people." Hannah stretched one leg out on the board and wiggled her toes. "People came to the bookstore for her, to chat with her or to say hi. Her enthusiasm was contagious."

I listened, not wanting to interrupt or give her a reason to stop talking, like at the bar when she told me about how she'd change the store if she could.

"What's your role in the store?"

"My dad still owns it and there's kind of an unspoken understanding that I'll inherit it one day. We don't talk about that stuff."

She was running the business single-handedly and it would probably be hers one day, but she had no say. That didn't sit right with me, but I pressed my mouth tight and kept it to myself.

"That's another thing I want to do before I turn thirty." She rolled her lips. "I want to make the business profitable again." She winced at me. "We haven't been doing great lately."

I frowned. Queen's Cove housed about two thousand residents but saw over a million tourists each summer. The summer months were when locals made money. If the store wasn't doing well in July, it didn't stand a chance through the winter.

But I thought about Hannah on her surfboard, bailing over and over again but not giving up. A smile lifted on my mouth. "You can turn it around."

She shot me a shy smile. "I hope so." She relaxed down onto her board again and closed her eyes. "Where's the first place you'd go if you got a sponsorship?"

I lay down on my own board and stared up at the sky. "Australia. There's a big surf competition there in January." I turned my head to face her. "You'd like it there. They have books and champagne."

I didn't know why I said that.

She smiled and opened her eyes, shooting me a skeptical expression. "They have sharks, too."

"We have sharks."

She snorted. "Shut up, please. I was doing a good job of not thinking about what's under the surface today."

A thought struck me. "Bookworm, when was the last vacation you took?"

She frowned, playing with the end of her ponytail, inspecting the ends of her hair. "I took a few days off at Christmas."

"And before that?"

She made a thinking noise. "The Christmas before that."

I blew a breath out. "Bookworm."

Her head snapped up and she looked like she was about to say something but instead, she reached over, grabbed my ankle, and flipped me into the water. In her attempt, she slipped off her own board. A surprised laugh burst out of me the second before my head submerged.

When I resurfaced, she wore a small, mischievous smile,

treading water a few feet away. "My feet are cold. Let's get breakfast."

Alright, so we were dropping the conversation about her taking a break from the shop. I suspected it wasn't just her dad who didn't want to change things in the store, but I'd leave it for today. I undid the leash, fastened it around her ankle, and ignored how smooth her skin was under mine. How delicate her ankle was. My fingers fit all the way around it.

"Thanks," she murmured, and I nodded at her before we paddled in.

When we approached the shop, we set our boards down and I unzipped her wetsuit, turning before I could see her peel it off.

"Say goodbye to this board." I listened to the sound of her pulling her wetsuit off and studied the siding on the shop.

"Why?"

"You've leveled up."

I turned to see her proud smile and I matched it. My gaze dropped to her swimsuit. The swell of her tits. The smooth skin of her stomach, and the flare of her hips. I pictured running my tongue up her stomach. My cock twitched again, and I blinked, turning away.

The door opened. "I'm going to change inside, be right back."

"Yep." My voice was tight.

What was *happening*?

Oh. It was because I hadn't hooked up with anyone recently. I usually surfed in the mornings but because I spent most mornings with Hannah, I surfed a bit later now, then spent the day at the shop, and then surfed until sunset to prepare for Pacific Rim. I didn't have time to see people these days.

I hadn't been thinking about it much, either. A few women had reached out, but I wasn't into it anymore.

It wasn't a big deal. It didn't mean anything. I wasn't her type and she was probably a virgin.

Shit. Was bookworm a virgin? The whole virginity thing was bullshit and it didn't matter, but I was still curious. Hannah was cute. Our date yesterday was her first.

Her date. Not our date. That wasn't a date.

Panic streaked through me.

If she didn't have any sexual experience, then she didn't have any standards.

The thought of someone messing up with Hannah made my skin too tight. A rock formed in my throat and I swallowed. Carter was off the table. There was no way Hannah would let him anywhere near her naked.

Holden wasn't interested in Hannah, I was pretty sure. I frowned. I'd talk to him later about that, make sure he knew that it was a practice date. It could be a practice date for both of them.

But Beck. A noise came out of my throat, frustration and disapproval. Beck would be all over Hannah. What if he went too fast? What if he pushed her and she didn't want to? What if he was selfish?

My fists clenched when I thought about him touching her, his hands on her waist or in her hair. I pictured them tangled together in bed and my jaw tensed.

Wrong. That was all wrong.

The back door of the surf shop opened and she walked out in her denim shorts and striped t-shirt. "I brought something for you." She blanched at the look on my face. "Jeez, somebody's getting hangry."

I cleared my throat and pushed the thoughts from my head. "Yeah. What did you bring?"

"This is my way of saying thanks for helping me." She pulled something out of her bag and handed it to me. It was a plastic inflatable book for babies, the kind they read in the bathtub, with words like CAT and DOG and BALL on it.

I raised a skeptical eyebrow at her and she shook with laughter.

"It's so you can read out on the water in the mornings." The giggles bubbled out of her and all the weird tension in me melted away.

"You're such a brat." I tugged on the end of her ponytail and grinned.

She returned my grin. "I know."

We smiled at each other for a moment. I had the urge to tell her I was reading *Pride and Prejudice*. The boring, weird cousin, Mr. Collins, had just visited their home. I had read late into the night, laughing to myself as Lizzy maneuvered the awkward conversation with him. For some reason, I held back from telling this to Hannah. I wanted to see how the story ended first.

"Come on," I said, tilting my head. "Let's get food."

On the walk to the food truck, I thought of something. "You've got more homework, bookworm."

Her eyebrows rose and her eyes brightened. "What is it?"

"Round up twenty of your favorite books."

She paused. "That's it? I don't need to run naked down Main Street or something?"

I laughed. "What? I would never make you do that."

Her shoulder lifted in a shrug and she shot me another smile as we approached the truck. "You're trying to push me past my comfort zone."

The idea of other people, people like Beck, seeing Hannah naked was past *my* comfort zone.

I had something else in mind.

She narrowed her eyes but her mouth twitched upwards. "What are you up to?"

I tugged on the end of her ponytail again. "You'll see."

9

Hannah

"GOOD MORNING, LIYA." His low voice made my ears perk up as I searched for a book at the back of the store. "Cool earrings."

"Good morning," Liya chirped back. Her earrings were two tiny copies of her favorite books—*The Hate U Give* by Angie Thomas and *Indigo* by Beverly Jenkins. She'd had a bunch made on Etsy and mixed and matched sometimes. She gasped in delight. "For us?"

"For you," Wyatt confirmed.

I poked my head around the corner. He held a tray of coffees and a white box with a familiar stamp on it. Beside him, the front desk was piled high with books.

I was struggling to narrow my favorites down to twenty. Last I counted, we were at nearly fifty.

My mouth fell open at the sight of the box. "Is that from the bakery?"

He winked at me, and my stomach flipped.

I took the box from him, set it on the counter, and opened it. Two perfect cinnamon buns were inside. I inhaled deeply before groaning with my eyes closed. When I opened my eyes, he was watching me with a little smile.

"Hi."

"Hi." His gaze skimmed over my face and my stomach flipped again.

Liya stuck her face in the bag and inhaled. "Oh my god. I haven't had one since April. The tourists snap them up so fast."

"Thank you," I told Wyatt.

He shrugged but his mouth slid into a satisfied grin. "No problem. You're going to need snacks. We're going on an adventure."

I hesitated. "What do you mean?"

Instead of elaborating, he pointed at the piles on the desk. "Bookworm, are these the books you've picked out?"

I nodded, wincing. "I'm sorry, I couldn't narrow it down."

He waved me off. "No problem. Liya, do you have yours?"

"Yep, got them." She pulled a small stack from a nearby shelf.

Now I was intrigued. What was he up to?

He handed me the coffee and cinnamon buns and picked up a stack of books. "Let's go." He proceeded to walk out the front door.

"What? Wyatt? Where are you going?" I called after him, staring as Liya gave an excited squeal and followed.

Outside on the street, the weekly farmer's market was in full swing. On Saturdays, the main street of Queen's Cove was open to foot traffic only, and local vendors lined the road with tables. The pizza place, Mateo's, was setting up for the lunch rush, the produce vendors had been open since I arrived at work, even the hairstylist had set up a chair for people who wanted a quick trim.

Wyatt led us to an empty booth and set down a stack of books. He gestured at me. "Hand me your phone."

"Why?" My stomach dropped. "Oh god. Am I going on Tinder? I've heard it's only for hookups now, and I'm not sure I'm ready for that."

He snorted. "No, we're not setting you up on Tinder." He pulled a tiny white square out of his pocket. "You're going to sell books." He plugged in the square and installed an app before handing it back to me to input the store's banking info.

My thumb hovered over the screen and I hesitated. My dad wouldn't like this. A phone with a credit card reader didn't have that small-town charm, he'd insist. This was different. This was new. A twinge of guilt hit me in the stomach.

I glanced at Wyatt, watching me carefully, waiting.

My dad wasn't here, though, was he? I was the one running the store every day. I was the one trying to keep the bookstore afloat. There were tons of people out today on the street, shopping and wandering around the town. We might even make a few sales.

I had to keep the store afloat, and what my dad didn't know for today wouldn't hurt him. I tapped in the store's banking info, and bang. We were set up for credit card payments.

Wyatt and Liya retrieved the rest of the books while customers milled around the table. Liya had brought out a small shelf that sat on top to display our favorites. We even brought the little *Staff Picks!* sign.

A woman with a straw hat picked up a copy of *So You Want to Talk About Race* by Ijeoma Oluo and read the back cover while her friend browsed the titles on the table.

"I loved that book," I told her. "She blends data with personal stories about race in America, and it's eye-opening. Her writing is beautiful."

She nodded and pulled her wallet out of her tote bag. "I'll take it."

Wyatt watched with a little smile on his face as I figured out how to use the square on my phone with her credit card.

The woman pulled out her phone. "Do you have social media?"

"We do." I rattled off our social media handles. "We're over there." I pointed over my shoulder at the bookstore.

"Found you," she said, lighting up. "Gorgeous photos. I'm so glad I found you."

"Oh." My face warmed but I grinned at her. "Me too."

"Do you have anything like *The Vampire Diaries*?" Straw Hat Woman's friend asked.

"Here," Wyatt said, taking the phone from me. "I'll do that. You do the books, bookworm."

I found the title I was searching for and handed it to the woman. "Hot vampires, a Southern waitress, a dangerous vampire king, and an unsolved murder. It's a long series so you can keep reading if you enjoy." I shrugged. "The books are better than the TV show."

While Liya was in an animated conversation with someone about a sci-fi romance series about blue aliens, I snapped a picture and posted it. I had caught Liya as she angled the book cover to the camera.

Pemberley Books is at the Queen's Cove farmer's market today. Come talk about books with us!

For the next hour, Liya and I helped customers find what they were searching for and Wyatt processed the sales.

"Do you have anything like *Bridgerton*?" a woman in her early twenties asked.

My eyes lit up. "Yes." I grabbed a historical romance off the table and thrust it into her hands.

A dad in cargo shorts and a baseball hat led his teenager up to the stand. "My kid is non-binary. Do you have any YA books with non-binary main characters?"

"Or trans," his teenager added.

I was already reaching for a couple books. "Do you read a specific genre, like fantasy or rom-com?"

They considered this. "I like fantasy stuff."

"You're in luck." I picked out two titles and handed them

over. "I have more in the bookstore over there in case these aren't what you're looking for."

They smiled big at me and the dad pulled out his wallet.

"I'll help you over here, bud," Wyatt said, beckoning them over.

From half a block away, I spotted Don hustling toward the table. "Oh, no."

"What?" Liya glanced where I was looking. "Oh, no."

"Hannah." He crossed his arms and surveyed the book stand.

"Hi, Don." My voice was tentative. I shot Wyatt a glance. He was helping the dad pay but a little smile pulled at his mouth.

Don nodded and leaned in, lowering his voice. "I'm happy to see you outside. Glad my rejection didn't send you into a depression."

My mouth flattened into a line. "Can I help you with something today?" Anything to move this conversation along.

He perked up. "I wanted to see if you had the second in that orc series."

"Oh. Um. Yeah, it's back at the shop. I'll go grab it."

When I returned to the stand with the second book in the series, Don had his camera up, snapping more pictures of Liya chatting with a customer.

He put his camera down when he spotted me and reached for the book. "Perfect, thank you. I lent the first one to Miri and she is *loving* it."

Miri Yang was Don's best friend. She also ran a popular social media account with town events. She had reposted one of my pictures the other day, an image of Liya in the window of the store as she placed a book up on the shelf.

And now she was reading orc erotica.

Okay.

After Wyatt put Don's book through, I was plugging my

phone into a battery pack Liya brought when Wyatt's mom strolled past.

I gave her a quick wave. "Hi, Elizabeth."

She was in her sixties, always wore a bold necklace, and stopped into the bookstore to buy a book or say hello or ask how my dad was doing. She wore a curious smile as she glanced between Wyatt and me.

"Hannah, honey, it's so nice to see you out here." She nodded to her son. "Wyatt."

"Hi, Mom."

They stared at each other while I bounced on the balls of my feet, and Elizabeth's eyes shimmered with excitement. "I didn't know you two were friends."

"He's teaching me how to surf," I explained. "And I'm running his social media."

Her eyebrows rose. "You are? That's wonderful."

I nodded and when she pulled out her phone, I showed her how to follow Wyatt's account. She scrolled through the page, shaking her head to herself with a smile. "Look at all these videos of you, Wy. So handsome."

He put his hand on her shoulder. "Okay. Time for you to leave."

I laughed. "Wyatt."

Elizabeth gave him a kiss on the cheek and winked at me. "See you two later."

The rest of the afternoon, Wyatt rang through the customers while Liya and I talked their ears off about books. Within two hours, the pile on the table was down to only a few books, so Liya watched the booth while Wyatt and I headed back to the store to gather more.

"This is the most books we've sold in one day and it's not even lunch," I told him as we carried the stacks back to the table.

"That's a good thing, isn't it?"

We had made Liya's salary for the day and probably mine

as well, not that I was paying myself these days. I'd save that money for utilities.

"A really good thing." I glanced up at him as we paused to let a family pass. "Thanks for doing this."

He shrugged. "I just gave you the idea, bookworm. You're the one matching people up with their books."

I couldn't help the smile that crossed my face. "It's my favorite part of my job."

"I can tell." His gaze was warm and constant, and my stomach did a delicious roll forward.

When we returned to the booth, Beck was there, chatting with Liya.

"There she is." He gave me that sunny smile. "Hey, Hannah." To Wyatt, he nodded. "Wyatt."

"Beck." His tone was casual but clipped. It had a weird edge I hadn't heard from Wyatt before.

"I was dropping by to tell you how much I'm loving *Pride and Prejudice*." Beck grinned down at me and gestured at the table. "I like what you've got going on here."

My face heated. Despite Beck being so friendly, it was hard for me to meet his gaze. "It was all Wyatt's idea." I nudged Wyatt and shot him a quick smile.

Beck's eyebrows lifted. "Nice job, Wyatt."

"Thanks." His voice was still clipped. "Is the clinic closed today or something?"

"Nope. Just dropping by to chat with Hannah about our date." Beck held eye contact with Wyatt and Wyatt stood up straighter.

I frowned. Something was off. A weird tension hung in the air.

Wyatt tilted his head, thinking. "Did you order a book about making friends? I saw it on the receiving shelf. *How to Make Friends With a Low Libido*, something like that."

I blinked at Wyatt. Neither Liya nor I had ordered that

book in. Liya shot me a bemused look before turning to help another customer.

Beck gave him a strange look before shaking his head. "Nope. I didn't order that."

Wyatt rubbed his chin. "Huh. Okay." He shrugged. "I swear it was for you."

Beck rubbed the back of his neck and glanced at me. "I have lots of friends and I don't have a low libido. It's normal. Everything is normal in that department." He shook himself. "This is a weird conversation. Anyway, I was thinking we could take the boat out on the water and I could pack a picnic. How's Wednesday night? I don't work early on Thursdays at the clinic so we can stay out as late as we want."

"I can open on Thursday at the store," Liya added from behind Beck before she turned back to the customer.

Wyatt crossed his arms over his chest. "She has surf lessons in the morning."

One of Beck's eyebrows rose and my stomach lurched. He was just being nice and Wyatt was making it awkward. My stomach did a weird flip. Underneath it, though, there was an excited little flutter.

Was Wyatt *jealous*?

No. No way. Wyatt didn't get jealous. He only cared about surfing.

"Wednesday sounds good," I told Beck with a nod.

He glanced between Wyatt and me before giving me a quick wink. "See you then. I'll pick you up?"

"I'll be coming straight from the bookstore. Meet you at the marina at seven?"

"Perfect." He smiled again. His teeth were so white against his tan, and his eyes were such a nice chocolate brown. He touched my elbow as he passed. "Have a good day, Hannah. Bye, Liya. Bye, Wyatt."

"Bye, Beck!" Liya called after him.

I waved as he left before spinning to face Wyatt. "What's up with you?"

"Nothing." He shifted, still crossing his arms.

"I thought Beck was your friend."

"He is." He cleared his throat.

I narrowed my eyes at him. "Why are you being so weird?"

He reached for his pocket and pulled out his phone, buzzing in his hand. "Sorry, it's Holden. One second. Hello?" he answered before he glanced at me. "Yeah, she's here." He handed it to me. "It's for you."

"Holden?"

"Hannah." There were noises in the background. A beeping noise as a truck backed up, people calling to each other. Water rushing? An alarm going off. "A contractor hit a water line at one of my sites." He had to shout over the noise. "I'm stuck here until it's finished."

"Oh." I glanced up at Wyatt, watching with a curious expression. "So I guess we're off for today."

"Looks like it. I'm sorry."

I shook my head even though he couldn't see me. "It's fine. I understand."

Relief settled in my stomach. Not that I didn't like Holden. I did. He was fine. I didn't really know him. But the market was going so well and we were selling so many books that I didn't want to leave Liya to deal with it herself.

"I'd ask for a rain check but today is the last day of the exhibit."

"I didn't know that." My mouth twisted. "It's okay. It'll come back, I'm sure."

"Ah, no, not there!" he called to someone on the other end. "I gotta go. Sorry again."

"It's okay. Bye."

I ended the call and handed the phone back to Wyatt.

His gaze skimmed over my face with concern. "All good?"

I shrugged. "All good." A woman with a little girl who looked about five wandered up to the booth. "Hi."

The woman smiled down at the little girl. "We were hoping you had some books with either princesses or penguins in them." The girl smiled at me before tucking her face into her mom's shirt and peeking out.

My heart flopped. The little girl and her mom were so cute. "We have books on both those things." I pulled a few options and showed them.

The next couple hours passed in a blur. At one point, we sold so many books that I was sending Wyatt back to the store to grab whatever he could find.

"Doesn't the surf shop need you?" I asked as he returned with another load from the romance section. "It's okay if you need to leave. You've helped us so much."

He shook his head. "They're fully staffed today. They got it handled."

When afternoon rolled around, the booths around us began to close up.

I turned to Liya and Wyatt. "Shall we pack it in? The market is over and we've sold a week's worth of books." I couldn't help the smile that grew on my face. We were so doing this again next weekend.

Compared to the bright sunlight outside, the shop was so dark. It took my eyes a moment to adjust before I re-shelved the few books we didn't sell. Wyatt leaned on the counter and I shot him a grateful smile. "Thanks for your help today. You're free to go."

He pointed at Liya. "Are you okay here on your own until closing?"

She nodded. "Absolutely. That was already the plan because Hannah was going to the gallery."

"Great." He straightened and gestured at me. "She still is. Come on, bookworm."

"Where are we going?"

"I'm taking you to the gallery. You shouldn't miss out because my brother's a workaholic."

Happiness flooded my chest and I grinned at him. "Okay. Let's go."

———

WYATT TILTED his head at the painting of a French countryside. "I thought her paintings were of forests around here."

"She spent most of her life in Vancouver and Victoria and that's what she's most known for, but she also studied art in San Francisco, London, and Paris." We studied the painting for a moment longer, all bright oranges and yellows, before moving on to the next. "People have the image of her being a reclusive artist in the woods with her pet monkey but she spent fifteen years not really painting after she finished school. Then she met a bunch of painters who inspired her, The Group of Seven, and it became her most prolific period."

I pointed at the painting in front of us, all lush greens, towering trees and swirling skies in the saturated, psychedelic style Emily Carr was most known for.

"That's when she began creating work like this." I stared at the painting, tracing the lines with my gaze. "It's amazing how you can meet people who bring something out in you." I caught Wyatt's gaze, embarrassed. "Sorry."

"Why sorry?" A little smile played on his features.

"I'm talking too much. I'm a bad date. I mean, not that this is a date or anything."

Hannah, shut up, I told myself. *Stop talking and making this worse.*

"I like it when you tell me about this stuff." He nudged me. "Talking about things you're passionate about on a date is a good thing."

My face warmed but my stomach fluttered again. "Which is your favorite?"

He pointed at the next one. "My aunts had a print of this one in their house."

"Married or sisters?"

"Married."

"Did they live nearby?"

He nodded his head. "I bought their house when my Aunt Beatrice moved away a couple years ago."

He shifted, crossing his arms, gaze locked on the painting. There was a story there but he'd tell me if he wanted to.

He glanced down at me with one of those quick smiles that people put on to make the situation lighter. A *this is not a big deal* kind of smile. The one I used all the time. "Her wife, my Aunt Rebecca, passed away when I was a teenager. I stayed with them the summer before she passed to help out with stuff. Rebecca had Alzheimer's." He cleared his throat and glanced at the painting. "She moved into a care facility at the end of the summer and went downhill pretty quickly from there."

My heart sank and my hand came to his arm. His skin was so warm. "Oh. I'm so sorry."

He shook his head and shrugged. His gaze lingered on the painting. "It's fine. It was a long time ago."

We wandered through the rest of the exhibit until we came to a self-portrait of the artist.

"You like this one," Wyatt murmured in my ear, and I shivered but nodded up at him. "Why?"

"It's just…" I sighed, organizing my thoughts, sifting through why I was so drawn to this painting. "I love artist self-portraits. So many of them are really harsh." I swallowed. "Like they're all their own worst critics. The rest of the world thinks they're incredible but they see themselves so differently. Like Van Gogh. His portraits show how depressed he was or how he had just cut off his own ear." I shook my head at the painting of Emily Carr, glaring out of the canvas with a haughty, challenging expression. Her clothes were plain, a cap hid her hair, and she had used muted colors, but her gaze was electrifying.

"Hers isn't like that, though." I chewed my lip. "It's like she's saying, this is who I am, and if you don't like it, go fuck yourself."

Wyatt's gaze flared and he shot me a roguish grin. "Language, bookworm."

"I wish I could be that bold. Did you know that she was an art teacher at a women's college but everyone hated her because she smoked and swore too much?" I laughed. "She didn't care what anyone thought."

Kind of like my mom, I realized. My mom didn't care what others thought, as long as she was having fun and doing what she loved. I glanced back up at Wyatt. His gaze was soft and his eyes were bright under the gallery lighting.

He lifted his eyebrows at me. "You're on your way. Look at you today, talking about books and getting people all excited."

I wrinkled my nose and shook my head. "They probably won't even read them."

"Yes, they will." We had come to the end of the exhibit so we headed outside. "The way you talk about the stories you love, it makes people want to read them."

I thought about Beck reading *Pride and Prejudice*. "Maybe you're right." And then I remembered something and gave him a little frown as we wandered down the main street. The day was still warm but not uncomfortable and a light breeze drifted off the ocean a block away. "Why were you so weird with Beck today?"

He didn't speak for a second but a muscle ticked in his jaw. "Was I?"

I scoffed. "You insinuated that he had no friends and couldn't get a boner."

A laugh burst out of Wyatt, and I slapped his arm.

"You're terrible," I told him, still laughing. "Why'd you do that? I thought you guys were friends."

He raked his hand through his hair and sighed. "I was jealous, okay? I'm jealous because he looks at you like he wants to fuck you." His jaw ticked.

Oh. My initial instinct had been right. I blinked a few times, mind racing with my interactions with Beck. He was nice, but he wasn't flirty. Was he? Oh my god. Had Beck been flirting with me and I didn't realize it?

"I've never been jealous in my life. And then one of my good friends made plans with you and it pissed me off." His Adam's apple bobbed as he swallowed and he pressed his mouth into a line. "I'm sorry. It wasn't cool."

My thoughts whirred. A hit of pleasure and warm feelings drifted into my bloodstream from knowing someone as inaccessible as Wyatt was jealous over me.

For a brief moment, I was more than the shy, invisible girl in the bookstore.

Things with Wyatt weren't going anywhere, though. He was going to place at Pacific Rim and then he'd be off, flying around the world and competing. I'd still be here, shelving books at my little store.

It was best forgotten. I gave him a tight smile. "It's fine. I'm sure it'll pass, anyway."

He watched me with uncertainty in his eyes before he nodded. "Yeah."

When we said goodbye, he hesitated and his arm twitched, like he wanted to hug me or something. His gaze raked over my face and my heart tripped. His gaze was so intense and focused.

"Bye," I blurted out.

"Bye, bookworm."

I whirled around and headed home, the back of my neck prickling until I turned the corner. When I got home, I caught my reflection in the front hall mirror as I kicked my sneakers off. I had been spending so much time outside on the water that a light tan washed over my nose, cheekbones, and forehead. Freckles dotted my skin. I hadn't had freckles since I was a kid. The apples of my cheeks were pink. Even my hair seemed brighter.

I was changing. I knew that. I didn't know if I liked it, though. My mom would have told me to find someone who liked me for me, whether it was the shy version of myself who didn't talk to guys or the girl who hid in the bookstore all day. But my mom wasn't like me, so it was easy for her to say that.

Who was this new version, with tanned skin, the one who got up on a surfboard and asked hot doctors out on dates?

My mom's laugh rang out in my memory, the loud, high sound stinging me with nostalgia in the middle of my chest.

I bet she'd like Wyatt. They both had that easy disposition, quick to smile and not take life too seriously. I swallowed.

My phone rang and my dad's picture lit up the screen.

"Hi, Dad."

"There's my Hannah Banana." His voice came through on the other end. "How was your day, honey?"

"Good." I wandered into the kitchen and leaned on the counter, staring out the window. "How's Salt Spring?"

"Busy but beautiful. These goats eat a lot."

I grinned. We visited my uncle a few times when I was a kid and I had fond memories of feeding the goats.

"Sell some books today?"

Another stab of guilt. This would be the time to tell him about the farmer's market, about all the books we sold, and how the store hadn't been breaking even for a while. My mouth twisted. "A few."

If I told him the store wasn't doing well, he'd worry, and there wasn't anything he could do about it from Salt Spring. A little spike of bravery rose in me.

"Hey, Dad, I wanted to ask you about something."

"Go for it."

Over the past few days, as I spent more time on social media, I had found a few accounts from local artists. One artist, Naya Kaur, had caught my eye with her paintings. Her style was colorful and whimsical, characterized by detail and nature. Her latest collection depicted people daydreaming in forests. One of her paintings was of a woman lying in a hammock, staring at the sky through the trees.

I'd been thinking about that painting for a couple days now. I couldn't get it out of my head. It reminded me of lying on my surfboard next to Wyatt, staring up at the sky.

Without a doubt, Naya was the right artist to redo the mural outside the store. If we had more days like today at the farmer's market, we could afford it.

"The mural outside the store is in pretty rough shape."

He didn't say anything, and my stomach clenched. I swallowed my anxiety.

"Um, and, like, parts of it are crumbling." I cleared my throat. Shit. I should have practiced this. "What do you think about someone fixing it up a bit? We don't have to change it, just fill in some of the faded parts. Revive it."

He made a humming noise and my heart sank. I'd heard that noise before.

"I don't know, honey." He made a huffing noise. "Did someone complain or something?"

"No, but—" I gathered my thoughts. My heart pounded in my chest. "It looks bad. I think it would be good for business to have a new mural."

"A *new* mural?" His voice went high.

"The same mural," I added quickly. "Fixed up a bit."

"I don't know," he said again. "I think we should keep it as-is. We can talk about it when I get back."

I exhaled through my nose and clenched my jaw. That meant no. He just didn't want to say it outright.

My dad would never let me make a single change to the store. That was clear.

"Alright, well, I have to make dinner now." My tone was sharper than I intended. "I'll talk to you later."

"Oh. Okay. Goodnight, honey. Love you."

"Bye. Love you, too."

We hung up and I stared at the phone a moment before I pulled up Naya's social media and wrote out a DM.

Hi, Naya. Your work is beautiful. Any chance you would be interested in painting a mural outside Pemberley Books?

10

Wyatt

HANNAH PADDLED hard through the water, hopped up on her board as the wave lifted her, and coasted toward the shore with ease. I rested my elbows on the board, floating in the water and watching her with a smile.

The day was already warm and there were a few advanced surfers behind the break, out in the bigger waves, but just Hannah and me closer to shore, the way I preferred it.

Just her and me.

It was Wednesday morning, and tonight, Hannah would go out with Beck. Something weird and grouchy simmered in my stomach. At the farmer's market on Saturday, she wasn't as relaxed and talkative with him as she was with me. The knot in my chest loosened. She was at ease around me.

Or she was so attracted to Beck that he made her nervous.

The tension was back.

"I still can't believe how fast I go once I catch a wave," she said as she paddled back to me. Her cheeks were flushed and her eyes were bright in the morning sun and I could do this all day, watch her when I should be training.

Right. Training.

I still went out every morning after Hannah and I were

done, and then again in the evenings. If everything at the shop was taken care of, I'd go in the afternoons as well. Mornings were for Hannah and me, though.

I paddled out after her and surfed a small wave.

"You make it look so easy," she called over.

I shrugged and gave her my cockiest smile. It *was* easy. The next wave, though, I hopped up and wobbled back and forth, pretending to be unbalanced, before pitching over into the water. I resurfaced, shook the water out of my hair, and opened my eyes to see her flat look.

"Is that supposed to be me?" Her chest shook with laughter, and her eyes shone.

"I'm trying to show you that even advanced surfers can fall." I flicked some water over at her and she splashed me back. "Let's call it quits for today."

"One more." She paddled past me, further out before the break, faster than before, and I pictured the muscles in her back moving as she swam.

And then I was picturing other parts of her under the wetsuit. Desire lurched in me and I frowned.

Things didn't seem to be awkward after admitting I was jealous a couple days ago at the gallery. She wasn't pleased, but she wasn't angry either.

It was like it never happened.

I had always thought Hannah had a crush on me growing up, even up until recently. The blushing, the way she couldn't make eye contact, how she'd disappear before she had to make any conversation.

But now? She splashed me, made fun of me, and didn't think twice about stripping down to her swimsuit in front of me. Something competitive and unsatisfied pinged in my chest. I should have been relieved that the bookworm didn't have a crush on me. It made things easier. Romantic feelings complicated everything.

I raked my hand through my wet hair, blew out a breath,

and my gaze returned to Hannah as she paddled with the wave, hopped up, and glided over the surface of the water.

"Okay, *now* we can call it quits." She swam over to me with her torso on the board. "I forgot to tell you. I booked an artist. She's going to fix up the mural."

"That's great, bookworm. What changed your mind?"

She pulled her bottom lip between her teeth and the motion stirred me. Her mouth looked so soft.

"I was talking with my dad on the phone and…" Her nose wrinkled. "He's so stubborn. He's never going to change his mind and he doesn't have a freaking clue about business." She made a frustrated noise in her throat.

I grinned and raised my eyebrows at her. I liked the fire she was spitting.

Her eyebrows pinched together in a frown. "Sorry, I didn't mean to get mad."

"I like it when you get mad. You should get mad more often."

Our gazes locked and my chest squeezed. A drop of water rolled down the column of her neck, into her wetsuit. She frowned at me. "What?" She smoothed a hand over her wet hair. "Did the seaweed get me again?"

"No, you look beautiful like this." The words flew out of my mouth.

She raised an eyebrow and laughed. "Like a drowned rat? Okay, weirdo. Did you hit your head on the rocks or something? Come on." She swam past me and paddled to our cove.

My mouth dropped and I watched her swim away. That was it? She brushed me off so easily. I called her beautiful and she called me a *weirdo*.

Well, there was my answer. She definitely didn't have a crush on me.

That's where I should have left it. I should have dropped it, continued helping Hannah become a hot girl or whatever, and kept things platonic. Friends. That's what we were. I should have left it all there.

That spark of competitiveness flared in my chest, the same one I felt every morning surfing. The same one I felt at competitions. I swam hard to catch up with her.

"When's your date with Beck?" I called over as I approached even though I knew the answer.

"Seven o'clock."

We drifted into the calm cove. She slid a hair tie off her wrist and pulled her hair off her neck before tying it up into a ponytail. I watched the movements, captivated, and I had the urge to run my finger down the back of her neck to see if she'd shiver. My throat worked.

"Are you going to kiss him?"

She blanched, and pink appeared on her cheeks. "I don't know." She blinked.

I should have shut up, but I couldn't. "When was the last time you kissed someone?"

She huffed, and the pink tinge spread. She was cute like this, all embarrassed. "None of your business."

I splashed her as she pulled herself up to seated on her board. "Tell me."

She laughed. "No. When was the last time *you* kissed someone?"

"A couple days before you held me down and blackmailed me."

She rolled her eyes and tried not to grin. "I didn't hold you down."

An image of us in bed flashed into my head. My bed. Hannah on top of me, holding my wrists down with a shy smile. Me pretending to be at her mercy.

Blood rushed to my groin. Thank fuck my lower half was under water.

This didn't happen. I didn't get hard-ons from chatting with a woman, both of us clothed, neither of us touching.

116

"University. Give me your leash." She held her hand out and I unwrapped it from my ankle before tossing it to her.

"Wait, university? Bookworm, that was years ago."

Now she *really* looked embarrassed, and I mentally slapped myself. Asshole.

My heart sank in my chest. "Bookworm."

She shrugged, studying the beach. "I know, okay? I could say that I haven't found anyone I liked but we both know I haven't tried. I tried a dating app a couple years ago but everyone on there was either a tourist looking for a threesome or someone I went to high school with." Her mouth pulled into a wince and she shuddered. "It wasn't for me." She grimaced, glanced at me, and chewed her lip.

"You look like you want to say something."

She pressed her mouth into a line before she took a deep breath. "Do you think Beck's going to want to…" She made a noise in her throat.

"Do I think he's going to want to what?"

"Have sex tonight?" Her voice was high and squeaky, like when we were on the sidewalk in front of her store and she was asking people out.

My brain skidded to a halt.

Beck. Trying to sleep with Hannah. With his hands on her. Touching her hair. Pulling the hair tie from her ponytail.

My skin was too tight. Frustration rolled through me with nowhere to go. I studied a scratch on my board. "I don't know."

Her chest rose and fell with another deep breath. "I don't like it."

"Sex?" My voice was hoarse. *Keep it together*, I warned myself. I had the bizarre urge to make Hannah feel safe, like she could tell me anything. I didn't want her to be embarrassed for asking me these questions.

She nodded. Her face burned red.

Well, that answered my virgin question. "There's a lot to unpack there."

"Ugh." She lay down on her board. "This is so embarrassing. Let's not talk about it."

"No," I said, too quick before catching myself and toning it down. "Let's talk about it." I cleared my throat. "Why do you not like sex?"

She shifted on the board, floating away, and I grabbed the edge to pull her back to me, despite the leash attaching my board to her ankle.

Her fingers dipped in the water. "Um. When I hooked up with that guy back in school, it—" She made a noise, a mix of anguish and frustration. "It didn't hurt, exactly—"

Rage. Yep. That was what this feeling was. Pure, white-hot rage rattled through my veins. Someone touched Hannah and they—

"It wasn't the magical experience that I always read about in books." She covered her face with her hands. "Okay, I'm going to go die now. My funeral is next week. Please bring flowers."

I was going to ask this guy's name, find him, and then beat the shit out of him.

Whoa. No. What the fuck? I wasn't the guy who got into fights. Deep breaths. Breathing. Calm. Safe space for Hannah.

"You didn't have an orgasm." I kept my voice steady and light, like we were talking about what we were going to eat for breakfast. Something neutral. Something that didn't make me want to fucking kill someone.

She gave a laugh of disbelief. "Not even close."

I didn't know where to start. "What did he do wrong?"

"I can't believe we're talking about this. I don't talk about this with anyone. Not Avery, not Liya, no one."

Pride washed over me. Pride and pleasure. She trusted me enough to talk about this stuff.

"We just didn't connect." One hand rested on her stomach, the other still dipped in the water, fingertips skimming the surface. The end of her ponytail had fallen into the water and fanned out, floating and following the motions of her board.

"Did you tell him what you wanted?" My gaze was glued to her face, watching for clues while she stared up at the blue sky.

"No."

"Why not?" Same casual tone. Just me trying not to picture Hannah in bed with another guy, that's all. Doing great. Not filled with a confusing horny rage.

"Um." She stretched a foot out.

I tried not to stare at the curve of her tits under the wetsuit. I failed.

"I guess I didn't know what I liked either? He—" She broke off with a noise of disgust. "It was like he watched too much porn."

A thousand images flooded my head and I felt sick. I hated this. "Explain." My tone was rougher than I meant.

She covered her face again. "Oh my god. Okay, he did this thing where he put his hands on me and like, pulled my, um, lady parts apart and it hurt."

I wanted to murder this guy. This fucking guy who didn't know what he was doing put his grubby little hands all over my Hannah and made her uncomfortable. He ruined an experience for her that should have been amazing. He should have rocked her world and instead, he made her not like sex.

"Was that too much information?" She lifted her head, shot me a tentative glance, and I quickly cleared my throat and shook my head.

"Nope. He sounds like a dumbass."

She laid her head back down on her board and snorted. "Yeah. He was."

We were quiet a moment. I had the urge to pull her board closer and put my mouth on hers. To race her back to shore, throw her over my shoulder, and take her back to my bed, where I'd give her a do-over of every sexual experience she had ever had.

With me, it would be better. Hotter. I'd make her writhe under me. I'd go down on her until she pulled my hair and gasped my name and couldn't handle how good it felt. I was desperate to see how she looked while she came, all hazy and flustered and breathless.

A twinge hit me in the gut. She wanted long-term. True love. If I did well next month, I'd be on a plane, and she'd still be here.

Beck, though. Beck would stay in Queen's Cove, same as Hannah. Despite wanting to smack the look off his face every time he smiled at her, he was a decent guy.

I wanted Hannah to be happy.

The thought of him touching Hannah made my fists clench, though.

"Wyatt?"

"Mmm?" My gaze snapped back to hers.

She lifted her eyebrows. "Is the third date rule real? Where you should sleep with someone on the third date?"

My stomach twisted and I could feel it all over my face, this anguish. This torn feeling.

"Bookworm, if you're worried about things with Beck, just do what feels right."

She frowned at me. The wheels turned in her head.

I shrugged, hoisting myself up onto my board so I could lie beside her. "Even if he does buy you dinner, you don't owe him anything. You don't have to sleep with him or even kiss him. The third date rule is bullshit. You can sleep with him on the first date or the tenth date or never, if that's what you want." We locked eyes. "You're the boss. Understand?"

She gave me a tiny nod.

"Beck is a good guy and he'll be patient with you. He better be."

She made a humming, thinking noise and let out a breath,

lying back on her board and gazing up at the sky. She relaxed and we floated, listening to seagulls, waves hitting the shore, and the occasional laugh of someone on the beach or whoop of one of the other surfers.

Later, as we padded across the sand back to the surf shop, Hannah grinned at me.

"I always feel so much better after being out on the water in the mornings with you."

My heart squeezed. "The water will do that."

She shook her head. "It's not just the water. I like hanging out with you. You always make me feel better about things I'm worried about."

Heart, meet sledgehammer. I had the urge to pull her in for a hug but I held back. Instead, I shrugged. Casual, like always. Noncommittal. "You can talk to me about this stuff. Hope you know that."

She nodded. "I know." She reached out and gave my arm a quick squeeze. The contact of her cold hand against my skin sent a jolt through me. "So, what's my homework, professor?"

"Professor?" I lifted an eyebrow and ignored the way my cock stirred when she called me that.

"You have a nickname for me." She shrugged, a cute little smile on her face.

I beamed at her, so hard my face hurt. "I like it."

"So, homework."

"Right. Uhhh…" I thought, narrowing my eyes. "Easy one today. When you go on the date tonight—" Even saying the words made me sick, "—only do what you want. Don't do anything you don't want to. Wear whatever you want. Drink champagne, not beer." I took a step closer to her and her mouth parted. "And if you don't want to kiss him, don't."

She nodded. "Okay."

I held her gaze for a moment. Her blue-green eyes were so pretty. "Okay."

There. Knowing her, she'd stick to her homework, even if

it was difficult. Even if he pressured her. The tension in my chest settled a fraction.

But what if she *wanted* to push things further with Beck? I remembered the way she laughed at the farmer's market, when he talked easily with her. The way she looked up at him, starstruck.

The tension in my chest was back.

———

I THOUGHT about Hannah's date with Beck all day. I thought about it as I taught surf lessons, as I helped a customer buy a wetsuit, as I ordered replacement surf boards, as I surfed that evening.

She was probably out on his boat now, I realized as I checked the time on my phone. Was he putting his arm around her, doing that cheesy yawn-and-stretch thing? No. No way. Beck didn't play games like that; he'd just ask her if he could put his arm around her.

And she might say yes.

Hmm. Didn't like that idea. Not one bit.

I thought about her when I scarfed down a late dinner in my kitchen. I thought about her as I finished *Pride and Prejudice*, setting the book on my night table and staring at it for a few minutes. I glanced at the time again.

I should go to sleep if I wanted to be up the next morning bright and early for our surf lesson. Antsy energy bounced around inside my head and through my limbs. I pulled a t-shirt over my head, slipped my shoes on, and headed out the door.

I was going to pay the bookworm a visit.

11

Hannah

"I THINK *you're on a date with the wrong guy, Hannah.*"

Beck's words replayed in my head as I lay in bed, staring at the ceiling in the dark. How he winced as he implied I was a bad date. I blew a breath out, frowning.

I had done everything right. With Beck, I still blushed under his gaze, but I forced myself to make conversation instead of clamming up like I wanted to. I asked him about the clinic, about his time in Vancouver going to school, about his volunteer work in South America in between university and medical school. I talked about the surf lessons I had been doing with Wyatt, about the social media stuff I had been doing for him, about the bookstore, something Liya and I had been laughing about the other day, about Wyatt's idea for me to do social media for the bookstore. I talked about the Emily Carr exhibit we had gone to. About the breakfast food truck we frequented after surf lessons. About the farmer's market book stand and how many books we had sold.

Wyatt. I had talked about Wyatt the whole time.

I groaned and covered my face with my hands. Poor Beck.

Between the disastrous date with Carter, the would-be date with Holden where he bailed, and the date with Beck where I talked about another guy the entire time, this whole dating thing was not going well.

My mom would find this funny. She'd find it *hilarious*. She'd laugh and tell me not to worry about it, that there were lots of other guys out there to go on terrible dates with.

I could picture it. "I just had the worst date of my life," I'd tell her.

She'd hold a hand up. "The worst date of your life *so far*."

Then we'd dissolve into giggles.

A month from now, I'd be thirty. Discomfort trickled through my stomach and I swallowed. I knew it was stupid, this rule I had imposed on myself, but I didn't want to be thirty and single still. I had to at least try to find something special, but I was even further away than when I started this whole thing.

A tap on my window startled me. I jolted and froze. I had the overwhelming instinct to hide under my bed.

Another tap. "Bookworm?"

I relaxed and opened the curtains to see his lazy grin on the other side of the glass.

"What are you doing here?" I whispered as I slid the window open. "It's late."

"Wanted to see how your date went." He gestured for me to move aside before he hoisted himself through the window.

I watched, mouth hanging open. "You can't be in here!" Why was I whispering? I was the only one home.

There was a boy in my room. I'd never had a boy in here. My gaze darted around my room, cataloguing my belongings, seeing them in a new light. Books everywhere, some of them in neat stacks, some of them lying face-down and open, my way of marking my place when I couldn't find a bookmark. My closet with my clothes hanging neatly. My bed with a fluffy white duvet and too many pillows.

Wyatt hovered over my dresser, reading the titles of the books stacked on top. He was so freaking tall. I had stopped noticing it when we were outside. What was one guy next to mountains and trees and the ocean? But here, in my tiny bedroom, standing so close to me, he towered.

Awareness fluttered through me. I shifted on my feet, unsure where to stand. In the small space, I could smell Wyatt, his deodorant or shampoo or body wash and a bit of the ocean, something unique and intoxicating. His back and shoulder muscles moved under his white t-shirt as he brushed his thumb down the spine of a book.

"So?" He picked up a necklace lying on the dresser—a silver chain with a tiny, light-blue stone.

"Avery gave me that for my birthday last year."

"I've never seen you wear it." His voice was low, his tone neutral. Not the easygoing Wyatt I knew.

He was being careful. Something was up with him.

"Did you wear it tonight?" He laid the necklace back down, turned, and leaned against the dresser. He crossed his arms and dragged his gaze down my form.

"Yes."

Even in the dim light, his gaze burned hot. My nipples tightened. The air between us charged with electricity and I didn't know how to respond.

He lifted his eyebrows and tilted his chin at my outfit. "That's what you wear to bed?"

I glanced down at my pink tank top and shorts. It was a warm night but I wasn't wearing a bra and the points of my nipples were visible through the thin fabric.

"You didn't answer me."

"Sometimes I wear a t-shirt."

That put a hint of a smile on his face. "I meant about the date. How'd the date go?"

"Oh. Bad."

His gaze flared. "What did he do? Did he touch you?" He stepped forward, looming over me. "Did he push you too hard?"

I shook my head and huffed. "I was the one who behaved badly. I was a terrible date. I'm better at surfing than dating and that should tell you everything."

"What happened?"

His authoritative tone made my stomach flutter. His dark gaze locked on my face and my skin tingled. I stared at the floor, hands clasped together, and shook my head. "The chemistry wasn't there."

His fist clenched at his side and I frowned. This was *so* not Wyatt. What was going on with him tonight?

"Did you do your homework?" he asked in a low voice, and my core fluttered. A clench around nothing.

I shivered, and goosebumps rose on my arms. There was something about that line, I knew I'd be thinking about it later. Wyatt didn't mean it in a sexy way but it sure came out like that.

Homework, right. Wyatt had told me to only do what felt right.

I gave him a tiny nod, and when I lifted my gaze to his, I saw fury flashing in his eyes.

"So you kissed him and there was no chemistry." He raked his hand through his hair, mouth pressed into a hard line.

"Kissed him? No." I made a noise of frustration. "We never got that far. I spent the entire time talking about—" I broke off before I said something embarrassing.

"Talking about what?" His dark gaze was back on me.

I shook my head, pressing my mouth closed.

"Talking about *what*, bookworm?"

"There's a weird energy in here," I blurted out, shaking my head. "Maybe that necklace is cursed," I joked, but he didn't laugh.

He took another step toward me and I backed up, the backs of my knees hitting the bed. "Talking. About. What."

I threw my hands up. "You. Talking about you. Oh my god. You're so pushy." I rolled my eyes, acting like he annoyed me, when really, my heart raced, my skin tingled, and my nipples pinched hard. I had all this energy and nowhere for it to go.

I put my hands on his chest to push him back a step but he grabbed my wrists and looked down at me. A smug grin grew on his features. Paired with his dark gaze, the effect was hypnotic.

"Me?" He raised his eyebrows, cocking his head. His hands scorched my wrists. It was like he ran hotter than normal people. Maybe that was why he was never cold in the water.

I rolled my eyes again. "You came up in conversation because of the surf lessons."

"Right. Because of the surf lessons." His gaze stayed glued on me, still heated. "So you didn't kiss him because it didn't feel right?"

I gave him another tiny nod.

"Interesting." His thumb brushed my wrist as if he didn't realize he was doing it. It sent tingles up and down my arm, making it hard to breathe. That could have been from his proximity, too. Or how he smelled freaking incredible.

I swallowed. Why was he here? What was going on? Having him here in my room, it was electrifying. It was dangerous and bad in a good way. Not wrong. Right. I liked him towering over my books and my bed and me. I liked him holding my wrists like that.

His gaze dropped to the front of my pajama top, where my nipples strained.

He exhaled through his nose, and a muscle in his jaw ticked. "Are you disappointed?" His chest rumbled against my hands as he spoke.

I chewed my lip. "No. Beck's nice——" His hands clenched my wrists at the mention of his name, "——but he's just a friend." I swallowed and met his gaze. "I was looking forward to making out with someone tonight, but I don't want to do it with the wrong person."

Well, *that* sounded suggestive. Wyatt's eyebrow ticked up, still watching me with that dark gaze, and a shiver rolled down my spine. His warm hands seared my wrists.

"And Beck would be the wrong person." His voice was low and thick.

I nodded again.

"Because you spent the entire date talking about me."

My heart hammered in my chest. I inhaled a shaky breath but it caught in my throat when Wyatt pressed his fingers into my wrist.

"Your pulse," he murmured.

I nodded again. Another flutter through my core, another clench around nothing.

He watched my face with heavy-lidded eyes. "It's been a long time since you've kissed someone."

Another nod from me.

"I don't want you to be out of practice." His gaze dropped to my mouth and he cleared his throat. "You know, for when you meet the right person."

"Right. I don't want to be out of practice either."

A pained expression passed over his face and he closed his eyes a moment, inhaling. His jaw ticked. His skin was so warm, and I wondered what it would be like to press my mouth to his neck, the spot where it met his shoulder. Would his skin be warm against my lips? What would he taste like? What could I do to make his head fall back, to make him groan?

I chewed my lip. That was all I could think of, now, making him groan. Hesitation and curiosity arm-wrestled in the corner of my brain while in another corner, embarrassment and desire battled in a thumb war. I drew myself up, summoning a bolder spirit. This was what I had been practicing all this time, right? Asking all those guys out, putting myself out there, embarrassing myself both on the street and on my surfboard, making a fool of myself. And for what?

Because I wanted to be a hot girl. Because I wanted to live a full life.

I swallowed again, watching the curve of Wyatt's mouth, noticing the rise and fall of his chest against my hands. My hands tensed, my nails dug into him, and his breath caught.

"So we should practice." I lifted a shoulder in a half-shrug. Casual, so casual. Like Wyatt.

He frowned like he was torn. He glanced from me to the window, then back to me, then to the bed behind me. My core clenched hard again and I almost whimpered. My underwear was wet. That *never* happened, and definitely not from standing beside a guy for a few minutes.

I watched his mouth again. I wanted a taste of him. Just one. That would be enough.

You know what? Screw this.

I raised up on my tiptoes and pressed my mouth against Wyatt's.

The first thing I noticed about Wyatt's lips were how warm they were. The slow brush of my skin over his, the gentle scratch of his stubble on my chin. His mouth was softer than expected for someone who spent most of his day outside. Kissing Wyatt was like sinking into a warm bath on one of those winter evenings where it rained all day, one of those days you felt like you'd never get warm again. I wanted to sink right into Wyatt. I sucked his bottom lip into my mouth and murmured with pleasure.

Up until now, Wyatt had been still, letting me press my mouth to his and test the waters, but the second I made that noise, something in him snapped. He squeezed my wrists.

"Fuck, bookworm." He let out a ragged breath.

"Was that okay?"

He growled. He *growled*. Wyatt. I opened my mouth but he covered it with his.

His mouth worked mine, his hands dropped my wrists, and one hand fisted my hair, tilting my head back. The pull against my scalp made me shiver. He was no longer a spectator in our kiss. His tongue demanded entrance into my mouth and I let him in, whimpering softly as his tongue slicked mine in a glide, lighting up every nerve ending in my body.

He groaned against me, long and low, and his other hand wrapped around my back, pulling me flush to him. He tasted me again and again until I was breathless. My head spun. Kisses were supposed to be sweet and loving.

Not like this. Not desperate and needy and demanding and drugging and *hot* like this.

I looped my arms around his neck. He nipped my bottom lip and the sharp, sweet pinch hit me between my legs. I made a noise, a combination of a laugh and a moan. His fingers loosened on my hair and rubbed my scalp in slow, firm motions, and I moaned against his mouth before his tongue slipped against mine.

I wasn't standing on my own but leaning into his arm, hanging with my arms around his neck, letting him hold me up while he took my mouth.

A ripple of delight moved through me at the idea of Wyatt using me purely for his own pleasure. An image flashed in my mind of his hands on my hips, thrusting into me hard, racing towards a release. My core throbbed at the idea.

"Jesus fucking Christ, bookworm, where'd you learn to kiss like this," Wyatt groaned against my mouth in between kisses. "I thought about you all fucking night. All day. I was going insane, thinking about his hands on you." His arm that had been around my back, holding me up, slipped lower until he was grasping my ass. My breath hitched again.

My fingers traced the skin on the back of his neck and he leaned his forehead against mine, breathing hard. He shivered as my fingers skimmed higher on his neck, threading into his hair.

"I love your hair," I whispered, combing my fingers through it. "Kiss me again." I tugged.

He made a low noise of frustration, his mouth came back to mine, and we were back underwater. His mouth was hungry, starving for me, demanding and needy and I loved every second of it. Nothing else was relevant, nothing else existed except Wyatt's mouth on mine, his possessive hands, and those low groans of pleasure and disbelief coming out of his throat.

I felt the sharp sting of his hand on my butt before I registered the noise of the slap, and I could barely gasp before his hand smoothed over the fabric of my shorts.

"How am I supposed to control myself around you when you wear little shorts like this?" His hand slipped beneath the hem, over my bare skin, and I whimpered against his mouth.

"I don't want you to control yourself."

My voice was raspy and breathy. Who was *that*? Who was this girl making out with Wyatt Rhodes, the most unavailable guy in town?

He lifted me into the air. My legs looped around his waist in some primal instinct that I didn't know lay dormant within me. We dropped, and he lowered himself onto my bed with me sitting in his lap, clinging to him, an iron bar pressing against me—

"Oh." My eyebrows shot up. My heart raced and my head swam with dizziness, but not in a bad way.

In a good way. In the *best* way. I made a noise of desperation and rubbed my center against Wyatt's hard length. My body took over. My body wanted more, more Wyatt and more of this achy tension building inside me.

When my center made contact with Wyatt's cock, something white-hot shot through me, right to my core, and I bucked and gasped. It was a fraction of a second but it was too good. My thighs jerked closed, snapping tight around his waist. Wyatt's length pulsed against me and his hands tightened on my bottom, so hard I'd have bruises tomorrow. The idea of his marks on me made me more turned on.

"Hannah," he gasped against my mouth. "You can't do that."

"Sorry," I whispered. "Didn't mean to. Just felt so good."

"I know, baby, I know." He chest rose and fell as he caught his breath, leaning his forehead against mine once again.

Right here. I wanted to pull his shirt off, push him down, and ride him right here. I gazed into his eyes, so dark, moody, furious, and desperate in this light. I ached for him. From the way his jaw tensed but his hands didn't move from my butt, I knew he wanted me too.

And then he was standing, I was in the air, and he was lowering me to the bed.

My body lit up with excitement and anticipation. This was happening. This was *so* happening—

He straightened up and my body screamed in protest.

"What—" I started.

"You're going to go on another date." His voice was low, his chest still rising and falling, and he crossed his arms over his chest.

Alarm shot through me. I didn't want to go on another awkward date with Beck. "I don't know if that's a good idea."

"By yourself."

"Why?"

He leaned over the bed, over me, and the mattress shifted as he placed his hands on either side of my head, caging me in. "Because you need to know what you like by yourself before you can enjoy it with someone else."

My eyes widened. Why did that sound so dirty?

His heated gaze locked on mine before it dropped to my swollen mouth. "And after the date, you're going to come home, crawl into bed, and touch yourself until you come."

Wetness flooded my center and my mouth fell open.

"Take notes." His gaze lifted to mine again. "You need to know what you like if you're going to show someone else how to do it."

I swallowed. My body sang for him, buzzing and achy and damp between my legs. He wasn't even touching me right now but I could come with a few brushes over my clit.

He raised his eyebrows. "Do you understand the assignment, bookworm?"

All I could do was nod.

"Good," he murmured, still hovering over me. He lowered his head but instead of kissing me, he put his mouth to my neck and sucked—hard.

I gasped and arched my back as the sting made my blood boil.

"Wyatt," I gasped.

"Tomorrow's surf lesson is cancelled. Sleep in, you've earned it." He placed a gentle kiss on the spot where he had sucked. "Goodnight, bookworm." He straightened up and gave me one last pained, lingering look, lying on the bed beneath him, before he climbed back out the window and slid it closed behind him.

I stared at the window for a long time after he left, my wet core aching and my mouth swollen. I brushed my fingertips over the spot on my neck.

What the absolute hell just happened?

12

Wyatt

I SHOULDN'T HAVE DONE it.

A wave roared past me as I hung out on my board behind the break the next morning, sun rising over the horizon and splashing the sky with colors.

Hannah was becoming one of my closest friends, and I was climbing through her window, making out with her, kissing her like it was curing me of something.

It did, kind of. I had been wondering for weeks what that sweet little mouth would taste like, what she would sound like as I stole her breath.

It cured me and in exchange, handed me a new ailment.

I could not stop thinking about that fucking kiss.

Her mouth.

Her tits in that thin top.

Her ass in those little shorts. Those shorts were a fucking crime.

The raspy moan she let out as she rubbed against me.

I rested my head on my board, closing my eyes, bobbing in the water.

Fuuuuuuuuuuuck.

Erections were uncomfortable at the best of times, but in a wetsuit? Fucking torture.

The yips and laughs of two surfers closer to the shore brought me back to the present. I inhaled a deep breath and let it out to center myself. I was out here to catch waves, not fantasize about her.

It was different with Hannah. I'd never been close friends with someone I hooked up with. I'd never noticed how their eyes looked in the sunlight or pictured their smile later in the day. There was a constellation of freckles over Hannah's nose and cheeks that I itched to trace with my fingertip while she told me about a book she was reading.

I had never told a woman she was beautiful before.

I had *definitely* never told a woman to take herself on a date, and then come home and make herself come.

I rubbed my chest. What did I always tell myself? Here for a good time, not a long time. There was no point in getting involved with Hannah. Even if I did stay in Queen's Cove, I couldn't imagine it lasting. We were so different. I had never pictured myself in something long-term.

The thought of some faceless guy with his hands all over her, towering over her in her bedroom like I did last night, scooping her up into his lap, it made me want to break something.

I shook the image out of my head. Focus, I told myself. Channel it back into the water.

The next wave approached, and I paddled hard to catch it, snapping up at the last minute and coasting along the surface. Adrenaline shot through me as I worked to keep my balance on the board, as my muscles tensed and gave to keep me upright. My heart beat hard in my chest and I threw my weight, turning the board and carving into the surf before coasting toward the shore. Adrenaline hit my bloodstream and satisfaction flooded my chest.

Fuck, that felt incredible. Almost as good as last night.

Again and again, I swam out behind the break and caught waves. I focused on my body, on reading the waves, and on listening to my intuition as they approached. Hannah crept into my mind a few times, but that only drove my focus. Pretending she was on shore watching me made my movements sharper, more intentional. It made each wave I caught worth more.

I swallowed, floating behind the break with my feet in the water. I wished she was here this morning, which made no sense because if she was, I wouldn't be training, I'd be floating off in the cove, staring at the sky and talking to her about her store or the town or some book she was reading.

A pang of something hit me in the chest. Homesickness, which also made zero sense, because I was right here in Queen's Cove.

Saying goodbye to all of this was going to hurt. Surfing the cold waters, the mountains, the forests, my little house on the beach. Hannah.

The way she gazed up at me last night in her room, so trusting, her eyes all hazy and fucking gorgeous, it felt fucking incredible. To have her look at me like she wanted me, it readjusted something in my chest and that piece wouldn't go back to where it was before. Now that I had tasted her, heard that little moan, I couldn't forget it.

I groaned and put my head on the board again, an ugly tightness trickling into my chest. She trusted me and I took advantage of that. I was helping her find someone. I was helping her come out of her shell, showing her it was okay to screw up, fail, and embarrass herself.

I thought about the expression on her gorgeous face after she got up on her board the first time she caught a wave. My heart squeezed in my chest at the memory of that huge smile, stretched ear to ear, her eyes lit up with pride and disbelief.

That was what we should be doing more of—surfing. Not making out. Not me squeezing the smooth skin of her ass. Not raking my fingers through her soft hair. Someone with my dating history hooking up with someone with her dating history? It had *wrong* stamped all over it.

It didn't feel wrong, but I knew better.

When I returned home that morning, my mom sat on the front steps, drinking a coffee with two more on the deck beside her.

"Hey, Mom," I called to her.

"Good morning, honey." She reached for a coffee and handed it to me. "No Hannah today?"

"Thanks." I took a sip and shook my head. "Not today. Tomorrow."

She smiled softly and raised an eyebrow. "You two have been spending a lot of time together."

I took a seat beside her and shrugged. "I've been giving her surf lessons."

She made a humming noise of acknowledgement. "And the farmer's market?"

I didn't answer her. Elizabeth was perceptive like a hawk. My chest twisted hard and I knew she knew. She knew I thought about Hannah *like that*. I didn't want to talk about it with her, though. Hannah was special and private right now. That hesitation I thought about in the water, about my history versus hers? Talking about Hannah meant people would point that out to me. I shrugged again.

She took another sip of her coffee and studied the ocean. "Hannah is a very sweet girl."

I thought about the way Hannah had ground herself against me last night. Not that sweet.

"She hasn't had it easy, since Claire passed. It's been hard on her and Frank, just the two of them."

Irritation prickled at the back of my neck. "You know she runs the bookstore basically on her own?"

She paused. "No. I thought she and Frank ran it together."

137

"He's stepped back in the past few years. She runs the entire business by herself." I gestured at the water. "She got up on her board last week. She surfed. She's terrible at surfing. She has zero balance." I shook my head. "But she kept trying and got up on her board and caught a few waves." My words rushed out with an edge to them. "She's not this wimpy little flower."

My mom's head reared back. "I didn't say she was."

"She works hard and she doesn't give up. People don't give her enough credit."

She watched me, a little knowing grin growing on her face. Busted.

I rolled my eyes, but a grin grew on my face too. "Don't look at me like that. We're friends."

It tasted wrong, saying it.

"Hmm." She leaned back on her hands, studying the sparkling ocean. "Friends."

"Yep."

We were quiet for a few moments.

"I don't know what's going on in that brain of yours, Wy." She gave me a sidelong glance. "I never have. You're like the water in that way, it's hard to see under the surface." She pressed her mouth into a line, nodding. "You were always so fearless." She laughed and rubbed her forehead. "Sweetheart, the years you have taken off my life with your stunts out there."

A smile lifted on my face.

She shook her head. "I don't know what I'm trying to say. I just hope you apply that same fearlessness to all aspects of your life."

I frowned. "Okay." What?

"What time is it?" She checked her phone and hopped up. "Avery's mother and I are going to visit Katherine and do some gardening." Katherine Waters owned an inn, The Water's Edge, and the past few years, she had been sick.

People in town helped her out around the inn, fixing leaking taps and weeding the garden. Holden had worked there for a few summers as a teenager and still dropped by often.

My mom stood and dusted off her pants. "Family dinner on Sunday. Bring Hannah. I want more women around." I opened my mouth—to say what?—but she was already down the walkway and out of my front yard. "Bye, honey!"

"Bye, Mom."

I sat there a few minutes, staring at the water, before getting up and heading inside. I had a missed call and a voice-mail on my phone.

"Hey Wyatt, this is Emilio Sanchez with Billabong. Saw you compete in Australia last year and loved what I saw. It's obvious that you have a presence in the surfing world, seeing how your social media has taken off. I'd like to speak to you about being part of the Billabong team. We'll be out in Queen's Cove for the Pacific Rim Worlds. Call me back."

I listened to the message a couple times, sitting on the step and staring at my phone.

Whatever Hannah was doing on social media, it was working. It was happening.

Surfing the best spots in the world. Surfing every day. The rush of catching powerful, crashing waves. I blew a shaky breath out. This was what I always wanted.

So why was my chest tight and weird like this?

13

Hannah

NERVES ROLLED through my stomach as I stepped through the back door of the surf shop to grab a wetsuit. I had been to the surf shop enough times now to feel comfortable walking right in, even at six in the morning, so I headed straight to where the wetsuits in my size hung on the rack.

"Not that one," Wyatt said behind me. His voice was still gravelly with sleep.

The nerves pitched in my stomach and that low voice traveled right down to my toes. The last time I heard that tone, his mouth had pressed against mine and he was taking it, claiming my mouth like it belonged to him.

You're going to come home, crawl into bed, and touch yourself until you come.

His low words echoed in my head. I shivered and turned.

Goddamn, he was hot. Even when he was still sleepy and his hair was a bit messy. His eyes shone bright, his skin glowed with a tan, his mouth was fascinating, and the sight of him set off a series of sparks in me.

I totally had the hots for Wyatt Rhodes.

I swallowed and lifted my eyebrows. "What do you mean?"

He gestured to the back room, where they kept extra inventory. "Got you your own."

Until now, I had been using one of the suits the shop rented to tourists taking surf lessons. The fit wasn't great. It was too long in the arms and legs, so I rolled the cuffs up. The mid-section was bulky and the zipper always snagged, but I didn't know any different, and I didn't want to complain, so I made do.

A new wetsuit hung in the back room, tags still on. The suit was shorter and way, way nicer. The spongey Neoprene was smooth, and the logo on the front wasn't a brand carried in the shop. I ran my fingers over it.

"This is my suit?"

He nodded, the corner of his mouth ticking up.

"You didn't have to do this." I glanced at him, leaning against the wall, looking so casual and nonchalant. Apathetic, even. "I don't mind wearing the suit I usually wear."

"That suit sucks. You've graduated past it." A smile lifted on his mouth. "Too many people have peed in that suit."

A horrified laugh burst out of me. "No! What?"

He nodded and winced. "Oh, yeah." He shrugged. "Now you can be the only person to pee in this suit."

I dissolved into laughter, shaking my head. "I would never."

His eyes sparkled. "It's fine, bookworm. You don't have to lie to me. Besides," he added, "you've been doing great lately. With everything."

Delight pitched in my chest at his praise and we smiled at each other.

I thought about our kiss for the millionth time.

His mouth against mine, the noise he made when his tongue stroked mine, his hard chest under my hands. His hand in my hair, taking control and tipping my head back.

His gaze dropped to my lips. Something zinged in me, an ache between my legs.

"We should talk about the other night." He was still staring at my mouth, gaze intense.

I swallowed and nodded.

"I shouldn't have done that." He raked a hand through his hair and I remembered tugging on it, and the sound of pleasure in his throat.

Wait, what?

"Why not?"

He winced. "I'm not supposed to be——" He gestured between us. "This isn't that."

I deflated like a balloon with a hole in it. A slow, pathetic sink.

Wyatt regretted kissing me.

I chewed the inside of my lip and stared at the floor. My face heated, and I knew a blush creeped down my neck. Wyatt was still the hot guy from high school and I was the shy, invisible girl standing on the sidelines. The nerd in the bookstore. Of course he didn't want to get involved that way with me.

I crossed my arms over my chest. My stomach tightened and I frowned but tried to erase it. The only thing more embarrassing than Wyatt regretting making out with me would be him pitying me.

"Bookworm?"

I blinked up at him as he leaned on the wall beside us. He watched me with curiosity, with something else behind it I couldn't place.

I thought about him in my bedroom. He had said it himself, he couldn't stay away. He couldn't stop thinking about me that day.

Because I had a date with Beck. So he was jealous because someone else was playing with his toy.

I blew a frustrated breath out of my nose. "I don't have any grand delusions, you know."

He frowned. "What?"

I shrugged. "It's not like I think you and I are going to get married on the beach and skip off into the sunset holding hands." I rolled my eyes and pulled my shirt over my head. I already had my swimsuit on underneath.

Wyatt's gaze dropped to my chest. His jaw ticked. He turned around and crossed his arms.

And *that* was how I knew he wanted to kiss me again. Because when we started surf lessons? He didn't react like this.

A zap of that boldness hit me, the same feeling as when the wave was right behind me and I was about to jump up on my board. The same feeling as when I reached out to the artist about the mural. The same feeling as when I lifted up onto my tiptoes the other night and kissed Wyatt.

Wyatt wanted me as much as I wanted him, but something held him back.

I wasn't going to make it easy on him.

I slipped off my shorts. "I needed someone to practice with."

He rubbed the back of his neck, still facing the other way. "Is that a new swimsuit?"

"Yes. Don't change the subject." I had seen the two-piece in the window of a shop in town targeted towards tourists with overpriced swimsuits, flip flops, and beach bags with Queen's Cove stamped all over them. The green palm print was so pretty, fun, and summery that I made an impulse purchase.

And it pushed my boobs up. It showed off my stomach, which had developed a hint of abs over the past few weeks from surfing and trying to balance on my board. I wanted to look cute. Not for Wyatt. For myself.

Wyatt cleared his throat. "You don't need practice. Do you need help with the wetsuit?" He glanced over his shoulder, took one glance at me, muttered, "*Fuck*," and whipped his head back around.

Interesting. A little smile grew on my mouth. "Nope."

"Then hurry up."

I suppressed a laugh at his impatient, frustrated tone, so unlike him.

This swimsuit was proving to be a worthwhile purchase.

My mind buzzed and I rubbed my lips together, narrowing my eyes at his back. What was this feeling coursing through me? I felt... strong, like I held the power in this situation. I dangled something in front of Wyatt like a cat, toying with him.

Thérèse flickered into my mind. I bet she held the power with men all the time.

"If you won't practice with me," I said, keeping my voice casual as I pulled the suit on, "maybe Beck will."

That was a low blow. Wyatt had admitted he was jealous and here I was, exploiting that. Wyatt was always so cool and careless, and I got a glimpse of another side of him in my bedroom the other night.

I wanted more of that version of him. Passionate, desperate, needy. Like he cared about something. Me. He wanted me, as much as I would give him.

I wanted more of that.

He turned, took a step toward me, and glared down at me. "Do not do that, bookworm."

"Do what? Make out with Beck?"

His jaw ticked. I gave him an innocent smile and blinked a few times. He made an angry noise in his throat and turned me around before he yanked the zipper up. "How does it fit." He spat the words out like a statement, and I suppressed another grin.

I had turned the most easy-going guy in town into a cranky asshole.

I rolled my shoulders and moved my arms around. "Fits great. Way better than the rental one I was using." When I turned, his gaze had softened a little from the hard glare. "Thank you, Wyatt." I reached out and gave his arm a quick squeeze.

I hadn't finished teasing him yet. I let my hand linger on his bare skin.

"Your skin is always so warm. Did you know that?"

He didn't answer me, but his throat worked as he swallowed, staring down at me with an expression on his face like he was in pain. He gave me a tiny shrug.

I nodded, letting my hand skim down his arm before I pulled it back. "That was the first thing I noticed when you kissed me. How warm you were."

I fought to hold eye contact with him. Deep in my brain, a version of myself was squealing and rolling on the floor at my boldness. A different version of me shushed her and gave me an encouraging wink.

Wyatt's jaw was so tight, his frown so intense as he stared down at me. His fists clenched at his sides.

"Have you done your homework yet?" His voice was low and tight, and I thought about another thing he had said in my bedroom.

I know, baby. I know.

I shivered and shook my head. "Tonight."

I was talking about the date. It was Monday, and I was going for a solo dinner at The Arbutus.

And of course, there was the other part of my homework. The thing I was supposed to do after, by myself in bed. The thing I had of course done many times before.

But this time would be different. I knew it.

I shivered again and a heaviness settled between my legs. I was nervous but I was also… excited? Was he going to ask me about it after? The thought should have terrified me but instead, it sent a new series of shivers down my spine.

I sighed and smiled at him before I tucked my bag into a lower shelf and walked through the door.

"Are you coming?" I called over my shoulder to where he stood. "We have waves to catch, professor."

I would pride myself for a long time in not laughing at his agonized expression when I called him that.

———

AFTER LUNCH THAT AFTERNOON, the bookstore was quiet so I pulled out my laptop and watched old footage of last year's Pacific Rim. The competition was always on Labor Day weekend, and it was the last rush of tourists before the cooler fall months. All weekend, surfers walked down the main street to the beach, wetsuits on and boards tucked under their arms. I didn't watch the competition last year but instead chose to work in the store.

This year, you wouldn't be able to drag me from it. We'd close the store if we had to.

My dad wouldn't be back until October. Hesitation pressed on my chest. I missed him, of course. Evenings at home had been even quieter recently without him sitting on the other sofa, reading his own book.

I rolled my mouth into a flat line and glanced at the little white square sticking out of the iPad I had bought for the store. We had gone back to the farmer's market each Saturday, selling more and more books each time. A few tourism accounts had reposted some of my content, including one of Liya at the market talking to a customer, and it drove business to us.

On his blog, Don had written a detailed review of each book in the orc erotica series. A website in Victoria had found it hilarious and reposted it, and we had sold out of all the books in the series. A new shipment was due to arrive the next day. Selling orc porn to my dentist was mortifying but I wasn't in the business of sex shaming people.

I was in the business of selling romance novels.

The romance section of the store grew with every ship-ment. Most of my social media posts revolved around romance, because that's what Liya and I read, and that's what we liked talking about. Each book I posted about sold out within a week.

For the first time in a long time, our finances were in the black. I still wasn't paying myself a salary but I was saving the equivalent funds for the mural.

"Hey, Hannah?"

"Mm?"

Liya tilted her head. "How come you never post photos of yourself on the store's social media?"

I hesitated. "Um. I don't know. I'm not very photogenic."

She set a box on the counter and sliced it open. "Well, I think you are, and you should post pictures of yourself as well. You're the heart of this place."

I didn't know what to do with that information. I wasn't the heart of this place, my mom was. It was her store.

"When are you meeting with Naya?" Liya asked, interrupting my thoughts.

"Next week. Tuesday night." I straightened up. "You should come with me. You're part of this store too."

She gave me an apologetic expression. "My sister's in town next week so I'm going to show her around. We're going to a comedy show that night. Show me what Naya comes up with, though."

"Of course." Excitement rolled through me and I gave a little squeal of delight and clapped my hands. "Liya. It's going to look so good." I beamed at her. "I can't wait to take a picture of you under the new mural."

She beamed back at me and pulled a handful of books out of the box. Her eyes widened at the covers and she laughed. "More hockey player romances?"

I shrugged. "People love them."

Liya studied the shirtless man on the cover. "I can see the appeal."

I snorted. "Pervert."

"You're a pervert, too." Her shoulder shook with laughter.

"We're both perverts," I agreed before gesturing around at the store. "Two perverts working in a store with perverted books. My dream come true."

She laughed again and headed over to the Sports Romance section to shelve the books. I thought about the mural again as my gaze swept around the shop.

In three weeks, we'd have a beautiful new mural outside the store, and the inside would still look like *this*. Dusty, faded wallpaper. Shelves held together with duct tape. Frayed carpet at the door to the stockroom. Peeling sign out front, barely legible.

When coming up with ideas for social media content, Liya and I had been getting more and more creative. I was hesitant to show our store in the images so we either did close-ups of the books, ourselves, or an image of us near the window. I tried to get as little of the store in the shot as possible.

A sharp, expanding feeling flickered in my chest. I didn't want to be ashamed of the store anymore.

A cascade of soft thumps came from the book stacks.

"Shifter Romance just gave up on life," Liya called over before emerging from the shelves with a handful of books in her arms. She dumped them on the desk. "Wyatt can fix that one next."

"What?" My eyebrows shot up.

She nodded. "He and Holden were in yesterday. They fixed Mafia Romance."

I wandered over to the Mafia Romance shelf and peered under the plank of wood. Shiny brackets now held the shelf up. "Huh."

"Somebody likes you," Liya sang as she passed.

The kiss, the wetsuit, and now the shelf.

A delicious warmth spread through my chest and I grinned. "No, he doesn't."

She cocked her head. "Oh? He goes around to all the local businesses fixing shelves with his hot brother?"

I rolled my eyes. I didn't know what to say. Wyatt fixing the shelf had made my entire day. My shoulders lifted in a shrug and I returned to the desk to clear the remaining books.

The stupid wallpaper caught my eye again. Liya cut the bottom of the box to flatten it and the knife caught the light from the window.

There it was again, the same boldness that made me buy the swimsuit. Same as when I kissed Wyatt. It filled my chest and raced through my blood. My chest rose and fell with a deep breath.

"Can I borrow that for a second?" I held my hand out for the knife and Liya handed it over. I turned to the wallpaper panel behind the desk, reached up, and dragged a long slice through it.

Liya stared in delighted shock. "Oh, she really did that," she whispered, nodding with wide eyes.

I stared at the giant cut. There. Now we *had* to change it. A maniacal giggle bubbled out of me.

I handed the knife back to Liya. "Thanks."

"No problem."

Spice Girls played in the background as we stared at the damage. There was no turning back now. My dad would hate it, but he wasn't here and I had a business to run.

"After lunch, let's look at wallpaper samples online." My voice sounded stronger than I felt.

Liya took her lunch and in between customers, I reviewed more old surfing footage of Wyatt's in case I could pull anything for his social media.

On my laptop screen, Wyatt carved and glided over the water, harnessing it like he was a god. He made it look so easy, like walking or breathing.

In the footage from last year, Wyatt paddled hard to catch a big wave. He hopped up and turned, carving into the surf—

And then he kicked his back foot out and fell off the board.

In the video, the crowd let out a collective groan of disappointment.

My eyes narrowed and I replayed the last ten seconds. Wyatt paddling hard, Wyatt snapping up, Wyatt carving into the surf, and then that weird kick.

That kick was unnatural. I'd seen him surf so many times, both in person and on video.

It settled in my stomach, heavy and uneasy.

Whether he realized it or not, Wyatt had bailed on purpose.

14

Hannah

I WAS WALKING home from the store that evening, thinking about the husky way Wyatt's voice sounded that morning in the surf shop, when I paused in front of the hair salon.

What was it that Div had said? *You should cut your hair. Something shoulder-length and choppy.*

My fingers toyed with my ponytail, pulling it over my shoulder and inspecting it. The ends were fried from the sun and saltwater. I glanced back at the hair salon, where the stylist was blow drying someone's hair, and then at my reflection in the window.

My hair had always been long and straight. I only ever had the ends trimmed. I never had a teenage phase where I did something crazy. I never cut my own bangs. I never ruined it with cheap box dye and then cried on my bed all night about how bad it looked. I never did anything interesting with it.

It was time to try something new.

An hour later, I walked out of the salon with something shoulder-length and choppy. I paused again at my reflection in the window, back straight and head held high with a little smile on my face. I bit my lip and sucked in a deep breath.

I looked good. Really good. Hot, even.

My stomach swooped. It was working. The store was doing better, I had been going on dates and kissing and surfing and placing orders for wallpaper with giant flowers on it, and now, I had this cute haircut. I felt more like Thérèse every day.

I had the urge to stop by Wyatt's place and show him my haircut.

I shoved the thought out of my head. I'd show him tomorrow morning before our surf lesson.

I took one last glance at myself in the window before walking home to get ready for my date with myself.

———

"WELL, HELLO," Avery said with a big smile as I stepped into The Arbutus. "Look at your hair! You look so chic."

My eyes widened and I tugged the shorter ends. I kept touching my hair, expecting it to be long still. I couldn't help beaming back at her.

She glanced behind me with a curious expression. "Is your dad here? I thought he was on Salt Spring still."

"He is." I only ever dined at The Arbutus with him. "Just me tonight."

My face warmed as I glanced around the busy restaurant, filled with, families, and friends, laughing and talking and reaching across the tables and sharing dessert. I swallowed.

Wyatt had pressed on a sensitive spot. I'd never eaten in a restaurant by myself before. He knew how to push me one inch past my comfort zone. I glanced down at my outfit—a summer dress I bought for my birthday last year and hadn't worn. It was white linen with blue stripes and a V-neck. The white fabric brought out my tan, I had realized, standing in my bathroom at home, staring at myself. I had fumbled my way through eyeliner application, swiped on mascara, and rubbed a pretty pink lip balm onto my mouth. The necklace

Avery gave me last year with the little blue stone hung around my neck.

Tonight, I felt pretty.

Avery led me to a table near the front window and I took a seat, placing my book on the table beside me.

"Does the owner always work as hostess?" I grinned at her as she slipped a menu in front of me.

"Only for very special customers." She winked. "Wine?"

I nodded. "Yes, please. Surprise me."

She smiled again and disappeared. My gaze swept around the restaurant again. I made eye contact with a man at another table and self-consciousness spiked in my gut. People were bound to notice I was alone. Did they think I was on a date with someone else, waiting for them? Would they think I got stood up? Would they think I was a loner?

I fiddled with my fingers, twisting and pressing on my bare nails before I forced myself to stop and laid them flat on my lap.

What would Wyatt say? He'd shrug and say, *who cares what they think, bookworm?* My mom would say the same thing. Thérèse would say something like, *the power of the male gaze is restorative.* I snorted to myself and took another glance around.

No one stared at me. Everyone had their own meals and conversations. I was the only one worrying.

My worry eased a fraction, and I opened my book.

Minutes later, Avery returned, set a wine glass in front of me and poured. "Veggie bowl?"

I paused. The veggie bowl was my standard order here. Always. Tonight wasn't about routine, though.

I thought about the rest of my homework, Wyatt rasping the words against my skin in the dark, and I shivered. Tonight was about me. Tonight was about indulgence.

"Tonight, I'd like a bowl of pasta. A big one." I nodded once. Yes. That was what I wanted. "With cheese, please."

Avery lifted her eyebrows, scratching the order on a pad of

paper. "And that is what you shall receive." She glanced at me, that curious expression back on her face. "What made you cut your hair?"

I shrugged and touched it again. The ends were so much healthier and less tangled, and whatever products the stylist had used smelled incredible. Light, fresh, and pretty. "It was time for a change."

"I love it. You look so cute. It's so you."

I shrugged again, smiling at the table. In my chest, a bubble machine spewed out fizzy, happy feelings.

"Something's different about you." Avery tilted her head and narrowed her eyes at me.

I bit my lip, self-consciousness rising in me, but forced myself to sit up straight. "What do you mean?"

"You just…" She hummed before shrugging. "You seem happier. I like it. Surfing must agree with you."

She put a weird emphasis on the word *surfing*. Like the word *surfing* meant something else.

I pretended I didn't notice.

"You must really like *surfing*."

I rolled my eyes with a grin and she let out a loud laugh.

"Stop," I told her, but couldn't hide my grin.

"Emmett said he sees you two on the water a couple times a week while he's out on his run."

Each week, I've spent more time with Wyatt than the last. We surfed almost every day, and he often dropped by the store to say hi to Liya and me. He brought us lunch on Saturdays at the farmer's market. After surfing, we always got breakfast sandwiches at the truck.

I spent way more time with him than with anyone else. More than most friends would.

Almost like he was my boyfriend.

I nearly choked. Wyatt wasn't my *boyfriend*. The thought was laughable. He was *helping* me become a hot girl so I could *find* a boyfriend.

"I'm helping him with his social media," I told her with a shrug. "For Pacific Rim."

"Right." She nodded, eyes still narrowed. "And he's teaching you to surf and become a hot girl."

I gave her a tight smile and quick nod. "Mhm. Exactly."

"Well, for what it's worth, which isn't much, I think he likes you."

I stilled. The bubble machine in my chest sped up. "Why do you say that?"

"Same reason I told you at Div's place. He doesn't hang out with people, he just surfs. He's kind of a loner, but people don't realize that because he's so hot."

A laugh burst out of me. "He is really hot."

"Also," she leaned in closer to me, "if he doesn't like you, how'd you get that hickey on your neck?"

I gasped and slapped a hand over the spot on my neck. Liya hadn't said a word today, and neither did the hairstylist.

Oh my god. I had been walking around town with a *hickey* on my neck all day.

Oh my god. Elizabeth had stopped in the store today to pick a book up and her gaze had lingered on my neck. She had done a little wiggly dance. I thought she just had to use the washroom.

I slapped my forehead and my face burned with fire but before I could make an excuse—any excuse—Avery straightened up with a big smile.

"That's what I thought. I'll put your order in. See you in a bit."

She disappeared into the kitchen and I opened my book, staring at the page but seeing nothing. My face was as a bright red stop sign.

And then I started laughing. I laughed into my wine glass as I took a big swallow of it. Who was this woman I had become, who chopped off her hair and walked around with hickeys on her neck?

I focused on my book, sipping my wine and turning the pages until my food arrived. Avery had delivered a bowl that looked like two servings. The tomato flavor burst on my tongue and the savory cheese made me hum with delight. Mmmm, fat, salt, and flavor. I worked at the enormous bowl of pasta until I couldn't possibly eat any more. Another glass of wine appeared in front of me, and when I glanced up from my book, half the restaurant was empty and it was dark outside.

My phone buzzed and I read Wyatt's name on the screen.

Took this of you today. Thought you should see it.

It was a picture of me in the bookstore through the front window, shelving a book near the window and laughing about something with Liya. A soft smile on my face as I reached up to place the book in its right spot.

I looked happy.

Avery pointed at my bowl and I slipped the phone away. "Are you done? Can I pack this up?"

I nodded and sighed. "I'm so full. That was amazing."

"Dessert?"

"Of course."

She laughed and whisked the plate away before returning with a square of tiramisu. I dove in with enthusiasm.

This was fun, I realized, grinning to myself. The second I stopped caring if people were staring at me, I started enjoying myself.

And so what if they stared at me? They'd see Hannah Nielsen with a cute haircut, wearing a pretty dress that made her look like she might have boobs, eating an indulgent dessert and reading a book. Maybe they'd think, *Hannah Nielsen's living a good life.*

Thérèse would say something like, *they would be lucky to stare at you, 'annah.* I took another bite of the tiramisu and my eyes rolled back in my head.

My skin prickled and I opened my eyes. Wyatt towered

over the table, arms crossed over his chest. His eyes were dark, gaze heavy on me, and he frowned like I had offended him.

It was the same expression he had given me in my bedroom.

"You cut your hair." He leaned down, resting his palms on the table, still watching me with that intense look.

All I could do was nod. My fork hovered in the air. My pulse pounded in my ears. My mouth might have hung open. What was—

He lowered his mouth to mine and the fork clattered onto the table.

The warmth of his lips and the quiet in my head—that's all I noticed. No music, laughter, clink of glasses, or creak of footsteps on the old heritage floors. Wyatt's mouth was hot, firm, and demanding, seeking and coaxing mine open, tongue slipping against the seam of my mouth.

He sucked on my tongue and I might have moaned.

In a restaurant.

Kissing Wyatt.

I'm pretty sure I moaned. Especially when his hand came to my hair and he fisted it, tilting my head back to open me up more. A ripple of something hot and languid moved down my body to my core and I throbbed. His other hand brushed my jaw, gentle and light, nothing like his mouth.

He smelled like the ocean. Fresh and clean with something masculine underneath.

He nipped my bottom lip but cut my tiny gasp off by laving the sting with his tongue. He tasted me, explored my mouth, using me to sooth something inside of him.

I'm not sure how long he kissed me before he broke away and rested his forehead on mine. We were both breathing hard, gaze locked on each other. I ached between my legs and pressed my thighs together.

"Don't practice with Beck." His voice was low, barely

above a whisper. His gaze locked on mine. "You want to practice? You practice with me."

I jerked a nod.

"And Hannah?"

"Mmm?" I could barely speak.

"Don't forget the rest of your homework." His breath tickled my mouth.

My core clenched around nothing and I nodded. He dropped another quick kiss on my mouth before straightening up and walking back out the front door of the restaurant while I watched, stunned.

Out of the corner of my eye, someone at another table fanned herself.

I fell back to earth and glanced around the restaurant. Except for the music, it was silent. Everyone stared at either me or the door with open mouths.

Avery stood at the bar with bright eyes and a look that said *busted. That's what I thought*, she mouthed.

Twenty minutes later, I flew through my front door, tossed my bag down, and headed straight to my bedroom. I slammed the door, whipped my dress off and crawled under the covers.

I thought about Wyatt while I did my homework.

I thought about his fascinating mouth, the way it ticked up at the corner, the way he watched me with that easy grin. The playful, roguish expression he shot me as he teased me. The hungry, furious look he wore tonight.

I should have been embarrassed at the sigh that came out of my mouth when my fingers found the damp spot between my legs. I wasn't, though. I was wet. Of course I was wet. I had been wet since the second Wyatt's mouth took mine. I had been aching, twitchy, and wound up the entire way home. I had never been so frustrated or needy until him.

My fingers moved fast, swirling over my clit, and in my head, I replayed Wyatt kissing me in the restaurant. I replayed Wyatt here in my bedroom, groaning against me and tugging my hair. How hard he was when I rubbed against him. Electricity shot through my limbs, and my fingers moved fast over my wetness.

Soaked. I was soaked. I had the bizarre desire to tell Wyatt, for him to be proud of me, and I almost laughed at the ridiculousness of it, but then I remembered kissing him, being kissed by him, and I let out a whimpery moan.

I thought about what it would be like for Wyatt to lie in the bed with me. For him to watch me do this. For his fingers to work my clit. For him to sink into me, for my core to stretch around his hard length. For his demanding, needy mouth to take another part of my body, to make me writhe and grind on his mouth.

My back arched and I cried out as I came, thinking of Wyatt the entire time. Lights exploded in my vision despite my eyes being clenched closed. My core pulsed around emptiness but it wasn't enough. It was the strongest orgasm I had ever had, and it still wasn't enough.

I blew a long breath out, relaxing into the pillows.

A different woman, indeed.

15

Wyatt

I HAD BEEN PACING a hole in the ground for ten minutes when Hannah arrived behind the surf shop the next morning.

"Good morning." Her smile was easy and cheerful and her new haircut swayed around her face.

I itched to reach out and touch it. The memory of her silky hair in my hands yesterday haunted me all night.

Her smile dropped and she shook her head. "No. No way."

I made a hoarse, unintelligible noise in my throat like *huh?* and my eyebrows shot up.

She pointed a finger at my chest and narrowed her eyes. The finger poked me and I glanced between it and her face with a mix of curiosity, surprise, and amusement.

"You're not going to grab me, kiss me, and then get weird on me. I'm not being weird. So it happened." She crossed her arms. "You kissed me. Twice. But you don't get to be weird."

Her haughty nature made me grin. The Hannah from a couple months ago wouldn't have told me to stop being weird. "Sorry."

She watched me. "You think this is funny."

"I think everything is funny, bookworm."

We watched each other for a moment.

Last night, I went for a drink at the bar after surfing. I couldn't sit at home and think about Hannah touching herself. I had already been thinking about it all day. Thinking about her letting out those little sighs, like the one she did when our mouths met in her bedroom. Thinking about her arching off the bed, pressing her lips tight so she wouldn't cry out when she came.

Fuck. It drove me crazy all day.

So I went to the bar to distract myself but it didn't work. When I walked home and saw her sitting in the window of The Arbutus, smiling softly to herself while she read her book and sipped her wine, she was so goddamn gorgeous. Her hair was shorter. Her foot tapped gently on the floor. She wore a dress, a white and blue one I had never seen. Did she buy it for the date? And why did that make me so happy?

Standing on the sidewalk, I had remembered her mentioning *practicing*. Possessive irritation had ripped through me. I hated the idea of anyone's hands on her.

Anyone but me.

I wanted to be on that date with her, but she needed this. She needed to love herself the way—

I swallowed hard, looking down at her outside the surf shop. "Did you have a good time on your date?"

A slow, shy smile crept onto her face before she nodded.

"I hope your date told you how gorgeous you looked."

Pink washed over her cheeks and she grinned harder. "My date was lovely. I even got lucky."

My cock reacted to her words. My head fell back and I closed my eyes, rubbing my forehead. My mind flooded with images of her in the dark. "Fuck, bookworm."

She laughed. She actually *laughed*. I was in agony, fighting an erection and trying not to think about her in bed by herself, and she was laughing.

After I got home last night, I headed straight to the

shower, thinking about her soft lips, the little sighs she made and the way she melted right into me while I stroked myself until I came.

"Where's my shy bookworm?" I asked, shaking my head as her eyes shimmered with laughter.

My. It slipped past my lips without permission. I gauged her reaction, but she just smiled. The apples of her cheeks popped. Fuck, she was pretty.

She shrugged. "Guess you embarrassed it out of me."

"Your hair looks nice."

She reached up to touch it. "I like it, too. And this way it won't get so tangled and in my face when I fall off my board."

"You're falling less and less these days."

She bit her lip and shot me a tentative glance. "Wyatt?"

"Mmm?"

"I like surfing with you."

Well, damn if that tiny compliment didn't make me feel like a million bucks. "I like surfing with you too, bookworm."

She rolled her eyes. "You don't do much surfing out there, you just float and watch me make a sad attempt."

"You know what I mean."

Her cheeks were pink again and I wanted to feel the heat of them under my mouth.

"Anyway. Um." She shifted, toying with her hands. "If I do find a, uh, boyfriend," she said the word funny, like it tasted bad, "I still want to keep surfing with you." She lifted her gaze to mine. "If you have time, I mean. If you're still here in Queen's Cove. And if you don't have training or whatever."

The thought of Hannah finding someone—someone who'd be sitting across from her at The Arbutus, someone who'd get to touch her hair and kiss her and make her smile like that—it made me sick. It made me feel like something had been taken from me.

Which was insane, because Hannah wasn't mine. I was helping her out.

162

Guilt wrenched my stomach into a knot. I was supposed to be helping her, and I was trying to keep her. She trusted me and I was trying to get into her pants, telling her not to practice with other guys. Fuck.

I was such an asshole.

My chin jerked in a nod at her. My eyebrows pulled together in a frown. "Sure, bookworm. We can surf together as long as you want." I gestured at the back door of the shop. "Shall we?"

We headed inside and retrieved our wetsuits. Hannah reached down and I watched as she pulled her shirt over her head.

Fuck. She was wearing that swimsuit again. The one that pushed her tits up into something incredible. If she knew how fuckable she looked in that suit, she wouldn't have worn it around me.

Or maybe she would have. Yesterday morning in the back of the shop, she toyed with me, trying to get a rise out of me.

I waved the thought away in my head and turned to face the other way.

Surfing. That's all we were doing today. I was going to be present with her, and with the ocean.

"Zip me up?"

I turned to see her standing with her back to me, wetsuit unzipped and smooth skin so close. I swallowed, and my throat was thick. I pulled the zipper gently, slowly, slower than necessary. Definitely slower than I would with a tourist doing a lesson. At the top of the zip, my fingers brushed the ends of her hair, and she shivered before turning and giving me a little smile.

"Hey, professor?"

Fuck, that nickname. I thought about her calling me that last night with my hand wrapped around myself. The soft, playful, teasing way she always said it made me come almost immediately.

"Mhm?" I closed my eyes and rubbed the bridge of my nose. *Deep breath.*

"You didn't ask me if I did all my homework."

Blood surged to my cock and I exhaled through my nose.

Helping her. Not fucking her. Helping. Not okay to take advantage of her. She was less experienced. Helping. Not getting hard in my surf shop while talking to her. Not jerking off thinking about her mouth on my cock.

I couldn't think straight right now. "I'm sure you did." I opened my eyes to see her watching me with a smug grin.

Fuuuuuuck.

My cock ached. That smug grin told me everything I needed to know.

"I thought about you while I did my homework." She gave me a shy but pleased smile before she walked to the door.

I watched her ass in the wetsuit and longed to slap it for what she was doing, teasing me and pushing me to the edge of control like this.

She was making me want her, and she knew what she was doing.

Hannah paused at the doorway and raised an eyebrow, still wearing that smug smile. "Are you coming?"

We didn't talk much on the water that morning. The cold water helped my erection subside and I focused on Hannah, hopping up on her board and catching waves. Sometimes, I threw out feedback, but I mostly let her figure it out herself. Her intuition was sharpening, she was learning the perfect timing of the waves, she was learning which waves to catch and which to let go because they were too messy, and when the ocean tossed her off her board?

She laughed. More and more, she laughed. She was learning it didn't matter if she failed. It didn't matter if she didn't nail that one wave, because there'd be another. There was always another. Each wave existed only in the moment and then it was gone forever.

Something panged in my chest but I ignored it.

The feeling swerved right back around, and I knew Hannah and I were like that. Spending time with her was the easiest thing in the world but come September, I might be leaving if the competition went well. The sensation sharpened, pinching me. Hannah and I existed in the moment like everything else in the universe. I thought about my aunts, how temporary it was for them, too temporary, and how heartbroken Bea had been when her wife passed. How heartbroken she still was. The woman wouldn't set a foot back in town since she sold me the house.

The thought of not surfing with Hannah, not spending mornings out here in nature with her? It made me feel like I was losing something important.

I swallowed and let a wave roll past me, taking the thoughts with it. I didn't want them. Didn't want to think about it.

Present. Focused. I was with Hannah this morning, so I turned my thoughts back to the now.

When this was all over, I could reminisce and deal with those emotions. But for now, I was going to enjoy the moment.

After an hour, she grew tired so we paddled to our cove and floated side by side on the water, soaking in the morning rays of sun.

She lifted her head. "Did that guy contact you?"

I opened one eye. "What guy?"

"The Billabong guy. Emilio something."

Right. I nodded. "He did." I called him back the other morning and he had walked me through what a sponsorship would look like. The company would pay me to wear their gear and take a couple pictures at a studio as long as I got to pro level and kept my nose clean.

She gestured, like *go on*. "Well?"

I flashed her a grin and shrugged. "It depends how I do at Pacific Rim."

"And if you do well…?"

I stared at the sky. "It sounds like I have a sponsorship." A splash of water hit me in the face and I burst out laughing. "What was that for?"

She beamed at me, so bright I thought my heart might crack open. "Wyatt. You did it."

"Not yet." It was so easy to rest my gaze on her. Like it belonged there. Like looking at her was healthy for my soul.

"You will. This is big. We should celebrate."

"What did you have in mind?"

She tilted her head and chewed her lip. "Will you take me camping?"

"Camping." I snorted. "With bugs and dirt and peeing in the woods?"

When she laughed, her chest shook, and mine flooded with warmth. "Yeah, that camping. But also with trees and sky and stars and a campfire. I used to go with my parents. My mom loved it. We're allowed to have campfires, right? I see people having them on the beach all the time."

During summer, there was often a campfire ban in our province because a hot, dry summer led to wildfires, which was where my brother Finn was right now. Every summer, he left to fight wildfires around British Columbia before returning in October.

"We're in the fog zone, so we can have a fire. Do you have camping gear?"

There was that big smile again. I'd do anything to keep it on her face. She nodded. "We have a tent and stuff in the garage."

We decided to go the next night. There were a lot of provincial parks in the area, campgrounds owned and maintained by the province, but they booked up months in advance. Besides, they were too populated. Hannah wanted nature, silence, and stars. I knew a spot further up into the forest where we could camp undisturbed.

The thought of having her all to myself for a night sent blood rushing to my groin. I shoved the thought from my mind. We'd have separate tents. It wouldn't be like that.

On her board beside me, Hannah let out a long sigh. "I'm very relaxed today."

Another image of her in bed flashed into my head and I stifled a tortured groan. She giggled.

On second thought, a night alone with Hannah, with her all to myself, teasing me and shooting me those smug looks?

It was going to be fucking agony.

16

Hannah

"I GOT YOU SOMETHING."

Wyatt flashed me a tentative grin from the driver's seat of his truck. "Oh, yeah?"

We were on the highway, his truck full of camping gear and a cooler of food, drinks, and ice. Music played on the radio and trees blurred as we drove past.

I fished the tiny figure out of the pocket of my jacket and hung it from the rearview mirror. Wyatt studied it with brief glances, alternating between the road and the swaying figure.

He snorted. "Is that supposed to be me?"

I grinned wide. "Yep."

I had contacted someone on Etsy with the Tula music video and commissioned a 3D-printed figurine of him, merman costume and silver body paint and all. The figure was about two inches tall. I didn't tell this to Wyatt but I had one made for myself as well. It sat on my dresser at home.

It made economic sense to buy two. The designer only had to create the design once. And this way, if Wyatt lost his, he'd have a backup.

Wyatt shot me a wry look. "I love it and hate it at the same time."

That made me laugh. I turned and watched out the window as he drove, smiling to myself and listening to the music. My stomach rolled forward. God, he was handsome. Even the crinkles around his eyes were hot.

He reached over and gave my knee a quick squeeze, making my stomach flutter. "Thanks, bookworm."

I thought about the way he looked yesterday in the surf shop, when I told him about doing my homework. The heated hunger in his eyes. The way his mouth pressed into an unhappy, unsatisfied line, like he was doing everything he could to hold back.

The way his gaze flared when I called him *professor*. I'd keep that in my back pocket for later.

"You're welcome." I smiled out the window.

Anticipation rolled through me and I pressed my thighs together. Maybe he'd kiss me again tonight. My stomach fluttered and I bit a grin back.

"You look cute in those glasses."

I hadn't worn them in a while. I rolled my eyes. "I'd rather wear my contacts but I didn't know if it was a good idea to put dirty camping fingers in my eyes."

"I brought lots of hand sanitizer." His gaze raked over my face with appreciation. "I like your glasses, though."

My chin dipped down and I played with my hair again. No one had ever said I was cute in glasses. I always thought I looked like such a dork. "Thanks."

"You want to put on Spice Girls? I don't mind."

"Are you sure?" I already had my phone out, fingers scrolling to the playlist. "We don't have to."

He jerked his chin at the radio and rolled his eyes with a grin. "Go on. I know you want to."

The opening notes of 'Wannabe' started and I sang loudly with them to make Wyatt laugh.

"You know all the lyrics."

I threw my hands up. "Of course I know all the lyrics. This song is a *classic*. It's carved deep in my brain."

Forty-five minutes later, Wyatt turned off the highway and the truck bumped up a series of gravel switchbacks, higher and higher. He pulled the truck off the road and parked on the shoulder.

"There's a clearing through those trees." He pointed into the forest.

We climbed out of the car and Wyatt led me along a small path, worn down by footsteps, through the trees.

"Oh, wow," I breathed.

The clearing overlooked the ocean. The area was flat with slates of rock underfoot. Fifty feet away, a cliff dropped down, too far for me to want to approach. Beyond that, deep blue water stretched all the way to the horizon. Trees towered around us.

Wyatt stood at my back, warm and solid, and I fought the urge to lean against him.

"See, down there?" He pointed to a spot. There were a few specks in the water. "That's the cove where we hang out after surf lessons."

"We're so high up."

"Mhm." His low voice rumbled in his chest.

A deep sense of calm settled through me, like when we floated in that cove in the mornings. The forest smelled so clean and my hair moved with the light breeze. At what point did I stop spending time out in nature like this? This was where I belonged.

Right. When my mom passed. My dad didn't want to go camping anymore because that was her thing. It broke my heart that he didn't want to be out here anymore.

The wind whistled through the trees and I inhaled a lungful of fresh air. She'd love it here.

I glanced around the clearing. A charred pile of ash encircled by rocks lay a few feet from us. Wyatt noticed me studying it and wiggled his eyebrows in that playful way of his.

"Not many people know about this spot." His voice was low as he watched my reaction.

"It's a secret?"

He nodded. "Super secret. We don't want some social media influencer ruining it for us."

I beamed and turned back to the water. I couldn't wait to wake up to this tomorrow morning. "I wouldn't dare."

We spent the next half hour unloading the truck, hauling tents, sleeping bags, a stove, and the cooler over to the clearing.

"Jesus, bookworm." Wyatt hoisted my bag out of the back seat. "How many nights are we staying out here?"

A laugh bubbled out of me. "I brought a few books."

He raised his eyebrows at me and I giggled more. "A few? How many do you think a few is?"

My shoulders lifted in a shrug and he pinned me with his bright gaze. I rolled my eyes. "Four. Okay? I brought four books." I threw my hands up in exasperation. My chest shook with laughter. "I couldn't decide. They were all sitting there like, *Hannah, take us with you! Don't leave us home alone. It's sad here. We love you.*"

Now, Wyatt was laughing, too. "You're adorable."

My blood turned warm and languid, and my laughter trailed off. His gaze dropped to my mouth and my pulse picked up.

He blinked and turned away. "We should keep unpacking."

"Right." Unpacking. Not staring at each other and feeling horny.

At one point, when I was carrying my tent from the car, a spider crawled out of it. It was the size of a dime but I still yelped in surprise, dropped the tent, and side-stepped towards Wyatt, whose arm came up around me protectively.

"Sorry." My face heated.

He squeezed my shoulder. "It's okay." He scooped the spider up and moved it to the forest. When he returned, he gestured at my tent. "Your tent is older than we are."

I nudged the rolled up bundle with my foot in case there was anything else lurking inside. "It is. It's been in the garage for years. It's one of those things we've always had and I've never questioned."

He nodded, grinning, before he leaned down to unroll it.

I held my hand out to stop him. "I can do that."

He shook his head. "It's fine. Can you grab the newspaper from the truck? I'll teach you how to make a fire once we set up the tents."

I raised an eyebrow at him. "I already know how to make a fire." My mom taught me as a kid.

His mouth fell open, crouched over the tent. "I'm sorry. I didn't mean—I guess because you don't camp anymore—"

"It's okay." I grinned at him. "I'm out of practice so might need your help, anyway." With that, I headed to the truck. When I returned to the clearing with the newspaper in hand, Wyatt wore a funny expression, standing over the tent with his arms crossed.

"Uh, bookworm, we have a problem." His mouth twisted and he frowned at the tent on the ground.

"What?"

He lifted it to show me.

Where the zipper should have connected to the rest of the tent, there was a big hole. The zipper lay on the ground.

"It's ripped?"

"Looks like it." His voice sounded strange. Kind of tight, and he wouldn't look at me. He just stared at the zipper.

"I should have known. My dad has so much stuff in the garage that he needs to get rid of." Anything to do with my mom.

Wyatt crouched to roll the tent back up. "You can sleep in my tent."

I watched his hands as he rolled the fabric. They were tanned from being outside, strong, with long fingers. Clean nails. I shivered. Sleeping in Wyatt's tent. A throb hit me between my legs and I clenched before sending him a tentative glance.

"I'll sleep in the truck." He stood up with the tent and walked past me, back to the truck, and I watched him walk away.

Disappointment twinged in my stomach but I waved it away. That wasn't what this camping trip was about. It was about celebrating Wyatt's sponsorship. It was about being out in nature because we lived in one of the most beautiful places in the world. It wasn't about me being horny every time I thought about Wyatt or caught a whiff of him or imagined his hands leaving marks on my ass.

I know, baby, I know. I heard his words again in my head and I shivered.

Wyatt strode through the trees, so tall and confident in the way he moved. He held a new bundle in his hands, something blue and woven.

"What's that?"

"This," he said, shaking the fabric out, "is where you're going to spend the afternoon."

It was a hammock. After we selected two sturdy trees with a view of the water, Wyatt and I strung it up and he helped me climb in.

"Lean forward for me," he said in a low voice, pulling me forward gently in the hammock with a little smile before placing a pillow behind my head. He dropped a blanket over me and tucked it into my sides. "Comfy?"

I nodded with wide eyes and a big smile, and he laughed and walked away. I sank into the pillow and let myself sway. I could have stayed there forever. The blanket was warm and heavy. Something about Wyatt bringing this for me, tucking me into the hammock and wanting me to lie here and read, it sent warmth through my chest.

Him taking care of me like I was something to be cherished made me never want to leave this campsite. Did he do this for other girls he hung out with? My instincts told me no.

The idea of Wyatt leaving after Pacific Rim made my heart hurt. Floating in the cove wouldn't be the same without him beside me.

I rubbed my chest and pushed the thoughts from my head.

While I read, Wyatt puttered around the campsite, setting up his own tent and making himself a coffee, asking me if I wanted one. At one point I glanced over and he was sitting back in a camp chair, feet up on the cooler, reading one of the books I had brought with a lazy grin on his face.

Like he was enjoying himself.

I must have dozed off because when I opened my eyes, the book was on the camp chair.

A *thwack!* caught my attention. I sat up and searched for the source of the noise.

A shirtless Wyatt lifted an axe over his shoulder and brought it down over a piece of wood, splitting it into pieces. His abs rippled as he moved, his obliques jumped and his pecs flexed. His arms were defined and strong and his shoulders broad. I saw him shirtless nearly every day, but seeing him chopping wood like this? So masculine, primal, sweaty, and so freaking gorgeous?

I was lost.

I got pulled under from how freaking gorgeous he was.

And I was very, very wet.

"Are you serious?" I whispered under my breath.

I watched Wyatt for some time, raising the axe over his head and bringing it down to split piece after piece. At one point, he glanced over and saw me spectating before flashing me a panty-melting grin.

He *knew* how hot he was.

Maybe this was payback for teasing him the other morning.

I snapped a quick video of him chopping wood for social media. His fanbase was going to lose their minds.

Late afternoon rolled around and I showed Wyatt my fire-building skills. I crumpled up the newspaper, laid the sticks of kindling on top, and watched the flames ignite before stacking progressively larger pieces of wood on top. Within minutes, we had a crackling fire in front of us.

"Nice work, bookworm." His voice was a low rumble and he flashed another one of those grins at me.

I melted.

———

"TO YOUR SPONSORSHIP," I said, raising my camping mug of red wine. The fire cracked and sent a flurry of sparks near my foot. Wyatt reached out and pulled my camp chair a couple inches closer to his.

Wyatt's mouth hitched at the side. "I don't have it in the bag yet."

"Yeah, but you will. And this is a big deal. Good job, professor."

His gaze flared with heat and he watched me over the rim of his mug. "Do you want another hot dog? I brought lots."

I shook my head. I'd already had two. "Where'd you find veggie dogs? I didn't think they sold them in the store in Queen's Cove."

"I drove to Port Alberni yesterday to grab them."

"They're surprisingly good. Even for hot dogs."

That made him grin. "We have to eat hot dogs when we're camping, bookworm. It's the rule."

We smiled at each other for a moment. The idea of sleeping in Wyatt's tent flashed into my head again. Would it smell like him in there? How would I sleep with that intoxicating, masculine scent in my nose?

Above us, stars winked down from the dark sky. Less light pollution in the woods made the sky look like someone had scattered a handful of glitter.

"It's so quiet out here."

"Mhm." He nodded, gaze on me. "No cell service. No background noise. Just quiet."

"I keep having the urge to check my phone. Oh, I didn't tell you. I set up an online store."

His eyes widened with surprise. "You did? That's great. When did that happen?"

"A couple days ago. My social media posts picked up a bit of traction and there were a couple customers from around Vancouver Island asking about purchases. Some people wanted to order books in so it was easier to set up the store online." I shrugged.

"Look at you." His grin was easy. "I'm proud of you."

My chest tightened in a good way, and my face warmed. I tried to hold back my grin but failed.

He nodded. "You've done a lot for the store recently. And for yourself." He tilted his head, still watching me. "I like seeing you like this."

"Like what?" I was fishing, but I didn't care. I needed to know what Wyatt liked about this new me.

"I like when you do things for yourself, and when you push yourself even though you're worried or nervous or scared." His eyes flicked to my hair and he smiled. "I like your haircut. You look cute."

Another flush of warmth to my face. I blinked down at my hands in my lap. "Sometimes I think that I'm turning into a new person." I chewed my lip and thought about it. "But then I wonder, maybe this is who I actually am, and I was holding myself back from everything good." I shrugged. "From trying things, from failing." I lifted my gaze to him, where he watched and waited. "I hate failing at things. Or hated." I frowned. "I don't know anymore. I'm getting better at being bad at things."

"Just in time for your birthday."

A shiver of unease rolled through my stomach. My birthday loomed in the background of my mind at all times. Sometimes I could ignore it, or pretend it wasn't there, but then I'd be paddling for a wave or reading my book or posting on social media or walking to the grocery store and it would pop into the forefront of my mind.

Thirty. I was going to be thirty in two weeks.

The store was back in the black this month. It was too soon to tell whether I had saved it or not, but the website, social media, and weekly farmer's markets were bringing in more sales. If sales kept up, we might stay in the black into the winter.

I felt pretty the other night when I was on the date by myself. I loved my new haircut. I could surf at a beginner level and had asked guys out on dates, even if none of that panned out. I could safely check off the hot girl goal.

But I didn't have a boyfriend, I hadn't found true love, and I wasn't sure if my mom would be proud of me.

I think she might, though. I was pushing myself, making changes and doing the scary things. I thought about kissing Wyatt, how I never would have done that before all this. I smiled to myself, playing with a thread on the arm of my camp chair. My mom would have loved to hear how I had kissed a boy. She would have been excited to hear that I had made the move.

Were all these things enough? Would my mom look down at me and say, yep, that's my girl, she's killing it? Or would she be disappointed still?

"What's going on in that head?" Wyatt's voice was casual but his gaze pinned me. He rubbed his jaw.

A corner of my mouth lifted in a half-smile. "Just thinking."

He shifted in his camp chair, getting comfortable and taking another sip of wine, giving me the option to tell him more or not. I felt a bizarre pull to divulge everything to him.

"My mom, she…" I narrowed my eyes at the blanket of stars. "She went for things, you know? She had such a fun spirit, so passionate about things, and she took control over her life. She loved books so she opened a store to sell them. She always had music on in the house and she loved going on adventures around the island."

A memory appeared in my head and a huge grin grew on my face. "I remember when the Spice Girls came to Vancouver. This was back when you either bought tickets in person or on the phone." I leaned forward to Wyatt. "She was on hold for *hours*."

"Did she get tickets?"

I shook my head, still smiling. "No, but that's okay. I still have that memory of her." I swallowed, and my throat was thick. "I want to do that for someone, one day. I want to shower someone in love and make them feel special. Like they're everything to me." Tears stung my eyes and I blinked them away, turning so Wyatt wouldn't see. My chest twisted hard with nostalgia.

"I remember her."

My gaze snapped to his and my eyebrows lifted. "You do?"

He took another sip of wine before answering. "Mhm. She came to my kindergarten class. She read a book about fish."

My face lit up. "She loved volunteering for story time."

"She was really good at reading the story. She did all the voices."

"That sounds just like her."

We were quiet a moment. My heart was about to crack open.

Wyatt studied my expression. "You look sad, bookworm."

I had the urge to smile and tell him it was nothing, but this was also Wyatt, and we didn't do that. I could be honest with him. I could tell him.

"I think my mom would look at me right now and be disappointed."

"Sitting in the middle of a forest with one of the Rhodes boys?"

I laughed. "No." I waved my hand at myself. "I'm living in her shadow."

"So that's what the whole birthday list thing is all about?"

I pressed my mouth into a line and nodded at him.

He made a noise in his throat, a mix between acknowledgement and disapproval.

I frowned.

"Now, bookworm, that bums me out." He rubbed his jaw, and when his eyes met mine, a spark hit me in the chest. "Because I think you're amazing. You're thoughtful, funny, and brave, and you're a good boss."

"I'm not the boss."

He lifted an eyebrow. "You are. You manage the store and it's clear Liya enjoys working for you. You run that place, however it's broken down on paper between you and your dad."

I didn't say anything. He was right, I did run the business.

"You're living life for yourself. You're starting to be willing to fail. Your mom wouldn't want you to be her clone. She'd want you to do whatever made you happy, whether that's working in the bookstore or falling face first off your board or eating a huge bowl of pasta, sitting by yourself in a restaurant, looking fucking beautiful."

My breath caught in my throat. He watched me so intently, so clearly, like I was all he could see. My heart squeezed.

"I think you're amazing," he repeated, softer this time.

"And I don't think your mom would be disappointed in you. She'd be proud."

I swallowed. My heart thumped hard in my chest. Wyatt's words etched something sweet into my heart. There was that sting of pain from the nostalgia, of memories that had passed, experiences I'd never have again. I'd never talk to her again. I'd never hug her and feel the warmth of her chest against my face. I'd never smell her light, floral perfume.

This was all I had, talking about her with Wyatt.

I wondered once if she would have liked Wyatt. Sitting there in the forest across from him, the fire crackling in front of us, him watching me with that warm gaze, I knew she would. I knew they'd get along, and that she'd give me a *he's cute!* look the second he turned around.

"What are you smiling at?" A teasing grin grew on his face.

I shook my head, letting myself smile wider. "Nothing. Talking about her with you is nice."

We watched each other for a moment. The light of the fire flickered over his face, lighting his eyes up. My gaze took him in as I memorized the moment.

"I'm going to miss you." I tried to smile at him but my mouth twisted. I cleared my throat. "When you leave, I mean."

He frowned but didn't say anything. His gaze swung to the fire.

The video of Wyatt surfing flashed into my head, and that weird kick he did.

"Question for you."

He met my gaze and nodded. "Go for it."

"Pacific Rim, last year." I tugged at my bottom lip with my teeth, not sure how to say it. "I was watching some footage." My knee bounced up and down. "For social media clips. Um." An uncomfortable laugh huffed out of my chest. "You fell off your board."

Wyatt watched me with an unreadable expression. His hand tightened on his mug.

I tilted my head with a wince. "It wasn't a big wave but you fell. And you kicked." I glanced up at him to see him studying me. "You kicked your leg back and fell off your board."

He cleared his throat and stared into the fire before he closed his eyes and exhaled a long breath. "Yep. I kicked."

"Did you—" My words broke off and his gaze snapped up to me.

"Say it."

I shook my head. What if I was wrong?

His eyes were bright. "Say it, bookworm."

"Did you do it on purpose?"

He pressed his mouth into a thin line before he nodded. "Yep."

"Why?" I breathed.

He raked his hair back and blew a breath out. "I don't know, bookworm. I've been asking myself that question for a year. I panicked out there. It was right there." His throat worked. "I was going to place well in the competition, and then I saw it all—surfing for a living, traveling all over the world, rubbing elbows with the best surfers." He met my gaze. "I'd be surfing with people I've looked up to since I was a kid." His hand tightened on his mug again and he shook his head. "It was so sweet that I couldn't even look at it. I had been working towards it for so long that the idea of finally having it, it was…" He shifted. "I panicked."

A log cracked in the fire and sparks flew.

"How are you feeling about it in a few weeks?"

I had asked him the question before but he knew what I meant this time. How are you *really* feeling, I was asking.

"Scared out of my fucking mind." He huffed a laugh and shook his head at me. "The idea of doing it again scares me and the idea of doing well scares me. What the fuck is up with that? I don't know why I'm acting like this."

My heart ached for him. In my mind, Wyatt held a shield in front of him with the words *everything is temporary* engraved on it.

"Bookworm," he said, and his gaze rested on me with such sad longing that it broke my fucking heart. "Hanging out with you on the water, it's been the best summer of my life."

He shot me a sad smile and my heart tumbled down a flight of stairs.

"Me too," I whispered.

I shivered and pulled my jacket around myself more. It was cooler up here in the mountains.

"Cold?"

I slipped my hands up into my sleeves. "A little."

"Come here."

My stomach rolled forward. He murmured it but the authority in it, the command, made me shiver. I stood and walked to him, and he pulled me into his lap. My pulse raced as his arms came around me. He warmed me as I sank into him, pressed against his thighs and chest. His arms locked around me and I leaned my head back against him. His scent teased my nose, fresh and masculine.

"Better?" His hand brushed my arm.

I nodded with a small, shy smile.

"I have an extra jacket and toque in the car for you if you want it."

"I'm okay like this."

"Good. I like you like this, too."

His mouth was so close to mine. Inches away. I had the urge to trace it, run my finger along the lines and soft skin of his mouth. The hair on the back of my neck prickled with awareness, and goosebumps rose along my skin under my jacket. The image of him shirtless that afternoon, chopping wood, flashed into my head and my pulse thrummed between my legs. A throb. Like I was empty and needed something to clench on.

I shivered. I needed *him*. I wanted to clench on *him*.

He shifted beneath me and my eyes widened when his hard length pressed into me. A muscle in his jaw ticked.

"Bookworm, you're making it real hard to be a gentleman when you look up at me like that." His chest rose and fell with a deep breath but his gaze dropped to my mouth.

"So don't be." The idea that he wanted me back made the heaviness between my legs intensify. The air between us crackled.

His jaw ticked again and his hands tightened on me, one on my thigh and one on my waist. The hand on my waist slid lower, to my hip. Sparks zinged up my spine.

"Bookworm." He groaned it like he was in pain. "I'm supposed to be helping you."

I wanted his mouth on mine again. I wanted his mouth all over me, and from the way he was looking at me like he wanted to devour me, he wanted the same thing.

I didn't want to be shy Hannah anymore. I didn't want to miss out on life anymore.

I shifted on his lap to get a better view of his face. I slipped my hand higher on his chest until my fingers brushed his warm, bare skin above the collar.

His eyelids fell closed. He exhaled through his nose and his fingers dug into my hip.

Something rustled in the bushes. I tensed and whipped my head around.

"What was that?" I asked, peering into the dark.

"Probably a bear." His voice was thick.

"What?" My voice squeaked and I lifted my legs off the ground, as if that would help. I was basically climbing him.

His low chuckle vibrated through his chest. "Don't worry. I'll keep you safe." His arm tightened around me, and I believed him.

Our gazes met. I was practically straddling him. "I know you will." A streak of boldness hit my bloodstream and I bit my lip. "We should go into the tent. So the bears don't eat us."

He snorted but his eyes darkened. His gaze dropped to my mouth again. "Hannah…" I could hear the hesitation in his voice. "I don't want to take advantage of you."

"I want you to." A tiny voice in my head screamed *what are you doing???* but I shoved that voice aside and pressed a soft kiss on Wyatt's mouth.

He made a noise of anguish and his fingers dug deep into my hip. I smiled against his mouth before I pulled back to gaze into his hooded eyes.

"Besides," I murmured, watching his pained expression with enjoyment. "Don't you think it's time you give me more homework?"

17

Wyatt

I PUT the fire out while Hannah got into the tent. I poured water on the flames and watched the steam rise into the sky. Once the hissing water had evaporated and only a few embers remained, I headed to the tent.

My pulse beat in my ears like a drum. I was so hard. So fucking hard.

This is not what you think it'll be, I told myself. This was Hannah. Sweet, innocent Hannah. It didn't matter that no guy had been smart enough to make her come. It didn't matter that I wanted to make her back arch, make her eyes roll into the back of her head. That wasn't my place.

So what the fuck was I doing, pulling her into my lap and touching her hip and smelling her hair like I wanted to keep her?

I knew this feeling. This was the *big wave* anticipation, the flash of uncertainty as I watched a wave approach in Thailand three years ago. I was new to the area and didn't know the waves like I did in Queen's Cove. I couldn't read it but I still went for it, and I bailed hard. The wave tossed me around like a rag doll.

This thing between Hannah and me, it wasn't normal. I'd

never wanted anyone like I wanted her. It wasn't like anything I'd ever experienced and I didn't know how to ride it.

The zipper purred when I closed it and I sat on the air mattress beside her. It was dark but I could make out her form in the dim light. "I should sleep in the car."

"No, thank you."

I huffed a laugh.

She settled into her sleeping bag behind me, and I swallowed. I undressed down to my boxer briefs and slipped into my own sleeping bag beside her, not looking at her. I kept at least a foot between us and closed my eyes.

My skin prickled with the weight of her gaze.

I thought about you while I did my homework, professor.

My throat worked again. Fuck. My hands made fists at my sides and I clenched my thighs to drain the blood from my hardening cock.

"Wyatt." Hannah's voice was barely above a whisper, and there was a light layer of something in it. Curiosity.

I ached at the soft tone of her voice. "Mhm?" Could she hear how horny I was?

She sighed and the air mattress moved as she shifted. I could still sense her thinking. I opened my eyes and from the dim light of the moon on the tent, I caught the glitter of her eyes as she watched me with a bitten lip.

"What is it?" My voice was husky. "What's wrong?"

"I want—" She worried her lip with her teeth.

"What?"

She hesitated.

"What, Hannah? What do you want?"

Her gaze pinned me. "I want you to make me come."

Lust rocketed through me. There was no distracting this hard-on away. My cock ached for Hannah and the needy way she said that. A shiver rolled through me.

"I don't know," I said, like a fucking dumbass.

This wasn't some woman I met in a bar. This was

Hannah. If we did this, if she pulled me under like a riptide, how could I walk away in September? Making her come, making her moan and twist and pant and whimper while rubbing her hot little center or thrusting inside her—fucking hell—I'd never get her out of my head.

One wrong move, losing focus for a split second, and she'd pull me under and swallow me up. There was a current within me, tugging me towards her. Wanting her.

I fucking wanted her, especially right now when she lay beside me, watching me with a hopeful, hungry look. I'd bet there was a blush on her cheeks.

She wiggled closer until she was inches away from me. Not touching me, but so close. "How can I know what I like if I don't get any practice?"

"You're supposed to practice on your own." Only on her own. Not with anyone else.

"I want to practice with you, like you said."

Fuck. I did say that. "You're making it hard to say no to you," I rasped, clenching my eyes closed. I could smell her shampoo and it reminded me of when I was in her room, her body pressed against mine. Another shiver rolled through me. Every cell in my body wanted to kiss her again, pull her hair gently to open her sweet mouth up to me.

"I trust you."

God, those words. *I trust you.* I groaned.

She sighed. "I need to come. I've been thinking about it all day."

My control broke. If that was what she needed, I would be her faithful servant. I'd do it well, too. I'd make her come harder than she ever had with her hand between her legs, late at night, all by herself. I'd make her remember me, even when she was madly in love with some other guy and I was on the other side of the world, thinking about her.

I yanked the zipper down on her sleeping bag and pulled her against me. Our legs tangled. She wasn't wearing pants.

My hand came to her hip again. She was in a t-shirt and tiny lacy panties that made me feel like I could come by her breathing on my cock.

I looked into her eyes. "You want to come?"

She nodded.

"Come here." I pulled her mouth to mine.

Her mouth was soft. Sweet, shy, a little curious, like her. I was slow with her, tangling my fingers in her silky hair, stroking her scalp as I kissed her slow and soft. I knew this feeling, too. Kissing Hannah was wading into the water every morning. Her mouth both gave me relief and turned up my need for more.

She nipped my lip with her teeth and rubbed against me. Her thigh brushed my cock.

"Hannah, *fuck*."

She laughed. She fucking laughed against my mouth. Here I was, trying to take it slow with this perfect woman and she was teasing me.

"Fine," I told her. "You want to come? I'll make you come so hard you see stars, bookworm."

I fisted her hair and pulled her head back to open her, dipping my tongue inside and tasting her. She moaned as I slid against her tongue and my cock swelled.

"Do you like that?" My other hand came to her jaw. "Do you like it when I take control?"

She nodded with a whimper and sucked on my tongue.

Fuck. I was done. I was so done.

My hand slid from her jaw down until I found one pinched nipple through her bra. She whimpered again as I rolled it, rubbed it, teased it.

"I hope you're taking notes."

She nodded against my mouth. Her hands were in my hair, and the pads of her fingers rubbed my scalp. Tingles shot down my neck.

"Are you warm enough?"

She nodded again. "Your skin is so warm, and I have socks on."

I laughed. "You still have your socks on?"

I felt her shy grin against my mouth. "I read that women had a better chance of having an orgasm if they were wearing socks."

My chest shook with laughter. "Okay, well, we keep your socks on, then." With my hand still in her hair, I pulled her back to me and kissed her more. "I don't think you'll need them tonight, though." My other hand moved to her nipple and she whimpered again.

"I like that," she breathed.

Jesus fucking Christ. That breathy tone had heat coiling around the base of my spine.

I tugged on the bottom of her t-shirt. "Off."

She pulled it over her head. I reached around and unhooked the back of her bra before tossing it aside.

I licked one of those perfect, pinched nipples and she arched against me, panting.

I sucked and she cried out. I grinned against her breast, my hands all over her skin. I couldn't get enough of her softness and warmth.

It was too late. The wave swept me under and my control was shot. We were doing this.

"Wyatt," she breathed, and I groaned. The way she said my name, it was pornographic, generous, sweet, desperate, needy, and grateful. All in a single word out of those fucking gorgeous lips.

My hands clutched her hips as my mouth worked her tits. "Are you wet yet, baby?"

She moaned her acknowledgement.

"Good. Don't let anyone fucking touch you between your legs until you're soaking wet. Do you understand?"

She nodded again, her eyes glazed and her lips parted. My dick was so hard it was going to puncture the air mattress.

This wasn't like me, this territorial, needy, lust-driven psycho. Hannah made me want to stake my claim, though. I wanted to be her first orgasm with a partner. I wanted her to remember me every time she came and compare every orgasm for the rest of her life to the one I was about to give her.

I wanted to be the best. A decade from now, I wanted her to shudder when she thought about tonight, and crave me like I craved her.

I skimmed my hands down her torso, down her stomach and hips, slow enough that she knew what I was doing. I watched her the entire time, watching for any hesitation, ready to stop the second she tensed up, but it never came. She only looked at me with wonder and lust.

Fuck, I loved the way she looked at me.

Over her underwear, I pressed my fingers to her heat and nearly blacked out.

"Fucking hell, you are so wet." Her underwear was damp. I pulled it aside and slid my fingers over her wet folds. Her head fell back.

I grazed her clit. My other hand made its way beneath her ass.

"Look at me."

She lifted her head and those gorgeous eyes were full of lust. I was driving her mad, and I loved it.

"You're going to watch while I make you come. Understand?"

She nodded and bit her bottom lip.

"Good. Good girl."

She shivered when I called her that and another wave of need hit me.

"Take these off." I pulled at her underwear and she lifted her hips to let me slide them down. My mouth was only a foot from her pussy and I groaned at the sweet scent of her arousal. I needed to taste her, like a man walking through a desert needed water. I needed her so badly, my balls ached.

I slid my fingers over her slippery center again and she moaned.

"You're a fucking goddess, you know that?" My voice was rough and demanding.

Her eyes widened a fraction at my words, watching me with parted lips like she was in a dream.

I stilled my fingers. "Answer me."

She jerked a nod and I rewarded her with more soft circles on her clit.

A wicked grin pulled at my features. She had no fucking clue how sexy she was, how fucking hard she made me. No clue. I'd break her, though. I'd work my way into that innocent little head until she knew the power she held.

When I was done with Hannah, she'd know she was beautiful. More languid brushes across her tight bud of nerves. Her eyebrows lifted in surprise and she arched back, closing her eyes.

"You are so fucking sexy," I told her. "Open your eyes."

She lifted her head again, wincing with hazy eyes. Her breath caught as I sucked a nipple into my mouth.

"You're going to come tonight," I told her, slipping a finger inside. Her breath hitched and she moaned, clenching me. Holy fucking hell, she was tight. On instinct, I ground my cock against the mattress.

The sounds of my finger moving in and out of her filled the tent, accompanied by her short, breathy moans. She clenched me as I worked her heat, and when she had adjusted, I added a second finger.

"Wyatt." Her voice strained with need, and my body shuddered.

Her eyes were closed again. She gripped the sleeping bag tight.

"I'm not going to tell you again, Hannah. Keep your eyes open while I fuck you with my fingers."

She propped herself up on her elbows, watching me. "It feels so good."

"I know. I know it does, baby." I curled my fingers until I found the right spot.

Her eyes widened and her walls clenched around me. Her abs tightened and I squeezed her ass.

"What is that?" Her voice was high and breathy.

I laughed, low and dark, before pressing a kiss to her stomach. "That's your G-spot, baby. That's the spot that's going to make you see fucking stars tonight."

"Wow," she breathed. "You're so good at this."

There was no happier man on the planet.

"*You're* so good at this," I told her. "Look at you, doing so well. You're going to come."

She nodded and winced. "I want to. I want to come with you."

"You will. I can feel it."

Her eyelids fell halfway before she snapped them back open to watch me.

"Good girl," I whispered, and her slick walls pulsed around me.

My fingers massaged her G-spot, and I brushed a thumb over her clit. Her hips bucked.

"Who's going to come tonight?" My tone was low.

She winced from the pleasure. "Me."

"That's right, you are."

She nodded and her soaking pussy clenched me again.

"You're doing so well, baby. So fucking well."

She moaned again and her hands clenched the sleeping bag. "I want to touch you."

"No. Not right now. I'm busy. Right now, we're making you come." I added pressure with my thumb on her clit and she moaned again. I slipped my hand out from under her ass and set it palm-up on her stomach. "Hold my hand, baby. Hold on to me while you come."

She fell back onto the pillow and grasped my hand with both of hers. Fuck, she was so sweet, so trusting and brave. Something expanded in my chest that had nothing to do with sex. She squeezed my hand and I squeezed back like she'd float away if I let go.

"Wyatt," she moaned. Her muscles tightened around my fingers and I massaged the spot inside her harder.

I pressed a kiss to her smooth thigh and scraped my teeth across the skin.

"Wyatt. Oh my god." She writhed under my hands, like in my dreams. Her legs shook.

"Be as loud as you want, there's no one around for miles. Keep fucking my hand until it feels too good. I've been dreaming about this."

"It's too intense." Her voice teetered on the edge, frantic and desperate. She writhed against me. "I can't."

"Yes, you can." She was soaking my fingers and my thumb swirled faster. "You're going to come harder than ever. Do you hear me?"

She nodded, an expression of pain on her face, and her eyes fell closed.

"I'm going to die," she whimpered. Fucking hell, her voice was driving me crazy.

"You're not going to die, baby. Let go and let it happen. Come on my fingers."

She pulsed again. She cried out and it echoed back to our tent from outside. Fuck, that made me even harder, that Hannah had no idea how loud she was. That I was making her lose control.

"You're going to come soon, I know it."

Her pussy clenched again. I lowered my mouth to her clit and sucked hard.

Her hips bucked against my mouth and I nearly came

from her sweet taste. A noise of pure pleasure rumbled from my chest.

She cried out as she started to come and a fucking devil unleashed within me. I pressed the button inside her, rubbing it hard as her pussy fluttered around my fingers, sucking pressure onto her clit. She ground against my face and made spectacular noises I would replay until the end of time. Her hands squeezed mine as she let out desperate gasps and I squeezed right back.

When she slumped back and her eyes opened, I ran my tongue up her slick opening. Now that I knew the taste of her, there was no going back. I had to have more.

"Oh my god." Her chest heaved and her eyes had this fucking incredible unfocused, dazed look.

"You did so good." I kissed the inside of her thigh. "So fucking good."

She let out a long, low, satisfied groan and her hands raked through my hair. Shivers rolled down my spine and I pressed my mouth to her soft skin again and again. I couldn't get enough of her.

I moved to lie beside her and leaned in to kiss her. Her mouth met mine and she sighed into me. My chest expanded with pride at how relaxed and satisfied she was. I looped an arm around her and tucked her into me.

Her hand came to my cock and I jerked. She stroked me hard over my boxers.

"Hannah." My voice came out strangled. "It's okay, we don't have to—" My voice broke when she stroked me again. "Fuck."

"I want to." There was a smile in her voice.

She squeezed me and a groan escaped my throat. My body curled toward her, and my arms folded her into me. "Fuck. Baby." I should have said no, should have pushed her away, but I couldn't.

Hannah slipped her hand past my waistband and cupped me. Heat shot up my spine.

"Jesus," I gasped, bucking.

"Like this?"

The noise I made was a combination of disbelief and laughter. "Yeah. Exactly like that."

She stroked my length while I pressed my mouth to her neck.

"You're so warm," she breathed. Every touch of hers added pressure to the base of my spine. "Your cock is so big."

My hips bucked again, shuttling into her hand. "Are you trying to make me come too fast?" I gasped into her hair.

She smiled against my shoulder and gave me a little nip with her teeth. "Yes." She squeezed me harder and her other hand came to my sac.

Not long, now. My body bowed around her. My pulse beat in my ears and my brain boiled with the need to come.

She tugged lightly on my balls and I groaned.

"Where the fuck did you learn that?" My voice was hoarse.

"In a book." She sucked on the spot she had bitten on my shoulder and sighed. "I like jerking you off."

"Uh huh," I moaned into her. One of my hands gripped her ass and the other was around her shoulder. I thought about thrusting into her wet heat, nothing in between us, how fucking incredible that would be. How good it felt with her hand wrapped around me. How her mouth would be so hot and wet.

Shit. Electricity shot up my spine.

"I touched myself, thinking about us having sex." Hannah whispered against my shoulder, her soft mouth brushing my skin while her hand jerked my soul out through my cock.

It was too much. I let out a low groan as heat ripped through me. Light exploded behind my closed eyes and I curled over her.

"Hannah, fuck. Hannah." I choked her name out again and again as I spilled hot liquid into her hands.

She worked my erection until there was nothing left in my balls, and I slumped over her. "Holy shit. I thought you were a beginner."

Her cute laugh shook into me. "I read a lot."

"Oh my god. You've been studying up. A-plus." I exhaled and my mind came back into focus. I slipped my boxers off and cleaned us up.

"Wait." She pulled her hand away when I tried to wipe it off. She slipped a wet fingertip into her mouth and sucked a drop of come off.

My cock twitched and my mouth fell open.

She bit her lip. "I was curious what you tasted like."

She was going to kill me. She had no idea how perfect she was. I made a noise like I was in pain and she chuckled.

Minutes later, once we were settled into my sleeping bag, she sighed in contentment against my chest. "I'm so relaxed." Her arm slid around my waist. "Great work, professor."

My fingers brushed her hair and I smiled in the darkness. Within a few minutes, her breathing turned slow and rhythmic.

I lay there awake for a long time, thinking. Everything changed with Hannah tonight. Or maybe it had changed the night I snuck through her bedroom window and kissed her. I couldn't stop thinking about her after that.

No, that wasn't right. I couldn't stop thinking about her before that. That was why I snuck into her room that night.

She made a soft noise in her sleep and burrowed further into my chest.

I was in the undercurrent, being tossed around, and there was no fighting it. Experienced surfers and swimmers knew not to waste energy flailing about. When the undercurrent was done, that's when you swam up for air.

Maybe I would let myself get swept away until I was ready

to resurface. My heart tugged. Lying with her in a tent in the middle of the woods, her warmth pressed up against me and the taste of her still on my tongue, the universe had aligned. Like she was home for me, she was right where I needed to be. We just fit.

I only hoped that I could swim up for air before I drowned.

18

Hannah

I OPENED my eyes the next morning with a heavy arm draped over my waist, tucked into a warm, hard chest. Naked. It was the first time I had woken up with a guy.

It was heaven.

Wyatt was still asleep, chest rising and falling against me. His lips gently parted, and I took the opportunity to run my finger along the edge of his mouth.

His mouth opened and he nipped my finger. A giggle burst out of my mouth and he opened his eyes and grinned at me.

"Good morning." His voice was low and raspy. His arm tightened around me.

"Hi."

"How'd you sleep?"

A soft, pleased smile pulled at my mouth. "Great."

He raised an eyebrow with a knowing smirk. "I bet."

Another laugh rippled out of me and my face turned pink. I couldn't stop smiling, though.

Last night. Ugh. Last night was... the best orgasm I'd ever had. It ripped through me like a tsunami. For a couple moments, my body wasn't my own. It was Wyatt's. He had complete control over me, and I loved it. The way he knew what to do, the way he touched me exactly how I wanted, it made me feel taken care of, cherished, comfortable, and so, so turned on. I wanted more, and yet I knew more would never be enough.

Keep fucking my hand until it feels too good.

I shivered against him. I was sore from his hand but I throbbed and ached for more.

"Are you cold?"

I shook my head, burying my face into his chest to hide my blush and his arm slid up higher so his fingers were in my hair. I shivered again, down my neck, all the way down my back. I wasn't usually like this, this turned on, aching, desperate-to-be-touched girl. This horniness was new.

I've been dreaming about this.

My core clenched and I made an unhappy noise in my throat.

"What's wrong?"

I exhaled against his chest. "Horny." My words muffled into his skin. God, he smelled good. His scent made my eyes roll back. I was slippery between my legs and I ached again for him. I pressed a light kiss to his chest and heard his own groan. He shifted and his hard length pressed against my stomach, sending another ripple of need through me. I pressed back against him and his breath caught.

"Yeah?" He sounded breathless.

I nodded against him, pressing another kiss onto his chest. His fingers tensed in my hair against my scalp and I hummed with approval.

"Tell me what you need, Hannah, and I'll give it to you."

His gaze was heavy, dark, and half-lidded. Pupils dilated. Hair messy.

I don't think I'd ever seen someone so handsome. I loved seeing him undone like this.

"I need your hand," I breathed.

He pressed a soft kiss on my mouth and his stubble scratched me in a delicious way.

I started to pull back. "I haven't brushed my teeth yet."

His hand came around the back of my neck and drew me to him. "Don't care."

My hand slid from his chest, lower on his stomach, tracing every defined ab. They jumped under my touch and I smiled against Wyatt's mouth.

"Your body is incredible, professor."

His mouth pulled into a grin against mine and he nipped my bottom lip. His hand stroked up and down my back against my bare skin. "It's yours."

Mine.

My core clenched again and my breath caught. Warm, languid feelings flooded my brain and bloodstream and I rubbed against him. The pressure of his leg between my legs made me whimper.

Wyatt must have liked me rubbing myself against him because he slipped his hand around to my front. His fingers found a pinched peak and he rolled it.

I whimpered again, arching into his touch. A low laugh rumbled out his chest.

"Feels good," I whispered.

"Mhm. I know."

The authority, the confident, knowing tone to his voice, like he knew he was in control, it made me clench harder. More heat, more wetness flooded my center. I grasped the steel length prodding my stomach.

He made a noise like he was in pain but even I knew better. I stroked him hard and he pinched my nipple in response.

"Slow down," he rasped.

I stroked him again. I wanted to see him lose his mind like he did last night, all over my hand. Wyatt was always so calm and cool, but last night, he was at my mercy. Like I was the boss. "No."

He jerked against my hand. "Hannah." His tone was warning.

"You said this was mine." I worked the heavy length, so thick in my hand.

He groaned into my shoulder. "Jesus Christ, bookworm, you're going to make me come before I'm ready."

I stroked him again hard and he sucked a breath through his teeth.

"Okay." He took his hand from my breast and pulled my wrist off him before he looked hard at me. He moved to hover above me, caging me in, nose an inch from mine. A little smile played at his mouth and I grinned back at him.

"You want to play a little game, bookworm?"

My grin grew and I nodded.

"Okay. This game is called 'who can make the other person come first.'"

I narrowed my eyes, pretending to think. "This game is new to me, but I think I'll be good at it."

He lifted his eyebrows. "Oh, yeah?"

"Uh huh."

His gaze dropped to my mouth. "I've been thinking about playing this game with you for a long time. A very. Long. Time." He placed soft kisses on my mouth in between each word. My center ached again. "I have more practice and I've been paying very careful attention. So what makes you think you'll win?"

His voice was so light and teasing. My heart beat hard and I bit my grin back. I shrugged and adopted an innocent expression. "I don't know if I'll win but I have to try. Isn't that what you've been teaching me?" My other hand reached up to touch his chest and he grabbed that wrist and pinned it down as well. He was holding me down, and I liked it. A lot.

He flashed me a wicked grin. "Mhm."

Another zing of confidence rushed through my blood. I wanted to make him slip. "I know your cock is probably too big to fit in my mouth but I want to try."

He laughed in disbelief and dropped his forehead to mine, resting against me. "Jesus Christ, Hannah, you're going to win before we start the game." He groaned before taking a deep breath. "Change of plans."

"What do you—oh." My words broke off as he shoved the sleeping bag off and pushed my thighs apart. I gasped as he leaned down.

His mouth came to my pussy and my head fell back. He groaned in appreciation and when his hot tongue slicked over my clit, I arched.

"This isn't fair," I whispered as his tongue ran circles over me, again and again, winding me tighter. I arched higher and higher, writhing against his mouth.

"Fucking hell, Hannah. You taste too good." His tongue dove into my wet folds and I whimpered. "Nothing sweeter than you."

Heat coiled in me and I itched to reach for him again but I couldn't, I was too overcome with how incredible this felt. His tongue was soft, fast, and slick, and I was soaking his face but he didn't seem to care. His eyelids fell halfway as his tongue glided over me and the pressure built, low in my stomach. We filled our tent with moans and gasps, and then he slipped a finger inside me and my mouth fell open.

My core clenched around him and he groaned against me.

I gasped a laugh. I could barely talk. He touched something inside me that made pressure build low in my belly.

He lifted his mouth to watch me, his finger still working that zone against my front wall. I met his gaze and something on my face made him grin wickedly. "You're taking my finger so well. And I bet if I slipped a second finger in, you'd take that, too, wouldn't you?"

I jerked a nod.

He laughed low and obliged, adding another finger and stretching me. My head fell back.

"Look at you, doing so well. You're so fucking beautiful, Hannah. I've always thought that." His voice was a caress against my skin and I reached down blindly. His hand met mine.

When he did that last night, grabbed my hand, it was what I needed. An anchor, something to squeeze, something to remind me it was him touching me. It wasn't just some guy.

It was Wyatt.

"Wyatt," I whined. My toes were curling.

"Mhm. I know. Tell me how good it feels." He studied his hand moving in and out of me.

"Amazing," I gasped, back going rigid. My legs were shaking. "Like I'm going to come."

"Good. Your pussy is clenching me, Hannah. Do you know what that means?"

I nodded hard and my eyes closed as the pleasurable waves approached.

"It means you're close, baby. It means you're doing everything right. Do you know how hard you're making me? Teasing me with that pretty mouth, telling me I won't fit?"

He lowered his mouth to my clit and licked me again, laying pleasure upon pleasure, and I wasn't sure how much more I could take. My hand gripped his.

"You're almost there, baby," he told me in between the circles he lapped on me.

The wave inside me crested and I could barely speak. I could barely breathe. "Wyatt." I choked the word out.

His fingers worked harder and he made a noise of approval against my clit.

It was that little noise, half-growl, half-groan, that tipped me over the edge. It was the same noise he made when we ate breakfast, when he was starving after a morning of surfing, and his eyes closed while he dove in. Him enjoying this, finding me so delicious and necessary, it shot electricity from my core throughout my body. I ground against his mouth, and everything was tight and hot and incredible, so fucking incredible. Pulse after pulse sparked through me and my focus darted everywhere and nowhere, all at the same time. My thoughts scattered in the air. I was weightless and floating.

When I came back to earth, I sank into the mattress and pillows, breathing hard. I let out a laugh. "You win."

He laughed and climbed over me, placing a sweet kiss on my mouth before pressing a trail of them down my neck. His erection hit my stomach. "I love how loud you get."

My face flushed with embarrassment. "Oh my god."

He laughed. "It's okay. There's no one out here."

I reached down for his length, prodding me with urgency, and he groaned when I wrapped my fingers around him.

"Oh, fuck." He broke off in a gasp when I stroked him hard.

"Consolation prize," I murmured against him, pressing a kiss to his neck before sucking on the tender skin. He shuddered.

I explored him with my hand, running along the length, all the way down to his sac, gripping it. He shuddered again. A bead of liquid appeared at the tip and I spread it over him.

"Fuck," he whispered against my hair, thrusting himself into my hand. "Fuck, Hannah." He thrust again and made a noise of pain in his throat.

I was going to take what I wanted while I had the chance. I sat up, leaned over, and took him into my mouth.

A high-pitched noise of disbelief came out of him as my lips slid over him and I moaned, as much as I could with him in my mouth. The drop that had beaded on his tip tasted a little salty, a little musky. His cock was harder than steel but the skin was so soft, like velvet, and there was something so satisfying about dropping further onto him, filling my mouth up with him. I glanced up to see him watching me with an expression of agony, disbelief, and pleasure.

"This is my first time doing this," I said to him, "so tell me if I'm doing it wrong."

He shook his head slowly, mouth parted. "Not wrong. Good. So fucking good." His chest rose and fell fast and I grinned at him before taking him again in my mouth. His eyes fell half-way closed. "Fuck, Hannah, you're taking me so well."

Delight shuddered through me when he said that and I bobbed up and down, running my tongue along the underside of him. He groaned.

This was fun.

"That's my girl. Just like that, baby." He lifted his hands to his own hair, raking it back. The muscles on his stomach tensed like they were carved from stone. I'd be thinking about this moment for a long time.

When I added suction, he pulsed in my mouth, and when I made a throaty noise of enjoyment, he gasped.

"Hannah. I'm gonna come."

I glanced up at him while I worked him in and out of my mouth, sucking hard. "Mhm."

He nodded hard, frowning like he was in pain, gaze locked on me. His mouth fell open and he thrust into my mouth. Hot liquid spilled all over my tongue in spurts and I listened to Wyatt's gasps and groans as he emptied himself.

When he was done, I gave him a big grin and wiggled my eyebrows. He was still catching his breath, lying back and watching me with a funny look.

Almost like he was afraid of me.

"What's that look for?" I snorted and he pulled me up to him, against his chest.

"I didn't know you could do that."

I shrugged. "Me neither. That was fun."

"Fun." He laughed. "Holy shit, Hannah."

"Any notes, professor?"

He groaned and closed his eyes. "Fuck. When you call me that…"

I bit my lip and snuggled in closer to his chest. "I know."

"You're a fucking temptress, you know that?"

I nearly laughed. Me, a temptress? I had the sexual prowess of a caterpillar. Temptresses wore long, flowing red robes with feathers, red lipstick, lingerie, high heels. I was the girl who hid in her bookstore.

The way Wyatt looked as I was about to make him come, though, like I held total power over him? Incredible. I could be my own type of temptress. I could just be Wyatt's temptress.

The thought made me laugh to myself. Wyatt's. *It's yours*, he had said about his body. I didn't even know I wanted to hear that until he said it. Mine. I'd never had someone's body to myself before. Never felt ownership over someone the way I did about Wyatt.

The thought shocked me. Wyatt wasn't mine. He didn't even believe in true love. He didn't believe in forever, for Christ's sake. A pinch of worry hit me in the stomach.

Wyatt believed in *right now*, though. Living in the present and enjoying what life provided. Letting things pass and moving on when it was time.

So maybe I should do the same. I should enjoy this time with Wyatt, enjoy fooling around with him and learning things from him. When it was time for it to end, I would let it.

The thought of this ending made me want to cry, so I shoved it away. That was future Hannah's problem. Right now, I was only concerned with the present. Like Wyatt taught me.

Wyatt squeezed his arm around my shoulders with his eyes closed, and I breathed him in, memorizing this moment.

"I need a nap," he murmured. "I need to recover."

I nodded, smiling. "Okay."

IT WAS early afternoon when we got back into town.

"Let's grab a coffee," Wyatt suggested, and I agreed. We parked and waited for a break in traffic before jogging across the street.

Miri Yang stood in front of the coffee shop with a stack of papers and a small group of people gathered around her. I recognized a few faces.

"…between ten and eleven at night." Her eyes were wide and animated. "We have almost no details but we do know she's in extreme pain."

"She may have slipped on a hike," Randeep Singh added behind her. He was a hiking guide for tourists. He crossed his arms over his chest. "On some of those trails out there, you take one step off the path and you're falling down a cliff. The way she was crying out, I'm sure she broke something."

They noticed us standing there and Miri shoved flyers at us. "Oh, good, you two. Here, take some flyers and pass them out at your businesses."

"What's going on?" I glanced down at the paper and read.

Missing hiker in distress in the Pacific Rim area. Thought to be unprepared and severely injured. Airlift may be required.

I frowned. "That's awful."

"We have search parties leaving in an hour to canvas the area," Miri told the group of us.

"If you and Holden are free," Randeep added to Wyatt, "we could use your help. You two are always camping in that area."

I froze and turned to Wyatt. It couldn't be…? He wore a funny expression on his face and my stomach plummeted through my feet to the core of the earth. His mouth ticked like he was trying not to laugh and he nodded, rubbing his jaw.

The woman they had heard crying out in pain was me. Crying out for a different reason.

A reason I did *not* want to have to explain to everyone.

"Sorry," I cleared my throat. My voice was thin and high. "Um. Why do you think there's a woman in distress?"

"I was camping out there last night and heard her," Randeep repeated with wide eyes. "She was moaning in pain. Again and again. Loudly, too. She was hurt. I'm sure of it. We have to help her." He shook his head. "There was *so* much moaning."

"What did the noises sound like?" someone asked Randeep.

He gestured to Miri. "Miri, go ahead."

"They were like *unh, unh, unhhhh*," Miri moaned, and my eyes bugged out of my head. "Right?"

Randeep shook his head. "Louder and longer, like *UNHHHHHHHHH, UNHHHHHHHH*." The crowd around Miri and Randeep grew as people stopped and stared at Randeep moaning. "She even said, *I'm gonna die, I'm gonna die*."

Wyatt's hand twitched on my shoulder, and I wished I *would* die right there. My face blazed with heat.

Don stuck his head through the crowd. "Like *unhhhnnn, unhhhhhh*? Or like *unh-unh-unh*?"

I cleared my throat. "I don't see why this level of detail is important." My voice warbled and Wyatt squeezed my shoulder.

Randeep pointed at Don. "The first one. Really drawn out."

Don nodded and made a note in his notebook. "Thank you for the clarification. Can I list you as a source?"

My head was about to explode from embarrassment. "Don, are you writing a blog post on this?"

He glanced up at me over his glasses with a frown. "Of course."

Wyatt rubbed his hand over his mouth and our gazes met, my wide eyes full of fucking mortification and his full of laughter and amusement. His chest shook and he covered a laugh with a cough.

"Excuse us a moment." He led me away, glancing over his shoulder at them.

We got all the way around the corner before he burst out laughing.

I slapped his arm. "Wyatt! You said we'd be alone." My voice sounded like a goblin.

His grin stretched ear to ear as he laughed and leaned against the wall. "I thought we would be."

"This isn't funny."

"Oh, bookworm." He wiped his eyes. "This is so, so funny."

I peeked around the corner, where the group around Miri grew in number. Randeep was explaining where to meet for the search and rescue, and I winced.

"They're sending out search parties," I whispered to Wyatt.

I wanted to hide. I wanted to run into my bookstore, lock the door, flip the sign to *closed*, and disappear into a book. The search parties would go out and find no one, because there was no one.

But that would be wrong. Super wrong. It would be a waste of everyone's day. A police cruiser pulled up, and then a firetruck came around the corner.

"Why the hell is the fire department getting involved?" I hissed over my shoulder at Wyatt, who stuck his head out to look.

It would be a waste of town resources. I had to say something. I wrung my hands and swallowed thickly, taking a deep breath. "We have to say something."

Wyatt's hand rested on the back of my neck. "You want me to take this one?"

I glanced up at him with hope on my face. "Would you?"

He nodded down at me with a smirk. "I owe you one after

this morning." He winked and dropped a quick kiss on my cheek. "Be right back."

I peeked around the corner as he approached the group and gestured to Randeep.

"Got a second?"

Randeep followed Wyatt a few steps away. "Do you have some info?"

"Uh, sort of." Wyatt chuckled. "That woman you heard last night wasn't in distress."

Randeep frowned and leaned in. "What do you mean?"

Wyatt cleared his throat and straightened up, looked weirdly proud. "That was Hannah and me."

Randeep frowned in confusion. "What do you—" His mouth dropped open. "Oh. So you two—" He raised his eyebrows.

Wyatt nodded. "Yep."

"Well, then." He put his hands on his hips. "Thank you for telling me. Guess I should call off the search party." He stared at the ground with a frown, thinking. "You and Hannah Nielsen?"

"Mhm." Wyatt shifted so I couldn't see his face.

My heart beat hard in my chest. The way he was talking, he was making it sound like we were...

A couple?

The thought melted into my bloodstream. A couple. Wyatt and I as a couple.

I mean, of course we weren't. We were practicing. He was helping me and I was helping him.

But the thought was nice.

Randeep clapped Wyatt's shoulder. "Good for you, Wyatt. I'm glad everyone's okay."

Wyatt nodded once and Randeep returned to the group.

"False alarm, everyone. There's no one in distress," he announced to the group in a loud, booming voice. "It was Hannah Nielsen and Wyatt Rhodes fooling around."

A strangled noise of humiliation gurgled out of my throat. My face burned so hot I might melt. Wyatt returned to my side with a huge grin while I watched in horror.

"Hannah Nielsen?" Miri asked. "And Wyatt Rhodes?" Her eyes were bigger than I had ever seen them. She grabbed Randeep's arms with force. She was a tiny woman of five foot two, but he reared back in fear at the savage fire in her eyes. "Tell me the truth. Are you kidding right now?"

"He told me himself."

Her sharp, interested gaze whipped to us, where I peeked around the corner.

Wyatt's hand slipped into mine and he tugged. "Let's get out of here, bookworm, before we have to answer some awkward questions."

He didn't have to ask me twice. We returned to the truck and Wyatt started the car. In the side mirror, I spotted Miri running towards us. Wyatt exited the parking lot, rolling down the window to wave at her.

"I'm so happy for you two!" she called after us.

Wyatt took one look at my face and burst out laughing again, the lines around his eyes crinkling and his grin reaching from ear to ear.

"I'm going to move to Newfoundland." I covered my burning face with my hands. "Everyone knows now."

He shrugged, still wearing that grin. "So what. Let them know."

Know *what*? What were we?

I was living in the present, or trying to, and those were questions for the future. I blew a breath out, glanced at Wyatt, and burst out laughing.

19

Hannah

THE NEXT EVENING, I sat at the counter in a bar in Port Kennedy, a nearby town, waiting for Naya and watching my phone as the video of Wyatt chopping wood went viral. I had sent him a screenshot of the video, pointing out the views and comments, and he responded with *nice work, bookworm* and a winky emoji.

A shiver rolled down my spine at the memory of what Wyatt had done with me. How he had touched me and made me moan.

And then I remembered Miri and Randeep re-enacting those moans and I cringed for the thousandth time that day.

"You must be Hannah."

I glanced up from my phone. Naya greeted me with a huge smile and a warm hug.

"So good to meet you," I said as she took her seat on the stool beside me.

Naya beamed at me and her brown eyes shone. "I'm excited to talk concepts with you. Thanks for sending over that Pinterest board."

Earlier in the week, Liya and I had trawled for images of

murals we loved, and they all had a common theme—vivid, striking, and colorful.

I nodded and swallowed as guilt caught me by the throat. I was sitting in a bar planning a mural to which my dad had said no. I was going to cover up the mural my mom had commissioned.

But the mural needed an update. The books in the existing mural were from a different time, and they didn't represent the world anymore. They didn't represent Queen's Cove, and they didn't represent publishing.

There was no doubt I was erasing her by painting over it, though. My heart twisted.

Naya pulled out a tablet and tapped through screens. "I've been thinking a lot about our conversation about your mom."

My chest was tight. "Oh?"

She nodded and shot me a wistful smile. "Yeah." She inhaled and sighed. "The way you talk about her, it's clear she's in every part of the store."

I nodded and swallowed past the rock in my throat. Naya could see this was a mistake, too.

"And I want to honor that in the mural."

My ears perked up. "You do?"

Her teeth flashed with her wide smile. "Absolutely. You have the same passion for books that she does."

"I do. I love stories. She showed me how incredible they were."

Her tablet screen glowed as she scrolled through images. "I was thinking about what she used to say, *there's a story for every soul.*"

"There is. There's a book out there for everyone. I love when people find the perfect book and come back and tell me about it."

"So, this is what I came up with. If you don't like it, that's fine, we can change it. It's just an initial concept."

She set the tablet on the table and I leaned forward to study the sketch.

The magenta letters looped and dipped in a swirling, whimsical font. Tropical flowers framed the text, growing thick and wild with emerald leaves and vines. Birds perched among the foliage, a racoon peeked out from behind a flower, and a deer grazed along the bottom of the image.

A story for every soul, it said. Tears stung my eyes. It was my mom in art. My guilt vanished and resolve took its place. I wasn't erasing her. The mural *was* her.

I nodded at Naya and rushed to wipe away a tear as it spilled over.

"Is this good?" she asked, watching my expression carefully.

I nodded and another tear spilled over. "Sorry. Yes. Good."

Her hand came to my arm. "It's okay. I'm so happy you like it."

"It's beautiful," I choked out, staring at the image. "So freaking beautiful, Naya. Can you send this to me?"

Her face burst into a beaming smile and she nodded.

We sat at the bar for a few more minutes, chatting logistics and schedule. Naya would begin the mural next week. My stomach fluttered with excitement as I studied the sketch. My mind whirred with ideas for social media posts of the mural. I couldn't wait for the town to see it finished.

My dad wandered into my mind.

He might hate it. No, he *would* hate it. Anything that Mom hadn't personally put her stamp of approval on, he hated.

Something sharp wrenched in my chest. He would just have to get over it, because the new mural was happening.

Naya slipped her tablet away and rose. "Well, friend, I'll see you next week." She shimmied her shoulders in excitement. "This is going to be fun."

My heart fizzed with happy anticipation. "See you next week."

I watched Naya leave and checked the time on my phone. It was about an hour's drive home.

"Can I get you anything else before the show?" the bartender asked. She had blue hair, shaved short on the sides.

"The show?" I blinked at her.

"The drag show. It's the first Tuesday of the month."

I gasped. "I've always wanted to go to a drag show."

She laughed. "Well, here's your chance. It's no *Drag Race* but it's a fun time."

A prickle of nerves rose in me at the idea of sitting here alone.

Who cares? a voice asked in my head. A voice that sounded a lot like Wyatt.

I shot a smile at her. "Sure. Can you make me something fruity and fun with no alcohol? I'm driving."

She winked. "You bet, honey."

She placed a magenta drink with a little umbrella in front of me as the lights dimmed and the music volume increased. A magenta drink, like the text on the mural. Like a sign. I smiled to myself and turned to the small stage area in the back corner. Rickety spotlights shook with the bass's low thump.

The bartender appeared at the side of the stage with a mic. "Good evening to all the girls, gays, and theys!"

The bar patrons cheered around me.

"We've got another great show for you tonight. First up, she's demure, she's elegant, and she'll never be caught dead without her pearls. She's singing 'Wouldn't it Be Loverly'—"

Someone near me groaned and set their forehead on the bar.

"—from *My Fair Lady* for the hundredth fucking time, it's Josephina Duvet!"

The black curtain separating the bar from the back swished aside and a tall queen strode out with giant platinum bouffant curls, theatrical winged liner, and a wide seafoam-green tulle dress. The audience cheered and whooped for her as she took the mic and stepped onstage.

"The rain in Spain stays mainly in the plain!" she boomed into the mic before she launched into an upbeat, pop version of Audrey Hepburn's classic show tune.

I sipped my drink while I watched her strut around the stage, dance to the music, and sing her heart out. Her makeup was so artfully applied, so fun and theatrical, and yet her outfit paid reverence to an era of women's fashion with precise detail. Her dress looked like it had taken time and effort. My gaze strayed to her cleavage. How did she make it look so real?

Josephina whipped her head to me and sang right at me. My eyes widened but my smile lifted. She swayed her hips and I stared in awe before I snapped a quick pic on my phone.

I should have taken hot girl lessons from her instead, I texted Wyatt.

Typing dots appeared and his response popped up.

You out there having fun without me, bookworm?

I grinned at my phone. *Yep. Sitting alone at the bar, like you taught me. Having the best time!*

Attagirl. Can't wait to hear all about it.

My stomach flopped and fluttered. Josephina finished her set and disappeared through the curtain.

The blue-haired bartender returned to the stage. "Let's give Josephina another round of applause!"

I clapped along with the other patrons. Next up was Rockstar Anise, who wore a huge eighties hair-metal mullet wig, fishnet stockings, and gave her everything to an air-guitar rendition of 'More Than a Feeling' by Boston. The music boomed from the speaker system as she lip-synced the lyrics. I was smiling so hard it hurt.

"Thank you, Rockstar Anise!" The bartender glanced at

the black curtain. "We've got an old favorite here tonight, it's—"

I gasped as the curtain swished aside, and a drag queen with a Union Jack minidress and giant red wig strode out. My hand came to my mouth.

She even had the red platform shoes.

"Wooooooo!" I screamed, clapping as hard as I could.

The queen glanced at me, paused with a little coy smile, and the opening notes of 'Say You'll Be There' played. My heart dipped as she sang and I danced in my seat.

During the chorus, she pointed at me. I sang along with the lyrics and everyone around me cheered.

I watched with fascination and admiration while she rocked her performance. She knew all the choreography from the music video and my smile reached ear to ear. She winked at me before she left the stage, and while I was clapping hard, familiarity struck me. I narrowed my eyes.

"Another pink drink?" the bartender asked, and I nodded with a big smile.

Two more queens performed in the little bar and I couldn't look away. I'd have to bring Avery here, she'd love this. Maybe Max and Div would want to come along. We could make a night of it.

"Hi," my idol dropped onto the stool beside me.

My eyes widened. "Hi." I was breathless. Her makeup was exquisite. Harsh, swooping brows, full red lips, insane lashes, and precise liner. She was perfection.

She waved at the bartender. "Can I get a water, please?"

That voice. I *knew* that voice. It clicked and I gasped.

"*Div?*" My jaw was on the floor.

She smirked at me.

"But you—" I shook my head, taking her outfit in. "How did... I didn't know. Oh my god." I beamed. "You're amazing."

She grinned a little wider. How could I have not seen it

before? It was in the smile. The bartender set a water and my second pink drink on the counter.

"Come on." She gestured for me to follow. "This wig is itching."

Through the black curtain, the other queens were in various states of disassembly. Div gently removed the voluminous red wig before setting it in a case. From a nearby stool, I watched as he pulled out wipes and removed his makeup in front of a mirror leaning on the wall.

"Where'd you learn to do makeup like that?"

He shot me a quick smile before he smeared off an eyebrow. "YouTube, mostly, but sometimes the queens help each other out before or after shows. Teach each other things, stuff like that."

"Why did you choose *her*?" My voice was awestruck.

One of his shoulders lifted and he studied the makeup wipe a moment before he peered into the mirror and worked at removing the rest. "She's girl power, she's femininity, and she doesn't care what people think."

I nodded. "That's why I love her too. She's so sexy."

We exchanged a smile that felt like friendship. "She is, isn't she?"

"Bye, honey," one of the queens called as two of them left. Div waved in the mirror at them. "Bye, new girl."

I flushed. I was a spectator here in their world, but it was nice to be seen instead of invisible.

"Why do you do drag?"

Div finished wiping off his makeup before he answered. He left the lashes on. "A couple years ago, my therapist asked me what I did for fun."

"And what did you say?"

He let out a flat laugh. "Nothing. I didn't know what to say. I thought it was a weird question. I worked. All I did was work. And before that, I went to school and studied." His throat worked and he tossed the wipe in the garbage. "It made me wonder, what's it all for? If all I do is work, and I don't do anything purely for me, what's the point?"

The last queens waved goodbye as they left and Div and I were alone in the stockroom. Music from the bar filtered through the curtain, and it swayed as the front door of the bar opened and closed.

"When I'm her, there's a point to it all." He pressed his mouth into a line. "It's just for me, it makes me happy, and I love it. It scared me at first but I'm glad I did it. It's my true self, or one of my true selves, up there."

He shot me a skewering glance, like he was daring me to laugh or make fun of him.

I nodded and swallowed with a smile. "Well, you're amazing."

His expression softened and he looked down at his makeup case. "Thanks."

"Can you show me how to do eyeliner?"

He laughed. "Sure. I can do that."

Div finished cleaning up and we walked to our cars together. Something daring streaked through me.

"Hey, Div?"

He sent a text on his phone and looked up at me. "Yes, Hannah."

"You should come hang out at my bookstore sometime." I shrugged. "I mean, I know you're busy working all the time, but if you have a day off or something. You don't have to—"

"Sure." He smiled. "That would be fun. Avery won't shut up about it."

A laugh bubbled out of me. "Okay. Cool."

He tilted his head. "So, you and Wyatt." He raised an eyebrow and his eyes glittered. "Camping."

I groaned. "Oh my god. Mortifying."

The corner of his mouth rose. "I expect all the details of what made you howl like a werewolf."

"I did *not* howl like a werewolf," I sputtered, shaking with laughter.

"Maybe, maybe not. Maybe that's what Miri's telling everyone. Wyatt likes you, and you should go for it."

I bit back a grin, flushed. "Maybe I will."

He lifted his eyebrows once. "Bye."

"Bye."

We climbed into our cars and I pulled out my phone. When I unlocked it, the picture Wyatt had taken of me in the bookstore was on screen.

Div had said he was his most authentic self up on stage in drag. He said it was scary but brought him happiness and made life worth it.

The bookstore made me feel like that. Not the old version of the bookstore, but the new one. The one where we sold mostly romance novels, had a stand at the farmer's market, and would soon have a huge, beautiful mural outside.

My bookstore.

Being with Wyatt made me feel that life was worth it. Pacific Rim was in a few weeks and he might be leaving but the memories of us camping and surfing and sitting at the bar, watching karaoke, would last forever.

My heart squeezed up into my throat. I opened my social media and posted the picture of myself that Wyatt took.

The girl behind the books, I typed.

20

Wyatt

HANNAH BEAMED at me the next morning, looking back to see if I had watched her catch another wave. I grinned back and rested my torso on my board as I bobbed up and down in the water. The sun had just risen and it was going to be a beautiful day.

For days, what Hannah and I had done while camping replayed in my mind. Her soft, sweet moans as I touched her. How she arched against me. How she tasted. The way she clamped down on me hard. Her dazed, sated expression after. That dreamy, lazy smile she had shot me as she sank back into the pillow.

How fucking incredible it felt when she wrapped her pretty lips around me.

I groaned and leaned my head on my board. Her eagerness and enthusiasm far surpassed any skill required and I had jerked off many, many times in the past few days thinking about her.

This was a problem, but I'd deal with it in the future, when it didn't make my chest hurt to think about not doing this every morning. All things came to an end, but they wouldn't end today. Today was all for us.

This morning, a registration email appeared had in my inbox for a surf competition in California in December. The conversation with Hannah over the fire while camping played in my head, where I had spilled my dark secret to her.

I watched her on the water, brilliant blonde hair catching the morning light. California wasn't that far away. I could go down for a weekend.

Hannah had never been to California. Would she want to come with me? I pictured us going out for Mexican food, sipping margaritas while she swatted my hand away from her food.

I rubbed the back of my neck and tried not to smile so hard at the thought. It was her birthday in a few weeks, on the last day of the Pacific Rim competition, and I'd been racking my brain for a gift for her. It had to be perfect, but everything I had come up with so far wasn't good enough.

She paddled back to me, pushing the wet hair out of her face with a big smile.

I winked at her. "You're getting good at this, bookworm."

She flushed under my praise and my heart squeezed.

She nodded over my shoulder beyond the break, further out in the ocean where the waves were bigger. "I want to try one of those."

The waves crashed hard as they broke. We didn't do lessons out there unless they were with intermediate surfers we had worked with before. Those waves required comfort with the ocean and intuition. I frowned, studying their height. They were a big level up from the baby waves she had been learning on. The period in between waves was long enough that she would have a decent recovery time if she bailed.

If she bailed.

I frowned and shifted on my board. She would likely bail. That's what life was about, though, wasn't it? That's what I always told her. Something pinched in my chest but I ignored it. Hannah wasn't a glass doll that couldn't be taken out of the case. That's what we were doing together, showing her she could get messy and fall down and still be okay.

I sucked in a deep breath and nodded once. "Okay."

Her eyebrows lifted with her smile. "Okay?"

That smile of hers filled my chest with warmth and made me feel like a fucking king. "Mhm. Let's go."

We paddled to the area where I'd hang out while she rode waves. It was louder over here since the waves were bigger, and she chewed her lip, but there was determination in her eyes. Pride hit me straight in the heart.

I knew it. Under all that shyness, buried under all those books in her brain, was the heart of a fucking lion.

"Have at 'er, bookworm. You got this. Trust yourself."

She nodded eagerly. She waited, watched a wave approach, and paddled as it caught up with her. Her arms dipped into the water in quick succession. She was so much stronger than a couple months ago. I thought about us laughing in the car yesterday about the entire town organizing a search party for her. She had laughed so hard tears rolled down her face. She was gasping for air. Two months ago, she would have disappeared into the ground with humiliation. Now, she just laughed about it.

That put a big smile on my face as I watched her paddle.

I didn't care if the town knew we were fooling around. Let them. Let every guy in town know to stay the fuck away from Hannah because she was mine.

Mine?

The thought jolted through me. Mine. Of course she was mine.

Hannah glanced over her shoulder at the wave. Her hands flattened on the board as she readied herself to snap up.

A bad feeling hit me. I shook my head. It was too early. The wave was going to—

The wave crashed over Hannah and she disappeared under the surface.

Fuck. Fear rattled through my veins.

I paddled hard, my head pounding with blood as my heart raced.

"Hannah!" I called, eyes darting around. Where was her board? "Hannah!"

Fuck. Fuck. Fuckfuckfuckfuck. My throat knotted and my heart was about to explode. This was my fault.

She gasped for air behind me and I whipped around. Blood dripped down her forehead. She blinked the water and blood out of her eyes and her chest heaved hard for air. Her board floated behind her, tethered to her ankle, and she reached for it.

In a shot, I was at her side, pulling her to me and inspecting her forehead while she coughed up water. My hands threaded in her wet hair, tilting her head to study the cut.

"Bumped my head on the bottom," she gasped. Her hand rested on her board, smearing another streak of red.

It wasn't too deep. "Did you lose consciousness?"

She shook her head and I studied her eyes. When our gazes locked, my heart jumped into my throat. Her eyes were wide but her pupils looked normal.

I grabbed her hand. Her palm glowed with bright red scrapes, leaking blood.

Rage rocked my veins. Fuck. She was hurt and it was my fault. I never should have let her do this. She wasn't ready. I pushed her too hard and now she was hurt. She might have a concussion.

Another wave approached.

"We have to get out of this area. Get on your board, baby. I'll tow you."

She shook her head. "I'm okay, Wyatt. I can swim."

My jaw tightened. "Get. On. Your. Board. Now." My voice was harsh and demanding and her eyes widened before she hoisted herself onto her board with one hand, keeping the scraped hand out of the water.

When we got to shore, my heart was still pounding.

"Leave the boards here," I told her, my hand wrapped around her arm and pulling her towards the surf shack with urgency.

She was hurt. She could have internal bleeding. She could have fractured something in her forehead or cracked a rib. Even if her pupils looked normal, she might have a concussion. She needed to go to the hospital.

"Wyatt, I'm fine, really." She laughed lightly. "It barely hurt."

I ignored her protests and pulled her all the way to the surf shop. Thank fuck my truck was here today. I yanked the passenger door open and pushed her in, taking care with her hand.

"Where are we going?" She laughed in disbelief when I reached across to buckle her seatbelt. "Can I take my wetsuit off, please?"

"You can take it off when we get there." I checked she was fully inside before I slammed the door and hurried to the driver's side.

"Get where?" she asked when I got in and started the engine. I backed out and threw the car in drive.

"The ER."

Her head fell back with a huff. "What? Wyatt, no, I don't need to go to the ER. I'm fine."

"You're not fine. You hit your head." It took everything in me not to press the gas pedal to the floor. *Get her there in one piece*, I reminded myself. I'd already done enough damage to her. My gaze snagged on the red gash on her forehead. It was about an inch long and didn't seem to be bleeding anymore.

She rolled her eyes and gave me a beseeching expression, reaching across and putting a hand on my knee with a little smile. "I'm okay. Really. I'm fine."

I turned back to the road and didn't say another word the rest of the way. My knee shook up and down, my heart raced, and my lungs were tight. When a family with small children crossed the street at a leisurely pace, I laid on the horn.

"Wyatt!" Hannah slapped my arm. "It's a red light."

The parents shot me a dirty look. I made a *hurry up* motion.

I pulled the truck up to the hospital doors, ignored the no-parking signs, and rushed around to Hannah's door, wrenching it open and hauling her into the ER.

The waiting room was quiet when we entered. The nurse at the front desk took one look at us, wetsuits dripping water on the floor, neither of us wearing shoes, and asked, "Surfing accident?"

"She has a concussion. She needs to see a doctor right now."

The nurse rolled her eyes and rage rattled through me. Out of the corner of my eye, Hannah gave her an apologetic look. I didn't care. I knew I was being an asshole, but I didn't care. Hannah was hurt. That was all I could think about. My Hannah was hurt and it was my fault.

Pain streaked through my chest. I'd deal with that later. Right now, I had to make sure Hannah was okay.

"Hannah?" Beck appeared at the reception desk, holding a clipboard.

My jaw clenched. This fucking guy again.

He frowned, studying her forehead. "What happened?" Then he glanced down at her wetsuit and at me. He reared back when our eyes met but he covered it up. "Surfing?"

Hannah nodded, wincing. "I'm fine."

"She's not fine. She hit her head. And her hand." I grabbed her hand to show him. "She has a concussion."

"I didn't hit my head hard," she told Beck.

I shook my head. "You don't know. You could have lost consciousness."

Hannah blew out a frustrated breath through her nose and gave a tight smile to Beck, who placed his clipboard down and gestured for Hannah to follow him. I took a step but the nurse put her arm out to stop me.

"You stay right there," she ordered. "Need you to fill out some forms."

Hannah shot me a reassuring smile over her shoulder before following Beck down the hallway. I swallowed with a thick throat.

"Is your wife pregnant?"

I turned back to the nurse with my mouth hanging open. "Huh?"

She repeated the question, slower.

Something woke up in my brain.

"Um." I blinked.

Wife. Pregnant.

My brain moved slow, like wading through water. I swallowed.

Hannah. Wife. Pregnant.

The corner of my mouth kicked up. A primal part of my brain liked those words together.

"No." I shook my head at the nurse. "She isn't."

She raised her eyebrows as if she didn't believe me. "You husbands drag your wives in for any little paper cut or tummy ache when there's a baby involved." She handed me a clipboard with a pen and pointed at the waiting area. "Take a seat and fill out these forms. Dr. Kingston should be back soon." She tossed me a towel from beneath the counter. I didn't want to know why she had a stash there. "And don't get any more water in my emergency room."

I nodded and sat quietly, reading the form while my mind raced. Hannah. Concussion. Hannah. Hurt. Husband. Hannah. Wife. Hannah. Pregnant.

I rubbed my hand over my face. Shut up, I told myself. Pregnant? Pregnant. That was the last thing I wanted. That was the complete opposite of temporary. Pregnant meant baby, and baby meant family and forever.

With Hannah.

I smiled. Husband.

No. Shut up, I told myself. No smiling at that. Look at what happened to my aunts. Aunt Bea was still broken after what happened. Hannah's father was a shell of a human, stuck in his ways after fifteen years, because he missed Hannah's mom so much. I was teaching her to be fearless so some guy could sweep her off her feet. I wasn't going to keep her for myself.

Professor.

The nickname rolled through my head and sparked down my spine. I raked a hand through my hair and focused on the forms.

Some of the information I knew, like her birthday, her address, and her phone number. Some of it I didn't know, like her personal health number. I left that one blank. Some I filled in for myself, like her emergency contact. Her dad was away, Avery was busy with… stuff. So I put myself.

Wife. Pregnant. Fuck.

We hadn't even had sex.

A sweet, pliant Hannah appeared in my head, under me in my bed. Naked and open for me. Me thrusting into her, her eyes falling closed as she flexed around me and I spilled into her. No condom. The warmth of sinking into her.

"Wyatt?"

My head snapped up. Beck stood in front of me. Hannah was at the front desk, talking with the receptionist. White gauze covered her hand and there was a bandage on her forehead.

Beck nodded for me to follow him. I didn't want to leave her but my worry overpowered my need to pick her up and tuck her under my arm, where she could be safe. Once we were in an exam room, I crossed my arms over my chest.

"Is she okay? What's going on?"

He nodded. "She's fine. I didn't see any sign of concussion. I cleaned her wounds, gave her a few stitches, and wrapped her hand up."

"You know she hit her head, right?"

He snorted. "Yep, you mentioned that about six times."

"This isn't funny!" I yelled, surprising both Beck and myself. "Sorry. Fuck." I rubbed my face and took a deep breath.

Beck reached out to put a hand on my shoulder but changed his mind. "It's okay, man. I understand. But if I thought she had a concussion, even the slightest one, I'd tell you. She's okay." He leaned against the counter. "I gave her a few Advil for the swelling and pain and I told her to take more tonight. She's going to have a bump on her forehead for a few days."

I nodded. Advil. Swelling.

"She can put ice on it if it's comfortable."

I nodded again, swallowing. My jaw was so tight it hurt.

Beck winced.

"What?" I asked.

He shook his head and laughed a little. "I didn't know."

My eyebrows shot up. "Didn't know what?"

He gave me a rueful smile. "That you two were a thing." He lifted one shoulder in a shrug. "I wouldn't have..." He narrowed his eyes, thinking. "But also, she asked me out. Right in front of you." He gave me a funny look.

I never should have told her to ask a bunch of guys out. What a stupid, stupid idea. She could have practiced asking me out, again and again.

Yeah. We could still practice that.

When I didn't elaborate, he shrugged. "Anyway. Sorry about that." He clapped me on the shoulder. "She's fine, okay? Lots of rest and keep her off the gnarly waves for a couple days."

Try forever. She was never going back behind the break. She could surf the baby waves within ten feet of shore.

"Thanks for seeing her so quickly." I cleared my throat, meeting his eyes. A hint of embarrassment hit me in the gut. "I know I'm being an asshole."

He grinned. "It's okay. You're taking care of your girl. I get it." There was something funny in his expression. Longing. Envy. "And I will keep looking."

Empathy flickered in my chest for the guy. He was my friend, and a good guy. Except for the whole hitting-on-Hannah thing.

Hannah was mine. He could find someone else, and I hoped he would.

He led me back to Hannah and I gathered her up in a big hug, right there in the waiting room. I tucked her into my chest the way I had been wanting to for the last half hour and breathed in her damp hair, pressing my mouth to her temple. She relaxed into me and my chest eased a couple notches.

Her hands stroked my back.

"Ready to go?" I said into her hair.

She nodded. "Yep."

We got back into the car and when we passed Hannah's street without stopping, she turned to me with a questioning look.

"Wyatt." Amused suspicion dripped from her tone and she raised an eyebrow before she winced in pain.

Well, that only settled my resolve.

"Where are we going?"

"My house."

Her eyes widened. "Why?" Her head fell back in frustration, but she still huffed a laugh. "He said I'm fine. I feel fine. Beck didn't see any sign of concussion."

I shook my head hard and pulled into my driveway. "He doesn't know what he's talking about."

Her chest shook with laughter. "He's literally a doctor."

I put the car in park and turned to her. "We don't know that." My mouth lifted in a grin.

She rolled her eyes. "You're impossible."

Beck was a smart guy and I trusted him but something deep inside me wanted Hannah near to me until this weird protectiveness went away.

"Your brain is addled," I said as we got out of the car. "I don't want you alone tonight. You might try to lick the light sockets or something." I reached for her and tucked her under my arm as we walked up to my place. I wasn't going to let her out of my sight.

Wife. Pregnant. I glanced down at her and my pulse picked up.

She snorted. "What's that look?"

I shook my head and unlocked the door. "Nothing."

We stepped inside and I rubbed a hand absently over my chest. I'd deal with these feelings later. For now, Hannah was my sole focus.

21

Hannah

THAT EVENING, Wyatt led me through the front door of Elizabeth and Sam's home. We slipped our shoes off and I could hear voices in the kitchen.

"Act normal and don't you dare make either of them feel awkward." Elizabeth's voice held a hard, challenging edge.

I frowned and exchanged a curious glance with Wyatt.

"I swear to god, if you ruin my chance for another daughter-in-law," her voice broke off and I got the sense she was shaking her head.

Daughter-in-law??? My face burned like molten lava and I refused to look at Wyatt.

"Why are you looking at me?" That was Emmett.

There was a derisive snort that sounded like Avery.

"You're already making us feel awkward," Wyatt called, grabbing my hand and pulling me into the kitchen.

Avery, Emmett, and Holden were lined up on one side of the counter and Elizabeth stood on the other side, shaking a wooden spoon at them. I could hear the sizzle of Sam barbecuing outside. Elizabeth turned and greeted us with a too-bright smile.

"You're here!" She rushed over and enveloped me in a

hug, pulling me into her and squeezing me. After a moment she pulled back to inspect my forehead with concern. "I heard you had an accident."

I shook my head, rolling my eyes. "A little bump. A few stitches."

"It's not a little bump. She might have a concussion." Wyatt opened the fridge and took out a beer.

"I don't have a concussion," I told him before turning back to the others with exasperation written all over my face. "We went to the ER and they shined a light in my eyes and said I was fine."

Elizabeth held up a bottle of white wine. "Would you like a drink?"

I shot her a smile and a nod. "Sure."

Wyatt shook his head. "She can't have a drink. Sometimes doctors miss things."

Avery frowned and tilted her head at me. "Who checked you out?"

"Beck."

She wiggled her eyebrows with an appreciative grin. "Lucky girl."

Emmett turned to her. "Excuse me."

Holden and I both snorted. Elizabeth ignored Wyatt and handed me a glass of wine.

"It's fine," I told him. He wore a pained expression, a mix of uncertainty and protectiveness.

Wyatt had been acting weird all day. First, this morning, he had been giving me heated looks that seared my skin and made me shiver. He was thinking about what we did while we were camping, no doubt. I was. It was *all* I could think about. His tongue on me, his fingers swirling, winding me tighter and causing my brain to explode with stars.

Since I bonked my head in the water, he had treated me like a cracked teacup. He wouldn't let me do anything all day except lie on the couch and listen to audiobooks. He had phoned Liya and made sure she was okay at the shop before he tucked me into the couch with a blanket and tea. He made me breakfast and lunch, and finally I got bored and took a nap. When I woke up, he was staring out the window at the water while his laptop played old footage from surf competitions on silent.

In Elizabeth's kitchen, I met Wyatt's protective, worried gaze. "I'm going to have one glass. I'm not going to drink the entire bottle. I'll be okay." I brushed my fingers over his tanned arm.

"One glass." His throat worked. His forehead wrinkled with worry.

Sam appeared in the patio door with a pair of tongs. "Food will be ready in five." He gave me a big grin and I saw Wyatt's lazy, casual grin in his expression. "Hey, Hannah. Heard you bonked your head."

I nodded and held up my glass. "I did and now I'm getting drunk."

"She's not getting drunk," Wyatt said, too loud, and everyone burst into laughter but him.

My arm snaked around his waist and I jostled him. "You're too easy."

He looked down at me with a strained expression before his arm came around my shoulders and a hint of a smile passed over his mouth. "You're taking years off my life here, bookworm."

Avery watched us with interest over the rim of her wine glass.

We headed to the table out on the patio and took our seats while Sam brought over the plate of burgers. Wyatt sat to my left and Avery to my right. Across the table, Emmett whispered something to Holden and the corner of Holden's mouth lifted. I caught the warning death glare from Elizabeth and they dropped it.

"How was the Emily Carr exhibit?" Holden asked, passing me the bowl of salad.

I nodded with enthusiasm. "Amazing. The paintings were beautiful and so different in person." I shot him a sympathetic look. "I'm sorry you missed it. I think there's another one next month you could catch by another local artist."

Elizabeth perked up and nodded at me. "I'd love to go to that with you. We could go for lunch after."

A funny, happy tightness prickled in my chest. "It's a date."

"Good." She wiggled her eyebrows. "Emmett, honey, you're holding up the salad."

Avery glanced between Elizabeth and me with a small, knowing smile on her face.

Wyatt leaned over and his breath brushed my ear. "Do you need another Advil? Your head feel okay?"

"I'm good," I whispered back with a small smile. "Thank you."

He glanced at the bandage on my forehead with a wince before his gaze met mine.

"I'm fine," I repeated.

He nodded and pressed a quick kiss to my temple before tucking back into his food. His mouth against my skin was comfortable, easy and normal.

Wait. Wyatt had kissed my temple in front of his entire family.

My gaze widened and I glanced around the table but no one had seemed to notice. Everyone was pointedly *not* looking at us. Holden stared at his plate. Emmett was very interested in the label of his beer. Sam studied something on the fence. Avery and Elizabeth's gazes locked on each other.

Huh.

Sam asked Holden about his latest construction project and they began discussing town permits. Emmett jumped in to explain all the bureaucracy he was eliminating from town hall.

Wyatt's hand settled on my knee. When I glanced up at him with curiosity, he winked at me.

That wink shot right down between my legs.

"When do you pick up your rings?" Emmett asked Avery.

She inspected her bare hand. "I'll drop by tomorrow and see if they're finished cleaning them."

He made an unhappy noise. "Good." His eyes lit up. "We should renew our vows. I should get you another ring."

She laughed. "What?"

Emmett nodded. "As a backup. I don't like seeing your hand without a ring."

Holden threw his fork down on his plate. "We get it, Emmett, you're *happily married*." Disdain dripped from his tone. "Good for you."

The table went silent and everyone gave Holden a strange look.

"Holden," Elizabeth chided. "Stop being so dramatic."

When we finished eating, the boys stood to clear the plates. I began to stand and Wyatt put a hand on my shoulder to keep me seated.

"We got it," he told me.

"But…" I started but he walked away with a handful of dishes.

Avery shook her head at me across the table. "Don't bother."

Elizabeth poured another glass of wine with a thoughtful expression. "I'm still learning about the patriarchy, but my takeaway is, we're dismantling it by *not* doing the dishes." She held the bottle out to Avery. "Top up?"

Avery nodded eagerly. "Yes, please. I'm not working tomorrow."

Elizabeth raised her eyebrow at me with a glimmer in her eyes. "No more for you, my dear, or my previously laid-back son will have my head." She wiggled her eyebrows with delight, like she couldn't imagine anything she wanted more.

I swallowed and a blush creeped over my face. Was it my imagination or was Elizabeth enjoying Wyatt's weird display of protectiveness?

"What are you reading these days, honey?" Elizabeth asked me and the endearment made my heart twist.

I began telling her about the historical romance I was reading, how it was so funny and inspiring and silly and the love interest made me swoon. She took down the title and I made a mental note to bring her my copy in case she wanted to read it.

The men returned to the table with plates of key lime pie, and Wyatt settled into his chair beside me before his arm came up around my shoulder. My skin prickled with awareness but I didn't dare move. I noticed a couple glances our way but perhaps Elizabeth's words in the kitchen had made their mark on everyone because no one said a thing.

If you ruin my chance for another daughter-in-law, she had said.

Daughter-in-law.

I nearly laughed at the idea of Wyatt and me married. Married was the exact opposite of what he wanted. Wyatt was all about impermanence and no tether.

Marriage was a legal tether, and an emotional one. Wyatt and me getting married would mean something.

Alarm spiked in my head and my gaze flared while I stared at my pie. What the absolute hell was I doing, thinking about marrying Wyatt? Maybe I had hit my head harder than I thought.

Elizabeth was just excited because she wanted good things for her sons. She was getting ahead of herself and dragging me with her. This was what moms did. Mine would have. A little smile grew on my face. My mom would love watching Wyatt wrap his arm around me and press kisses to my temple and bark at people that I couldn't drink.

"Speaking of town news," Emmett said, and the look he gave Wyatt was full of mischief before he glanced around the table with an innocent, concerned expression. "Did they ever find that missing hiker?"

I froze.

"What missing hiker?" Holden took a pull of his beer.

Emmett glanced between Wyatt and me, gaze snagging on Wyatt's arm around my shoulder, before he shot us a wicked smile. "That missing woman shrieking in the woods."

Avery's chest shook with laughter but she stared at her plate, Holden put a fist against his mouth but his eyes were bright, and Emmett beamed openly at Wyatt and me. Sam chuckled and Elizabeth glared.

My face was red like a stop sign. "Does *everybody* know?" I asked the table, mortified all over again.

Everyone started laughing, even Elizabeth. She shot me a sympathetic look. "Oh, honey. Yes. Everybody knows."

I buried my hands in my face and Wyatt rubbed my arm. His chest shook with laughter.

"It's okay, bookworm." His teasing grin was back and his teeth flashed. "I don't mind everyone knowing what I can do."

"Ew." Avery threw her napkin at him.

"We're just giving you a hard time, Hannah." Sam grinned at me. "This is what we do."

I rolled my eyes, despite my burning face. "I know."

Wyatt cleared his throat and addressed the table. "You know when I was in Europe last year?"

Holden raised an eyebrow. "Yeah?"

"I filmed a music video while I was there where they smeared me in silver body paint." His expression was unreadable. "I had to wear a merman tail."

"What?" Holden asked, blinking.

The entire table stared at him with open mouths, including me.

"What are you doing?" I whispered. "Why are you telling everyone?"

Wyatt nodded to Holden. "Yep. You can see me dancing in the background."

Emmett's eyes glowed like this was too good to be true. "Name. Artist. Now." He unlocked his phone, fingers hovering.

"'Depths of Love' by Tula." Wyatt took a bite of pie and ignored me gaping at him.

The opening notes played through Emmett's phone.

"Oh my god." Emmett stared at the screen with wide eyes. Avery peered over before she snorted. "First the chopping wood video and now this? Oh my god. This is amazing."

Emmett made everyone watch twice before Elizabeth and Sam returned to their seats.

"I've already sent it to everyone I know," Emmett informed Wyatt. "I'm dressing up as you for Halloween."

Wyatt shrugged with a small smile. "Okay."

I pinched his side and he shot another wink down at me. It dawned on me.

Wyatt told everyone about the video so they'd forget about the search party thing.

"You might as well post it on social media," he told me, reaching over and stealing a bite of my pie.

Elizabeth straightened up and gestured to me. "Honey, I forgot to tell you. I love the photo of you in the window."

A smile pulled at my mouth. "Wyatt took that one." One of my shoulders lifted in a shrug. "I'm trying something new."

Wyatt squeezed my shoulder. "It's working."

Did he mean with the store, or with my hot girl plans, or the finding true love thing? I wasn't sure.

Sam took a sip of his beer. "You're breathing new life into that place."

"I walked past today and someone was painting the wall," Elizabeth added.

I nodded. "That's Naya and her team. She's going to paint a new mural."

The light shifted in Elizabeth's eyes and she watched me with a small smile. "It's time. I can't wait to see it."

"I'll post progress pics on social media. I'm thinking about doing a time-lapse." This morning, while Naya and her team rolled primer over my mom's mural, I took videos.

Before Naya arrived, I had taken about a hundred pictures of the wall, including a selfie in front. My heart still twisted at the idea of painting over it, but Elizabeth was right. And my instincts were right. It was time.

"I bought wallpaper," I blurted out. "I pick it up tomorrow morning at the post office."

Avery's eyes lit up. "I didn't know that. You need help applying it?"

"If you have time, sure. I don't know what I'm doing." I frowned. "I don't know if it'll look good but I'm sick of the store looking straight out of the nineties." I rolled my eyes. "I'd still like to rip the carpet up, but one step at a time."

Wyatt shrugged. "Let's do it."

"Do what?" I raised an eyebrow.

"All of it. Let's rip the carpet up, fix the shelves, and put wallpaper on. We can get a bunch of plants for the front window."

Holden turned to Emmett. "Do we still have that flooring from the Ucluelet house?"

Emmett frowned in thought, tilting his head. "The one that was boat-access only?"

Holden nodded.

"It should be in the warehouse."

Holden tilted his chin to me. "We did a reno on a big house last year and the owner changed his mind about the flooring color but we couldn't return it." He sat back with his arms crossed over his chest. "It's nice, it's a dark cherry wood that would look good in your store."

Emmett nodded. "We could install it in a day."

I blinked. "You could?"

Holden shrugged. "Sure. It's just taking up space in the warehouse anyway."

Excitement flopped around in my stomach and I bit a smile back. "Okay."

Wyatt squeezed my shoulder again and shot me an amused smile. "We could do the shelves and wallpaper at the same time. Then you wouldn't have to close twice."

Avery raised her hand. "Elizabeth and I can help."

"I've got some odds and ends in my garage for shelves, Hannah," Sam added. "I'll make you some new ones. Do you want some flower boxes for outside?"

I could barely speak, it was happening so quickly and images flashed in my head of a beautiful new bookstore. The same store but better. The same store but with my stamp on it this time.

Wyatt snorted at my baffled expression. "Yes. She does."

The family made a plan and we decided that on Monday, we'd close the store and make the changes.

Deep in my chest, something ached. Two months ago, I ate dinner alone in my kitchen or with my dad, reading my book.

Now I sat at the dinner table with people who felt like family, people who were helping me make the store beautiful again.

My heart twisted. I didn't even mind that they teased me. Holden and Emmett treated me like they were *my* brothers. It had always just been my parents and me, and then it was my dad and me, and this was so much different. Louder and more stimulating and more chaotic, more emotional. I studied the Rhodes family, discussing Avery's restaurant and whether she wanted to rent a food truck for Pacific Rim or not, and a sense of home struck me.

My throat tightened. Next week, I'd turn thirty. I was spending time with a guy who was going to leave. I was still wasting time but in a different way. Maybe I hadn't changed as much as I thought. A weird pressure formed behind my eyes and I stood.

"Just going to grab some water." I shot Wyatt a tight smile before my gaze darted around the table. "Anyone need anything?"

Everyone shook their heads and I stepped back into the kitchen, where it was quiet and I was alone and could think. Where I could shove these emotions back down where they were safe.

Wyatt stepped into the kitchen with a worried frown. "You okay, bookworm?"

I nodded, pulled a glass down from the cupboard, and ran the kitchen tap to fill it. "I'm fine."

He stepped up behind me and placed both hands on the counter, caging me in. He warmed my back and it took everything I had not to lean into him. He stepped forward and didn't give me the choice. His arms wrapped around me and his mouth dropped to my neck below my ear. I shivered at the sensitive contact and he made a pleased humming noise against my skin.

"We can leave whenever you want," he murmured, his hands brushing my arms, sending goosebumps up and down my skin.

I nodded. "I know. Let's stay a bit longer."

"I like you being here."

I hated how much I loved those words. I hated how welcome and wanted I felt with him and with his family. I never felt like he didn't want me around. Never. Not once.

"I like being here." It came out as a whisper. "Even if you're being crazy and overprotective."

He grinned against my neck.

I tilted my head. "Stop worrying about me so much."

"I won't." He leaned down and stole a quick kiss and my breath caught. "I have to tell you something."

My stomach lurched. Here we go. "Okay."

He brushed his hands up my arms. "The nurse at the ER thought you were my pregnant wife."

A laugh choked out of me. My eyes were saucers. "Oh."

He lowered his forehead to my shoulder with a sigh. "I can't get it out of my head."

My mind raced to process this. "Why did she think that?"

He shrugged and kissed my neck again. "Don't know. And I didn't correct her."

"Does Beck think I'm *pregnant?*" I whispered the last word.

"I corrected the nurse about that. But not about the other part."

"The wife part."

"Mhm." Another soft kiss on my skin.

"Why not?" My heart thumped against the front wall of my chest.

His voice was low in my ear. "Because I liked the idea of it."

My brain skidded like it was slipping on ice. "But you…" I wasn't sure how to word it.

"Yeah, I know." His teeth scored my skin and I sucked a breath in. "Just wanted you to know that."

Between my legs, pressure built. The same pressure that happened when I saw Wyatt chopping wood without a shirt, muscles rippled and sweat dripping down his forehead.

"You getting hurt was my fault, bookworm." His voice was low and my center clenched. "And now I'm going to take care of you." He dropped his voice to a whisper. "All night long." He slapped my ass and I yelped with surprise. He headed back out the patio door with a sly wink and I stared after him with my mouth hanging open.

My center ached and I had the urge to drag him out of here, not caring who saw or what his family thought.

I groaned and downed half my water. I couldn't get turned on in my mother-in-law's kitchen.

Wait, mother-in-law? I shook my head hard. No. No, no. Stop, Hannah. She was *Avery's* mother-in-law.

He thought about us *married*, though. Wyatt. The guy who didn't believe in long-term love.

"I was thinking," Elizabeth said, stepping into the kitchen through the patio door, jarring me from my thoughts. "We should start a book club."

"A book club?" I raised my eyebrows and blinked.

"Well," she winced. "More like, you recommend books, I read them, and we talk about them over lunch."

"Oh." I blinked more. "Sure. I was going to bring you that historical romance I was telling you about anyway."

She smiled wide at me. "Wonderful. That would be wonderful." She watched me for a moment with a wistful expression. "I just adore you, honey. Your mother would be so proud of you."

My throat closed up and I couldn't breathe. I started to turn away but Elizabeth's hands came to my arms and she turned me to her. I couldn't hide.

"I forgot you knew my mom." My voice wobbled and I cleared my throat.

"I sure did." The apples of her cheeks popped when she smiled. "I remember how proud Claire was of you as a little girl and then as you grew up, as a teenager." She nodded. "Oh, yes. If she saw you today, running that shop and chopping off your hair and camping and surfing, she'd be thrilled."

I didn't say anything, just let her words settle. They rolled around in my mind as I considered them.

Maybe she would be proud.

"The only thing she ever wanted was for you to be happy. That's all I want for Wyatt." She shrugged. "Doesn't matter what that looks like, as long as he lives a life that's good for him." She raised an eyebrow and that wolfish gleam appeared in her gaze. "But it sure looks like what's good for him is you."

My mouth fell open. "I don't—"

"It's none of my business." She rubbed my arms again and stepped away with a smile and a wink. "You don't have to explain anything to anyone." She disappeared through the patio doors and I stood there, feeling seen, special, confused, and torn.

We sat out on the patio until it got dark. Holden had to head home because he had an early morning the next day and Emmett wanted to get up for a run and Wyatt was sending me more of those worried glances, so we said goodbye, exchanged hugs, and headed home.

Holden's reaction to Emmett and Avery's ring discussion popped into my head. "Do you think Holden's lonely?"

He made an amused noise of disbelief. "No. He could date if he wanted to."

I thought back to who I was before this whole thing with Wyatt started. How I wanted someone but didn't know how to go for it. I had hid in my bookstore with my nose pressed up against the glass, watching the world go by. "What if he doesn't know how?"

When he pulled the truck into his driveway, anticipation fluttered in my stomach.

We hadn't discussed where I would sleep tonight. Mid-afternoon, we had stopped at my place and I had packed a bag of clothes and books. He'd probably offer his bed to me like a gentleman and sleep on the couch.

I didn't want that, though. I wanted more of what we did while camping.

I smiled to myself. I was going to be brave and go for what I wanted.

22

Hannah

WE STEPPED in the front door of Wyatt's home and slipped our shoes off. The air radiated with tension.

"Are you tired?" His hand came to my arm and he peered down at me, searching my face.

It was only nine thirty. I smiled and shook my head.

"Great. Go sit on the couch and I'll bring you a tea."

My heart squeezed. Staying over, him making me tea, dinner with his family, it was like I was his girlfriend. Like I was his. Like he was taking care of something precious to him.

Hannah, shut up, I told myself. It was just tea. Avery had made me tea before. It wasn't a big thing.

I plopped down on the couch in Wyatt's living room. His home was small and tidy, with sparse, minimalist furniture, and I got the sense he didn't spend much time in the living room. He was either on the water, in his shop, or hanging out with his brothers. He had a TV though, and a few accent items like a sansevieria plant and a framed vintage surf poster. Perhaps Elizabeth had brought those over.

Wyatt returned from the kitchen with mugs of tea, and I remembered something Avery had said to me.

Tea is the least horny beverage.

I held back a snort. This cup of tea dashed any hopes I had of Wyatt and I re-enacting what we had done in the tent. No one had an orgasm with a stomach full of Sleepytime Tea.

"What are you snickering at, bookworm?" Wyatt set the mugs down on the coffee table and flashed me a curious look.

"Nothing. You want to watch a movie?"

"You're not supposed to look at screens."

My head fell back in exasperation. "You're so stubborn."

The corner of his mouth kicked up and he reached for the book I'd set on my bag. When he dropped down onto the other end of the couch, he pulled my pink-socked feet into his lap.

"Wyatt." I raised an eyebrow.

He cracked the book open to where my bookmark marked the page and cleared his throat. "Watching TV before bed isn't good for sleep anyway."

And then he began to read my book out loud.

My heart melted in my chest. His bare feet rested on the coffee table and his free hand settled on my ankle in his lap. The way his sharp jaw moved as he spoke mesmerized me and I longed to run my mouth over the scrape of his stubble again, but then I'd have to move and ruin this perfect moment.

Wyatt's lazy drawl put a new tone on the sweet romantic comedy. He made every sentence sound sexy, languid, and suggestive. In the scene he read, two teachers bickered with each other, and I smiled, watching as he read, listening to his low voice narrate. When his hand stroked my ankle, sparks of electricity shot up my leg.

The two characters began kissing frantically. His thumb stilled on my ankle and I froze, listening as he described the hungry, desperate, needy way the characters touched each other.

My heartrate sped up and heat pulsed between my legs.

This book was supposed to have closed-door sex scenes, but now the male main character was sucking on the female main character's tongue. My core throbbed at the memory of doing that to Wyatt and the tortured noise he made after. I had the urge to squeeze my legs together but held back. Wyatt continued reading about the characters now tearing each other's clothes off as if it was nothing. Like he was reading furniture instructions.

This was a bad idea. A bad, bad idea. My toes curled and Wyatt glanced at me out of the corner of his eye, then down at my toes, and paused with a tight jaw.

He took a deep breath and continued reading.

God, he was so sexy like this. Before dinner, he had showered and put a bit of product in his hair and the dark blond looked so... unf. And his strong, tanned hands, one clutching the book and one making warm contact with my ankle. I remembered the noise he made when I ran my hands over his chest. How warm he was. He seared me, and I always needed more.

And that mouth. As he read the dirty words, his mouth turned up and his eyes grew heavy-lidded.

The ache between my legs intensified and I shifted. My foot brushed something hard in Wyatt's lap and my breath caught. He paused, pressed his mouth into a firm line, and closed his eyes.

My body warmed from my core out and my blood surged with something bold. I twitched my foot against his erection again and his head fell back.

"Hannah." His tone was warning, and his hand tensed on my ankle.

I bit a grin back and shivered. "What's wrong?"

"You know what's wrong." He sounded like he was in agony.

Wyatt took such good care of me all day, even though I was pretty sure there was nothing wrong with me other than an ugly scrape on the forehead. My heart pounded in my chest.

It was time for me to take care of Wyatt.

"I'm tired."

His head snapped up and he closed the book before tossing it on the coffee table. "Okay." He nodded to himself. "Let's go to bed."

I snorted. The way he said *let's go to bed* was the way someone would say *sure, you can pull my tooth out*. It would hurt me, him acting this way at the thought of us going to bed, but his jaw ticked and his gaze dragged over me. He was turned on, same as me, but he was going to try to be a gentleman tonight.

He stood over me, raking his hand through his hair. His gaze was unreadable. "I would offer to sleep on the couch, but I want to be near you tonight. In case you aren't feeling well or something."

I nodded. "Because I hit my head."

"Because you hit your head." His voice was low, his gaze dark. He held his hand out. "Come on."

We spent the next few minutes going through the going-to-bed motions: brushing our teeth, me taking out my contacts, changing into our pajamas. Wyatt didn't wear pajamas, but I brought the tank top and short set from the night he crawled through my window because I wanted to play with fire. He wandered through the house while I changed, locking the doors and turning off lights before I heard his footsteps go past the bathroom door.

In his room, he lay in bed, shirtless with his arms propped behind his head. His gaze wandered down my pajamas. My nipples pinched and his nostrils flared. He groaned and closed his eyes with a pained expression.

I laughed.

"Fuck, bookworm, you're going to kill me." His throat

worked as his gaze snagged on my chest, on the hem of my shorts, on my bare collarbone.

His bedroom was like the rest of his house—small, tidy, sparse, and masculine. Clean lines, like him. It even smelled like him in here, a masculine, fresh scent that made my blood hum. A book on his bedside table caught my attention.

"*Pride and Prejudice?*" I shot him a questioning look as I picked it up and studied the cover. My mouth opened to form another question but nothing came out.

He lifted one shoulder with a little smile. "You were right. It was good."

My brows snapped together. Something sweet wrapped around my heart. "Why did you read it?"

His expression softened. "It's your favorite. I wanted a peek inside that brain of yours." He pulled back the covers and gestured for me to get in. "Come on."

Wyatt read my favorite book. For me. If I thought too hard about that, I would... I didn't know. It was just a book. Beck read the book, too.

But this was different. Wyatt was different.

"Did you like it?" I asked softly, sliding under the covers beside him. His arm tucked around me and pulled me to his warm chest and my breath caught.

It was me standing in Elizabeth's kitchen all over again, seen and wanted and loved. My throat tightened and my hands came to Wyatt's hard chest. I peered up into his eyes, so gray and kind and full of affection.

He nodded with a small smile. "Mhm. You were right about the scene with Mr. Collins."

I pressed a soft kiss to Wyatt's neck. He inhaled and his chest rose under my hands.

"We should sleep. Your head—"

"I think you should give me another lesson." I brushed my lips over his stubble and he shuddered. "Professor."

In a split second, I was on my back, Wyatt's mouth pressing hot, fast kisses down my neck.

"You know exactly what to say to make me lose it," he murmured against me, and I shivered again. His fingers found a tight nipple through the thin fabric of my top and I arched.

A soft whimper escaped me, and I reached for him but he batted my hands away.

"Not yet. Let me do my work."

I smiled and his mouth covered mine, lingering a moment before his tongue coaxed me open. The slow glide of our tongues melted my brain like an ice cream cone in summer and I let my consciousness sink, sighing against him. Wetness pooled between my legs, warm and slippery, and after a few moments of us tasting each other, exploring each other's mouths, me reaching for his length and him holding my wrists, finally, finally, he touched me.

"Oh, Jesus, bookworm, you are so fucking wet for me," he rasped. I nipped his bottom lip. "I love how you get so worked up."

His fingers slid over my center and my head fell back. More. I needed more. I pulled my shirt over my head and his mouth fell to my breast, tasting and rolling and tugging. A strangled noise came out of my throat. My core clenched around nothing and my hips thrust harder towards his hand, needing more.

"I love how soft you are." His fingers found my clit and I moaned. "Mhm. Like that?"

I jerked my head in a nod. "Like that. Like that." I was babbling but the heat coiled low in my stomach and I didn't care. Wyatt's hands on me made me mindless, and I didn't want it to stop.

"Why don't you show me your homework?" His voice was so low and soft. "Show me how you touched yourself after your date."

A streak of self-consciousness shot through me, and I bit

my lip and opened my eyes. Wyatt watched me with something dark and hungry in his eyes, and a cruel little smile on his mouth.

"I've thought about you touching yourself so many times." His throat worked and he began to slide my shorts off. "Show me the real thing." He lifted his gaze to mine. "Please, baby."

My hand slipped to my center and I began to rub slow, soft circles on my clit while Wyatt watched with hungry fascination. The warm heat coiling around my spine and the intense way he watched drowned out my self-consciousness. I moved a little faster and pressed my lips together with a wince of pleasure as the pressure grew.

"Jesus fucking Christ," he breathed and pressed a kiss to my inner thigh. "You are so fucking gorgeous, Hannah. I've been thinking about this nonstop. I wanted you all day."

"Me too," I gasped. "You make me come so hard."

Those were the magic words. He grabbed my wrist and pinned it to the bed. "Lesson's over." He slipped a finger inside me and began to work my center. He located that spot within me and white-hot electricity shot through my limbs.

"Wyatt," I gasped. My legs shook and everything seized with pleasure. I grasped the duvet. Wyatt's gaze swung from where his finger entered me to my face in fascination.

"I should draw this out and torture you for scaring me this morning." His eyes seared me, half-teasing, half-furious. "I was so worried, bookworm. I never want to see you hurt. You're too important to me."

"Not hurt," I gasped again, arching. I frowned and winced, it felt so good. All the waves of pleasure radiated from where his finger pulsed. My body squeezed him. "Doing just fine."

He laughed low and pressed another kiss to my inner thigh. "I can see that. Now, what do you need to come?"

"More."

"More what?"

My chest heaved as I pulled in deep breaths that weren't enough. His finger slowed inside me, with less pressure, and I groaned with frustration. "Wyatt."

"Bookworm, what do you need to come?" His tone was teasing and knowing.

A noise of furious anguish wrenched out of my throat. "Hand." I held mine open on my stomach and he pressed his palm into mine.

His warm skin, the intimate contact of our hands pressed against each other, it did something to me. Anchored me. Connected us.

He ran his velvet tongue up my inner thigh, inches from where I wanted him. My head spun and my clit ached for friction and pressure.

"What else?" His voice was so low and controlled.

My head swam but he dangled what I needed in front of me.

"Mouth." I heaved another breath and spared him a glance. His eyes were dark and heavy. "On me."

A pleased noise rumbled from his throat. "I was hoping you'd say that." His head dipped, he set his mouth on my clit, and my head fell back.

A string of words flew out of my mouth at the heat of his tongue on the bud of nerves. He worked my G-spot while I twisted and writhed on his mouth. My free hand came to his hair, and when all of that wasn't quite enough, I set his hand that had been resting on my stomach against my breast. He pinched, I arched, he rolled, I whimpered. I tugged his hair and he groaned into me, increasing the speed at which his tongue slicked over me and burying his face further into my center.

Heat grew in my stomach, tightening and creating pressure. I was close. Close and yet I couldn't completely get there.

"I love you under me like this, writhing and mindless," Wyatt murmured against me. His breath tickled me. "I jerk off thinking about this, about how you taste and how you look when you're about to come." He sucked on my clit and I bucked my hips against his face with a cry.

"I don't know if I can." I could barely get the words out.

My body was wound so tight it might snap, but there was something missing. Frustration flicked at my brain and distracted me.

"It's okay if you can't." Wyatt licked me from my entrance to the top of my clit and I let another breathy moan slip out at the electricity that shot through me. "This is for you, and whether you come or not isn't important. Watching you react like this is making me fucking hard." He did that licking thing again before adding suction to my clit and I whimpered. "We can do this for as long as you like." His teeth lightly scored my clit and my eyes widened as I bowed off the bed.

Him taking the pressure off me, telling me it was okay not to come, it lifted a couple weights off me, and when he sucked harder on my clit, I forgot what I was thinking about. I forgot what I was worried about. My body was his to play with and my brain crackled with sparks. I filled his bedroom with my breathy moans while I ground onto his face and tugged his hair.

Regular me would die of embarrassment but horny, almost-there me didn't care. I wanted to come.

"Yes, baby, yes," he groaned when I pushed harder into his face. "Like that. Give it to me like a good girl. Come for me."

And I did. I tipped over the edge and every muscle in my body tensed. I was suspended in time as wave after wave rolled through me. Wyatt groaned and gave encouraging *mhm*s against my folds as I shook under his desperate mouth. My hips bucked and when my thighs squeezed him, he moaned like I was the one giving him pleasure.

I fell back into the bed, heaving for air. He crawled up the bed beside me and pulled me into his chest, pressing kiss after kiss to my temple and cheeks and lips. His face was wet and something very bad inside me flushed with pleasure. I sank into his warmth, my heart still thumping hard.

"You smell amazing," I said, inhaling him.

One of his hands came to my hair and he stroked it, sending shivers down my back. "I love having you in my bed."

He reached down to adjust his boxer briefs. They strained with his erection. He made a choking noise when my hand encircled him through the fabric.

I stroked him and he bucked.

His face contorted into a look of pain and he groaned as I explored his length. He was warm, rock-hard, and heavy, and when I slipped my hand inside his briefs, his skin seared my hand.

"Jesus, baby." He choked the words into my hair as my hand skimmed up and down, running my thumb over the swollen tip and dragging through the bead of liquid that had appeared there.

So many times, I had pictured Wyatt sinking this length into me, stretching me and making me feel amazing. I wanted to feel him shudder into me. I wanted us connected, experiencing it together instead of one after the other.

I wanted Wyatt to lose control.

I sat up and began to slide his briefs down, but his hands came to my shoulders and he pulled me back to him.

I gave him a questioning look.

"I don't trust myself to be gentle with you." He sucked a deep breath in. "I want you too much."

Need sparked within me.

"You already made my head explode a few minutes ago," I grumbled.

"I lost control there." He grunted as my hand returned to his cock and began to stroke.

"Like that?" I watched his gorgeous face before running my mouth over his stubble.

He jerked a nod. "Just like that." He grabbed my other

hand and brought it to his sac, and when I squeezed lightly, he sucked a breath in. "Fucking hell, bookworm, I'm never letting you leave."

His words washed through me and made my heart lift. I stroked him faster. I loved the noises that were coming out of his throat, loved the way I had complete control over his body. Watching his face, my head swam with power, pleasure, and desire. He opened his hazy eyes and watched me. Something sweet, twisting, and heavy struck me.

"Baby," he gasped. His hand covered mine and he stroked himself faster with my hand, gripping tight. "Oh god. Hannah, you're going to make me come."

His eyes clenched closed, his mouth fell open, and he used my hand for pleasure. With a shudder and a groan, he spilled hot liquid all over our hands and his stomach while I watched in fascination.

He exhaled long and low. "Holy shit. You made me come so hard from a hand job." He said it like he didn't believe it and I beamed.

His grin was sluggish and lazy with a hint of casual cockiness, as always. He rose up and met my mouth. Pure affection and gratitude replaced any urgency in me, and my heart expanded in my chest. His intoxicating scent teased me. The soft duvet brushed my bare skin, and his skin warmed me all the way to my toes. My brain hummed with comfort.

"I need to clean up," he whispered. "One sec, okay?"

I nodded and he rose, stepping into the bathroom before returning with a washcloth. He shot me a wink as he wiped my hand off and I sighed.

When we crawled under the covers, he pulled me to him and I smiled into the pillow. My body tucked into his like we were made for each other.

"I'm falling for you, bookworm." He whispered the words against the back of my head in the dark.

Alarm spiked in my brain. Those words were all I wanted to hear, so why was my chest tight?

"I'm falling for you, too." I swallowed hard at the half-truth.

I wasn't *falling* for Wyatt. I was in it. I was in love with him. The thought of him leaving—

"What are we going to do?" I breathed.

"I don't know."

23

Hannah

"OVER HERE, BOOKWORM."

My paintbrush stilled and I shot a smile over my shoulder at Wyatt down on the sidewalk. He snapped a picture of me on the ladder in front of the store, painting *Pemberley Books* over the stencil.

Instead of a faded gray like before, the front of the store was now a deep forest green. Even in the late afternoon golden hour glow, the color was magnificent. Rich, lush, and comforting.

Chatter, laughter, and the whir of a drill traveled through the open door below me. When I saw the new flooring Emmett, Holden, and Sam had installed, I had no words. The deep, cherry wood was a stark contrast to the gross old carpet, lying in a heap in the dumpster behind the store. Pemberley Books looked like a real store now.

It wasn't even finished yet. The books stood in stacks in the stockroom, waiting for placement once Sam finished fixing the shelves in the alley. Naya worked beside him, painting the mural with headphones on, lost in her work.

My heart squeezed with gratitude. I never could have

afforded the flooring or installation. I never could have done all this work by myself in one day.

Wyatt stepped back to capture another picture. "Nice choice on that color."

I smiled to myself as I applied the petal-pink paint to the store name. It *did* look great, and if I changed my mind, I could paint over it.

Because everything was temporary, like Wyatt had said.

His words from the other night echoed in my head and my heart tripped.

I'm falling for you, bookworm.

Falling for Wyatt didn't seem temporary. My stomach knotted and I shoved the thought away as I brushed more paint onto the sign.

In my back pocket, my phone buzzed. The music video clips had gone viral on Wyatt's social media and the comments, likes, and messages had been rolling in. His fans thought the clips were hilarious and even Tula had commented and reposted. More brand sponsors had contacted me and he had a call with an agent tomorrow.

Holden stepped out the door and looked up at me. "You want me to install those lights now?"

"Oh. Sure." I made my way down the ladder and Wyatt was at my side in a flash, ready to catch me if I fell.

The nurse at the ER thought you were my pregnant wife, he had told me days ago at his parents' house. *I liked the idea of it.*

Wyatt's gaze made my skin prickle with awareness. "Careful," he said in a low voice, and I shivered.

If he was this protective now, what would he be like when I *was* pregnant?

My brain jolted. *If. If* I were pregnant. Which I never would be with Wyatt. We hadn't even had sex. And it wasn't like that. It wasn't forever with him, as much as that pinched to think about.

His thumb brushed my jaw and I leaned into his touch. "You got some paint on you."

Our gazes met and I bit my lip. He had woken me up this morning with his tongue, drawing slow, intoxicating circles on my clit. Heat streaked through me at the memory.

Beside us, Holden folded his arms over his chest in exasperation. I flushed and Wyatt laughed and slapped me on the butt before I followed Holden inside.

Elizabeth and Liya had almost finished applying the wallpaper. I covered my mouth to hold back a squeal. The giant flowers were like something out of *Alice in Wonderland*. Holy crap. The store was almost unrecognizable.

"Sorry," I told Holden. "I know you have better things to do."

Holden managed the construction company now. He hadn't done wiring in years, but he was here in the store, helping me out along with his entire family.

He waved me off. "It's fine." He pointed at the boxes near the door. "Are these the lights?"

I nodded, pulled the box cutter from my back pocket, and sliced the box open.

When I pulled out the feathery orb, Holden grimaced. He regarded the light like it was about to bite him before he sighed and took it from me.

I stifled my laugh. "Thank you."

"Ohhh, pretty lights." Avery appeared behind me with a potted plant with big leaves. She held it up. "Chinese evergreen. Dana at the garden store said this would be good for low light." She tilted her head as Emmett walked in the door carrying another potted plant. "We have a whole bunch in the car."

I beamed at them. "Thank you. Do you want to set them outside until we move the bookshelves back in?"

I led them outside as Max and Div turned the corner.

"Whoa." Max stepped inside the store.

Div studied the newly painted storefront with a small smile on his face before nodding once at me. "Looks good." His gaze swung to my hair. "And your hair does too, I forgot to mention that the other night."

My fingers came to the ends of my hair. My face was going to be tired tomorrow from all the smiling I'd done today. "Thanks."

Div put his hands on his hips. "How can we help?"

———

"*CONNOR FLIPPED her onto her back and kneeled at her soaked entrance,*" Emmett read in between bites of pizza as we collapsed in giggles.

"Jesus Christ." Holden's eyes were wide from where he scrutinized the sturdiness of the hanging chair in the window. "I thought this was a hockey book."

It was just after nine at night and pizza boxes lay open on the floor. Avery and Emmett sat with their backs against the desk. Div and Liya lounged in the squashy blue chairs we had dragged to the main area. Holden tested his weight on the hanging chair and studied the mounting brackets. Max returned from the washroom and took a seat on the arm of Div's chair. Sam and Elizabeth had called it a day once the last book was on the shelf.

"It's hockey romance," Liya told Holden, as if that explained everything.

The store was like a fairy dreamland greenhouse. Like something out of a book, just like I wanted but better because it was real. Twinkle lights sparkled along the top of the book-shelves. The rich brown of the cherry floors matched the trees in the wallpaper, and the soft lighting doused the store in a warm glow. Avery had placed viney plants near the hanging chair in hopes that the vines would grow up the support to the ceiling.

The Main Character chair, I had called it. People could sit there and feel like the lead in their own story. I hummed with bliss.

"*'I'm going to make my pretty little wife come hard tonight,' Connor growled, dragging a meaty finger through her wetness,*" Emmett read. He took a bite of pizza, scanning the page. "Wow. This is a lot. Meaty." He shook his head to himself.

Holden stared at Emmett in horror. Liya and Avery were laughing so hard they couldn't breathe. Wyatt and I exchanged a grin. Even Div wore a little smirk as he wrote an email on his phone.

"*'Connor, please,' she begged. He delivered a sharp slap to her quivering folds and she gasped with pain and pleasure.*"

Avery let out a loud cackle and stuffed a piece of crust in her mouth.

"A sex slap? Oh my god." Max shook his head at me. "You sell porn." He looked to Div. "Are the straights okay?"

Div didn't look up from his phone. "They were never okay."

My face glowed red but I couldn't stop laughing. "I'm so glad your parents left," I whispered to Wyatt.

He cringed and shuddered.

Emmett turned a page. "Throbbing, thrusting, aching cocks, yada yada yada." He turned another page. "Here we go. *Connor roared as his orgasm raced through him and his engorged member sprayed seed like a firehose, all over his wife's ample breasts.*" He closed the book and regarded us all with a satisfied sigh. "What a scene."

Holden's eyes were huge with disbelief. "This is what women read?"

"And Don," I added.

"Firehose?" he whispered to himself.

Wyatt cut him a look. "Romance makes people happy. Things aren't dumb because women like them."

"I didn't say it was dumb." Holden blinked and rubbed the back of his neck. "It's just horny."

"Women are horny, Holden." Avery held up the pizza box. "Who wants the last piece of this one?"

Wyatt pulled me closer to him on the window bench. "How you doing?"

I rolled my lips. My face hurt from smiling so much today. "Great."

He nodded, hot gaze searing me. "Great. You look happy."

"I am. This place finally feels like…" I sucked in a breath, surveying everyone. "Mine." Sitting here with Wyatt, I knew I was meant to be here in the bookstore. Like all the uncomfortable stuff I went through to make the changes was worth it. Like it was fate.

But I also couldn't wait to get back to Wyatt's place tonight.

"Are you tired?" he asked in a low voice.

I matched his heated gaze. "Not *that* tired."

He smirked.

My phone buzzed in my back pocket. When I peered at the screen, my dad's picture flashed there.

Tension cracked my good mood and my spine went rigid.

"Just a sec," I told Wyatt with a quick, tight smile as I stood and wandered to the back room. "Hi, Dad."

"Hi, honey."

"Um, what's up? How's Salt Spring?" My voice was weak and watery and I squeezed my eyes closed in frustration. I hadn't thought about my dad once today.

I hadn't really thought about my mom, either.

I slumped against the wall in the storeroom, glancing down at the stack of crime thrillers on the table. When we re-shelved the books, I had made the decision to leave anything non-romance back here. Romance books made up the majority of our social media posts and accounted for ninety percent of our sales these days. Over the summer, with the social media taking off, Pemberley Books' brand had become all about romance novels. It didn't make sense to take up valuable real estate on the shelves with books that didn't fit our brand.

"It's good. Keeping busy. It's quite beautiful here." He laughed. "They have a great ice cream shop down the road, we like to walk there every night after dinner."

"We?" I frowned. "Is Uncle Rick back?" The idea of him and my dad walking to get ice cream was kind of cute.

His tone changed. "Um. No. Uh, the neighbor. Anyway, how's the store?"

Oh, the store that was unrecognizable from when he left? That store? "Fine." My voice strained.

My heart hammered in my chest. I couldn't do this. I couldn't lie like this to him. It was wrong.

"I have to tell you something."

He paused. "Okay."

"Um." I blinked and sucked a breath in before I let it out, nice and slow. *You got this, bookworm*, I could hear in my head. "I started social media for the store. We, um…" I cleared my throat and rubbed my forehead. "We weren't doing that well."

"Okay." He drew the word out in three syllables.

"When people visit Queen's Cove on vacation, they check out certain hashtags and the town social media pages to see what there is to do here." I swallowed. "Um. So it's important that we have an online presence and at least show people that we exist." I dragged the toe of my sneaker along the edge of a cardboard box full of biographies. "It's helped bring the store back into the black."

My pulse beat in my ears while I waited for him to respond. He sighed.

"I didn't know the store wasn't doing well."

"I wanted to fix it. I didn't want you to worry." My mouth twisted.

He hummed, thinking, and I could picture his uncertain expression. "I should have been around more. I should spend more time in the store once I get back."

I could hear the reluctance in his voice.

I didn't want him here, either. Having him in the store more would be a step backwards. The store had my stamp all over it now.

"I don't think that's necessary." I picked at a drop of dried paint on my jeans.

This was the part where I should have told him about the renovations.

Wyatt stuck his head in the storeroom and gave me a questioning look with a thumbs up. *Everything okay?* he mouthed.

I nodded. "Dad, I have to go."

Baby steps, I told myself. Today, social media. Next week I'd tell him a few more things.

"Okay. Call me if you need anything."

"I will. Bye, love you."

"Love you, too."

There. That wasn't so bad. Maybe he wouldn't totally lose his mind when he saw that I had erased my mom completely.

Wyatt stepped into my space and I breathed in his scent.

"Everyone's packing up." He towered over me, looking down into my eyes with warmth. "I'm so proud of you."

"For what?" I looped my arms around his waist.

He tilted his head out at the store. "For everything. Look at you go, bookworm, riding the wave. Shooting forward."

His head dropped and he pressed a soft kiss to my mouth. I melted into him.

"Let's go home," he whispered, and I nodded against his mouth.

24

Wyatt

I WOKE up a few mornings later with a smile on my face, Hannah in my arms, and the sun streaming into the bedroom.

And I thought surfing was heaven.

She was still sleeping, curled up against me, her chest rising and falling softly, and I studied her face, replaying the past few nights with her under me in bed, writhing and gasping.

I had always enjoyed making women come. Seeing a woman's pleasure turned me on, but with Hannah, it was more.

It was ecstasy. It was all I thought about. I was showing her a new side of sex she hadn't experienced before, and when she grabbed my hand and squeezed it as she came, she showed me a new side, too. I craved seeing her lose her mind and enjoy herself. I wanted to leave my imprint on her, on both her body and her mind.

I wanted to leave a lasting impression.

My throat tightened. For whom? I didn't want anyone else to touch her ever again. But I didn't know what to do with that thought.

Hannah. Wife. Hannah. Pregnant. The nurse's words had

been playing in my head on a loop since we left the ER all those days ago. They played as Hannah napped on the couch that day. They played as we sat around the dinner table with my family, everyone laughing and talking with her and welcoming her with open arms. And they played last night as I fell into the deepest sleep.

With Hannah, those words didn't sound like they used to. Before her, they didn't apply to me. They were for someone else. But when I watched her sleep beside me, my heart ached for those words. Hannah living here. Moving all her books in, them taking up space everywhere in organized piles and filling up bookcases. The thought made me smile.

Deep in my chest, something cold and sharp poked me. My summer with my aunts flashed into my head. This thing with Hannah wouldn't last. She'd bring her light, happiness, and radiance into my home and then she'd leave, it would be over, and I'd be left with a hole in my life. Like my Aunt Bea. Like Hannah's dad.

I swallowed. I wasn't going to worry about it now.

I slid out of bed, careful not to wake her, and padded to the kitchen, stretching and opening the fridge.

Twenty minutes later, she wandered in with a cute, sleepy expression on her face and rumpled hair. I grinned at her from my place in front of the stove and she stepped up behind me and slipped her arms around me.

Yeah, she wasn't leaving. Not when I could have her like this, all comfortable and sleepy and sweet.

"What are you doing?" Her mouth brushed the bare skin of my shoulder.

"Making breakfast. You want a coffee?"

She nodded and I reached for a mug.

"I can get it." She shot me a smile and poured herself a cup before taking a seat at the kitchen island. "Let's go surfing today."

Hesitation twisted in me and I made a face. My gaze snagged on her forehead. I frowned at it.

"Wyatt." She rolled her eyes.

I crossed my arms over my chest and wandered over to the living room. Out the window, the water sparkled in the early morning light.

She stepped up beside me. "We don't have to do the big waves today. We can take it easy. I want to get out there with you." Her eyes pleaded and her pretty mouth curled into a smile. "It's the perfect way to start the day."

I sighed. "I can't say no to you." I pulled her into my chest and we watched the water for a moment before heading back to the kitchen.

After we ate, we changed into our swimsuits but got distracted. We fell back into bed, reaching for each other and getting each other naked again. I couldn't get enough of touching her. Her smooth skin, her soft curves, the way her breath hitched when I touched her nipples or squeezed her ass or scored her neck with my teeth, it drove me insane. It was everything I wanted and yet never enough. I could never have enough of her.

We hadn't gone all the way yet. I wanted more than anything to sink my aching cock into her warm, wet core while she squeezed me the way she had squeezed my fingers each time she came, but something held me back.

She wasn't ready.

Maybe I wasn't ready.

Which made no sense. Sex wasn't a big deal to me.

I guess with her, it was. It wasn't just me in this. It was her too, and I wanted to make sure she didn't do anything just because I wanted her to. She had to want it for herself. She had to ask for it.

We finally made it out onto the water, paddling straight to the cove we hung out in after surf lessons.

She stretched out on her board and closed her eyes. Her

mouth turned up in an expression of contentment. "If I were more cynical, I might think that you wanted to fool around this morning so I wouldn't put up a fight about not surfing." She opened one eye at me and I grinned.

"I will always want to fool around with you, bookworm."

We watched each other for a moment, floating there, bobbing up and down in the water, and something passed through our gazes. Something warm, languid, comfortable, and understanding. My heart tugged toward hers and I swallowed with a thick throat.

A splash nearby stole our attention and she lifted her head with a frown. We saw them at the same time.

"Oh my god." She jerked up and her board swayed in the water, threatening to tip.

"Stay still." My voice was calm and I reached out to take her hand. "Stay where you are and breathe."

She gripped my hand and we watched the black fins skim through the water fifty feet away.

"Are they going to attack?"

I laughed softly. "No, they're just curious."

The pod of orcas swam closer and she squeezed my hand.

"I'm scared." Her voice was a shaky whisper.

I kept my tone calm and steady for her. "They're not going to hurt us. They're coming to say hi." My thumb stroked back and forth on the back of her hand. "I've got you."

One of the orcas blew out a breath and Hannah inhaled sharply. My gaze swung between the orcas in the water and her astonished expression. Her eyes were wide and her mouth parted. Neither of us would forget this moment. I'd seen orcas before in the water—they migrated up to the coast every summer and the town ran whale-watching tours—but never this close, and never with someone like Hannah squeezing my hand.

After a few moments, the whales grew bored or hungry

and swam away. Hannah exhaled a long breath and lay back on her board, staring at the sky.

"Holy."

My mouth lifted in a grin. "You okay?"

"Uh huh." She glanced at me with bright eyes and a smile grew on her pretty mouth. "That was so cool!"

I nodded at her, smiling. My chest was tight and I couldn't take my eyes off her as she watched the surface for more.

We floated out there for an hour before heading back in.

"I'm going to open up the store," she told me as we stepped inside the house. I started to protest but she held up a hand. "If my head hurts, I'll come home. I promise."

I nodded, my mouth set in a firm line. She had referred to my place as *home*, and that might have been the only reason I let it go. "Okay." I cleared my throat. "I was thinking…"

She raised an eyebrow. "Mhm?"

"We're going on a date tonight." I stepped up to her and put my hands on her upper arms. One hand skimmed up her shoulder and played with the strap of her swimsuit. She shivered under my touch and I grinned.

"A date?" Her eyebrows lifted. "Where?"

"Let me handle that." I leaned down and pressed a kiss to her neck.

She made a soft moan. "Wyatt. I can't think when you do that."

I huffed a laugh against her skin and kissed her again. "Be ready at seven." I thought about her sitting in The Arbutus by herself, wearing a pretty dress. "Wear something that makes you feel beautiful."

———

THAT EVENING, I finished up at the surf shop, locked the door, and walked to my parents' place. That was one of the things I loved about Queen's Cove—nothing was more than a half-hour walk away. The evening was warm and while I walked, I thought about Hannah. I thought about this morning in my bed, about last night in my bed, about seeing the pod of orcas, about how the second she left for the bookstore, my home felt empty.

"Hello again," my dad called as I stepped into his workshop. He lifted his safety goggles and gave me a big grin.

"What are you working on?"

"Your mom thought the community center could use a new bench." He gestured at the plywood he was measuring. "We're going to put it in front of the walkway, near the rose garden." He took his gloves off and gestured for me to follow him. "Come on."

I followed him out of the workshop, through the backyard where we all sat the other night, to the kitchen.

"It sure was nice to have Hannah here," he said, standing at the sink and washing his hands.

"She had fun."

He continued washing his hands. I liked this about my dad. He said his piece and left it. I appreciated the restraint. I knew where he stood but he didn't push. I was grateful, because there were a lot of thoughts at the forefront of my brain, confusing thoughts, and if I started talking, I might say a lot more than I meant to.

"You want to borrow the Porsche?"

I frowned. "How did you know?"

My dad was not a materialistic guy. My mom bought most of his clothes. He wasn't showy or flashy. He valued his family, his community, working in his workshop during the day and drinking a cold beer with my mom in evenings on the patio he had built himself.

But he had this car.

He bought it when my brothers and I were teenagers. For years, he'd searched for a specific make, model, and color, and when it was finally available, he called the guy that day, test drove it, and rolled it into our garage.

He loved that vintage, emerald-green Porsche 911. He forbade my brothers and me from driving it. In our mid-twenties, he had allowed us to drive it while he sat in the passenger seat. This car was his fifth child.

I had come here today with the intention of asking him to borrow it for my date with Hannah tonight. I wanted to make her feel special. I wanted her to know she was worthy of effort and something memorable.

His mouth hitched into a grin as he dried his hands on a tea towel. "You have that look about you."

"I'm afraid to ask."

He moved to the cupboard and pulled down a glass. "Water?"

I shook my head. "No thanks."

He turned the tap on to fill the glass.

"Okay, I'll bite. What look?"

The grin on his face was ear to ear. "Same one Emmett had last year."

My heart wrenched in my chest. I wanted that with Hannah. Hearing it from my dad, the possibility of having what Emmett and Avery had, it choked me up with a mix of feelings. I waded through them in my head but they clouded my mind.

My dad clapped me on the shoulder. "Don't overthink it."

"What do you mean?"

"Don't talk yourself out of it. Trust your instincts."

Holden walked into the kitchen. "What are you doing here?"

I snorted. "What are *you* doing here?"

"Mom said the tap was leaking in the guest bathroom."

I made a face and pointed at our dad. "Why can't Dad fix it?"

My dad shrugged. "She likes to create problems for Holden to solve to lure him over for lunch."

A laugh burst out of me and Holden scowled. "Are you fucking kidding?" he asked.

My dad's tone was warning. "Don't tell her I told you that."

Holden grunted and rolled his eyes. "I won't."

My dad opened the drawer where he kept the car keys and tossed them to me. Holden watched with a frown.

I caught them and leaned against the counter, crossing my arms at Holden. "Jeez, no wonder half the women in town are afraid of you with a mug like that."

He frowned deeper, gaze snagging on the keys in my hand. My dad started pulling things out of the fridge in preparation for dinner.

"Say it." Defensiveness clawed up my throat. If he said one negative thing about Hannah or what we were doing, I didn't know how I'd react.

He lifted one shoulder in a shrug, the tension easing a fraction from his features. "It was nice to have Hannah here for dinner."

The fight left me. "Oh. Yeah."

"You're clearly head over fucking heels for her so don't fuck it up."

I choked out a laugh. "I'm not going to fuck it up."

Holden snorted. "Okay."

"We're…" My voice trailed off and both my dad and brother stared at me, waiting.

"You're what?" Holden asked.

"Hanging out." The second I said it, it felt wrong, like a lie. I frowned. I had told her I'd thought about us married, about her pregnant. That I was falling for her.

How could I explain it to them, though? If I said it out loud, it was real. Panic rose in me, tightening around my chest. "I have to go." I backed out of the kitchen and held the keys up to my dad. "I'll return it in the morning. Thanks."

He waved me off and Holden watched with a skeptical expression.

In the garage, I lifted the protective sheet off the car, started it up, and eased it out of its spot.

As I drove through the streets of Queen's Cove, waving to people I recognized, I thought about my aunts. Aunt Bea used to bring Aunt Rebecca coffee in bed in the mornings. I remembered her moving around the kitchen that was now mine, humming to herself, pouring coffee and adding cream right up to the rim.

The day she dropped Aunt Rebecca off at the care facility, her sobs traveled through the bedroom door. I had grabbed my board and left because I couldn't bear to listen.

In the Porsche, I passed The Arbutus as Avery walked out and her mouth dropped when she spotted me in the car. She pointed at me.

Maybe this was a bad idea.

The bookworm's beaming smile flashed into my head and my throat knotted. Fuck.

Husband. Pregnant.

When I spoke with the agent on the phone, she told me to plan to be away for most of the year. "Oh yeah," she had said. "When you're not competing or training, you'll be doing work with sponsors. You should get a roommate or someone to watch your place."

Hannah could move into my place while I was away. I could come home to her in my bed.

And expect her to wait for me? A couple times a year, drop my bags at the door and pull her to my chest, show her how much she meant to me before I left the next week?

Have her put her life on hold for me? Her life had been on hold for years. Finally, she was living for herself, taking big swings and going for what she wanted.

And I wanted to keep her here waiting for me, suspended in time like a butterfly under glass in a museum. My throat was a knot when I swallowed.

I couldn't do that to her. She wanted true love. So I had to either let her go, or—

I almost drove off the road when the idea rose in my head. She could come with me.

I had pictured it before, us laughing over chips and salsa at a made-up Mexican restaurant in Northern California. She could do a lot of her work online, like ordering, social media marketing, and payroll. She could hire more help for the store.

She could come with me.

My mouth kicked up in a smile.

Tonight. I'd ask her tonight when I took her out on a date.

The house was quiet when I arrived. Hannah had texted me that she was going to stop by her place to get a few things, so I suggested I pick her up there. Even through text, I could tell the idea made her excited.

I had never been on a real date, I realized. I had met women at bars for drinks and had hookups, but never gone to the effort to take out someone special with the intention of making them happy.

The idea of making Hannah happy made my heart swell.

I showered, threw product in my hair, and put on a nice shirt. Emerald-green, like the car. Maybe it was too matchy. Whatever. I looked good in this shirt, and I wanted to look good for Hannah.

I drove over to her place with my pulse in my ears. My fingers drummed a beat against the steering wheel in anticipation. It had been what, less than eight hours since I'd seen her? And already I couldn't wait.

Head over fucking heels for her.

Something caught my eye in front of the corner store, and I pulled over and parked without thinking, heading back to the car a few minutes later with the bouquet.

I pulled up in front of Hannah's house, grabbed the flowers, and knocked on the door. I tensed and flexed my free hand at my side. This nervous simmer in my stomach was rare for me. I couldn't remember the last night I felt jittery and excited like this.

Relax, I told myself. *It's Hannah.*

She opened the door and shot me that shy smile I loved so much. My heart rose into my throat.

She wore a sparkly gold dress that hit her mid-thigh. It had a V-neck with a little cleavage. Smooth, tanned skin. Freckles stood out on her face and her pretty eyes glowed with excitement. Her hair fell loose around her face, wavy from the water this morning.

I'd remember the look on her face until my dying breath. She was lit from within, radiant like a fucking goddess, chewing her lip with a hint of hesitation, but her eyes danced, like she knew what she was doing to me.

My breath caught in my chest.

Head over fucking heels indeed.

276

25

Hannah

I VIBRATED with anticipation as Wyatt drove through the streets of Queen's Cove. Beside me he stretched out, one hand on the wheel and one arm propped on the door. He was wearing a dark green button-up shirt, a step up from the t-shirts and wetsuits I'd seen him in before, and sunglasses perched on his nose. He had swiped some product into his hair.

He was gorgeous. There was something about the way he held himself, like he was so comfortable in his body. Like he knew how hot he was. And maybe he knew how hot *I* thought he was.

I paused and peered at my reflection in the car's side mirror. I looked pretty tonight. My hair seemed brighter from the sun. I wore mascara and a brush of highlighter, had rubbed a tinted gloss onto my lips, and I felt pretty. This sparkling dress put a spotlight on me, and a corner of my consciousness wanted to panic, crouch down behind something and hide, but I needed to do the dress justice. Twice, I had tried it on before taking it off, talking myself in and out of wearing it. People would think I was too dressed up. People would wonder where we were going. People would make comments.

I remembered Thérèse's words to me when she gave me the dress.

What if people look at me? I had asked.

So let them look, she had told me with a shrug.

Tonight, I would let them look.

Besides, Wyatt's heated gaze when I opened the door made any self-consciousness worth it. The skin on the back of my neck prickled and I smiled at the shops we drove past.

"Where are we going tonight?" I asked.

One side of that cruel mouth hitched with his grin and he wiggled his eyebrows. "It's a surprise, but first, we have to make a stop."

He turned down the Main Street toward the bookstore. The green storefront drew my eye immediately.

"Did you forget something there?"

He shook his head and parked in front of the store. "Come on." He jogged around the car before opening the door and pulling me out. His hands came to my shoulders, he made me face the alley, and my breath caught when I saw it.

"Oh, wow."

Naya had finished the mural. It was even better than the sketches. I pressed my hand to my mouth, blinking hard.

A story for every soul.

I nodded to myself, swallowing past the lump in my throat, blinking away the tears in my eyes. "Sorry," I laughed, wiping my eyes. "Don't know why I get so emotional when I see this thing."

Wyatt's arm wrapped around me. "Because it's a big deal."

I nodded and we stood there, staring up at it. "Yeah. It is."

He pressed a kiss to my temple and I closed my eyes, drinking this moment in when everything was right and happy. The mural wouldn't bring my mom back, but it was as close as I'd ever get.

Wyatt's warm hand came to my lower back and he gave me a gentle push forward. "Go ahead." He pulled his phone out. "I want to get a picture of you."

I skipped over to the mural and craned my neck up at it. My smile reached from ear to ear. I glanced over at Wyatt as he snapped a picture. The phone came to his side and he tilted his head at me.

"Get enough pictures?" I asked with a grin.

"One moment." His gaze rested on me, memorizing me. "Okay. Yeah."

I was the luckiest woman in the world, and I'd love Wyatt Rhodes until the day I died.

———

"I THINK I'm too full to have a drink," I told Wyatt as he ushered me through the door of the bar.

"Too full, even for champagne?" He shot me a cocky grin and I laughed, turned to find an empty table, and froze.

Every person in the bar stared at me. Jaws were on the floor and beers hovered inches from mouths.

I took a deep breath and pulled myself up to my full height. Thérèse wouldn't shrink. My mom wouldn't. Neither would I. Wyatt's hand came to my lower back and the tension in me eased a notch.

Right. This was fine. It wouldn't kill me for people to stare.

"Grab a seat and I'll get us some drinks." His breath tickled my ear as he murmured the words, and then he dropped a quick kiss on my cheek before giving my butt a playful tap.

Well, if they weren't staring before, they sure were now.

My face heated but I zeroed in on an empty table off to the side and I took a seat there. My hands itched to pull out my phone and mindlessly scroll but I resisted, clasping them together in my lap and tentatively taking in my surroundings.

A group of young women sat at the table beside me, sipping drinks and whispering, sending me side glances. My stomach clenched up. Were they whispering about me? I took another deep breath. I wouldn't wilt. Not tonight. Tonight, I was going to have fun. For me, but also for Wyatt. I didn't want him to play the role of my mentor or teacher tonight. Tonight, he was my...

Boyfriend?

My stomach fluttered at the thought.

In the bar, I caught the eye of one of the women at the next table before I quickly looked away. They were in their early twenties.

"Your dress is really pretty." She had long black hair that cascaded down her back in curls.

I glanced over at her. They were all smiling at me.

Another one of them nodded eagerly. "Super pretty. I wish I had the confidence to wear that."

I gave her a tentative smile. "Oh, I'm not—" I broke off and shifted in my seat. "Are you on vacation?"

"We're from Seattle." The third woman sipped her drink and played with the little paper umbrella. "This town is so cool, we love it."

"You're so lucky to live here." The fourth one leaned her chin on her palm and gazed at me with a dreamy expression. "It's like a TV show."

"Oh," I laughed. "Sometimes, I guess. But yes, I'm lucky to live here."

"Did you grow up here?"

I nodded and told them about the town, about the funny festivals we had and about my bookstore.

"Oh my god, Pemberley Books is *your* store?" The dark-haired woman's eyes widened and she gestured to her friend.

"Tasha showed us the mural photos. We were going to go see it tomorrow."

"It's so cool that you sell romance," Tasha added quietly. She rolled her eyes at herself. "I mean, I know they're dumb."

I held a hand up to stop her. "They're not dumb, they're awesome. Things aren't dumb because women like them."

The women blinked at me and I realized how forcefully I had said the last part.

"You are *so* right," Umbrella Drink said. "It's like when my coworkers make fun of me for drinking pumpkin spice lattes. Like, just let me like them."

I nodded. "Absolutely."

Something behind me caught their gazes and their mouths dropped open. I turned as Wyatt set two drinks on the table and slipped into the seat across from me.

"Thanks." Both of our drinks were pink with salt rims. "What's this?" I licked the rim and his gaze dropped to my tongue.

"Paloma," he said, still staring at my mouth. "Grapefruit and tequila."

"It's good, thank you."

Out of the corner of my eye, the table beside me sat very still and stared at each other. I held back my laugh and gestured to them.

"Wyatt, meet my new friends. They're visiting from Seattle."

They all turned with big bright smiles and chorused their hellos.

"And I'm Hannah," I said to them.

They introduced themselves—the dark-haired woman was Shima, Umbrella Drink was Cassidy, and the other two were Harneet and Tasha.

"We saw you at the surf shop yesterday." Was Harneet blushing? "We booked a lesson for tomorrow."

Wyatt nodded and smiled at them, listening as they talked while sending me little amused glances.

Movement in the corner of the bar caught my eye. Olivia was setting up a microphone.

"Oh, it's karaoke night." I wiggled in my seat and gave Wyatt an excited smile. "My favorite."

He winked. "I know."

"They do karaoke here?" Tasha interjected. "Are you freaking serious? I love this place!"

Cassidy clutched her hands together in excitement. "We have to put our names down. Are we doing a group song?"

"Of course we are." Shima pulled out a paper from her purse. "Start thinking of songs and I'll grab a pen from the bartender."

Wyatt turned to me and lifted his eyebrows. "What do you say, bookworm? Is tonight your night?"

I nearly choked on my drink. "No. No, no. I don't think so."

He didn't push it, he just shrugged. "Okay." His gaze dropped to my mouth, and he reached out and brushed the corner of my mouth with his thumb. I shivered. His gray eyes darkened. He pulled his thumb back and sucked on it. "You had a bit of salt on your lip."

Maybe we didn't need to stay for karaoke night. We could go straight home, I could yank this dress off, and Wyatt could rub the part of me that was thrumming between my legs right now until I gasped his name against his chest.

Maybe we could finally have sex tonight. Maybe he wouldn't hold back on me.

I watched him, nodded without a word, gaze locked with his.

He winked at me and I pressed my legs together.

"Have I told you how beautiful you are?" He leaned forward on his elbows, his voice low. "I've been thinking about doing terrible, terrible things to you since you opened the door."

Oh my god. We were *so* having sex tonight. My insides somersaulted. His words made my blood thick, turning warmer and slower and more languid.

"Uh huh." My voice was soft and my thoughts floated in the air around my head. Swooning? I think this was what swooning was. I had always read about it but had never experienced this light-headed, floaty deliriousness like I did with Wyatt. "I would like that."

A wolfish look came over his features before he took a sip of his drink. "Lots of time for that later, bookworm. For now, you have fun." He smirked.

I slid my foot so that it rested against his. We watched each other for a moment.

The door of the bar burst open and Miri Yang appeared in the doorway, chest heaving for air like she had run here. Her head whipped around as she surveyed the bar, eyes narrowed, before she spotted us and her eyes widened.

Wyatt shifted and surveyed our two nearly full drinks. "I'm going to get us some more drinks."

I put my hand out to stop him. "No, Wyatt, don't leave me here—"

He shot me a teasing glance, walked away, and Miri rushed into his seat.

"Hannah Nielsen, as I live and breathe."

"You're breathing really hard. Did you run here?" I raised an eyebrow at her.

She waved my words away with a scoff. "Run? God, no. Someone texted me that it was karaoke night." She nodded. "Yeah. That."

I narrowed my eyes at her with suspicion but a grin crept onto my face.

Miri *thrived* on juicy gossip. It was her life force. And she was here for another hit of the good stuff.

STEPHANIE ARCHER

"So." She gave me a sweet smile but hunger lurked behind her eyes. "I heard you and Wyatt went camping."

I groaned and put my face in my hands. "Straight to it, huh?"

Her eyes sparkled. "Are you two an item?"

"No. We're—" I sucked a breath through my teeth, scrambling. "Surfing. He's teaching me how to surf."

Somewhere in heaven, my mom laughed at how obvious the lie was.

Miri blinked. "Sweetheart." Her tone was skeptical.

I squirmed in my chair.

"Miri, please stop interrogating my girlfriend." Wyatt towered over the table with two new salt-rimmed drinks and a smirk.

Girlfriend? My stomach rolled forward.

"Girlfriend," she breathed, biting her lip. She stood quickly to give Wyatt his seat. "Girlfriend," she repeated to herself before glancing between us with delight. "Very well. Carry on." She turned on her heel and practically skipped over to a table where her husband, Scott, sat.

"You've created a monster," I told Wyatt. "She's going to be disappointed when you leave."

My heart stopped as I realized what I said. Wyatt and I stared at each other for a moment, his mouth slightly parted at the acknowledgement of him leaving soon if he placed well at Pacific Rim.

"I mean…" I trailed off. I had nothing.

"I'm going to miss Miri, too," he said, and the side of his mouth lifted in a sad smile.

My heart clawed up my throat and I heaved in a breath, letting it out as a sigh.

Just as I started to like a guy, he was going to leave.

He put his hand on mine. "I want to talk to you about something."

My heart lifted. "Okay."

"Alright, drunks of Queen's Cove!" Joe crowed into the microphone and a laugh bubbled out of me as the bar patrons cheered. "Are you ready to sing your hearts out?"

Another big cheer, half of it coming from the table of women beside us. A big smile stretched over my face and I glanced over at Wyatt, easing back into his chair and stretching out.

"We'll talk later." His eyes sparked with amusement.

"Tonight is not just karaoke night, folks," Joe continued. "It's Queen's Cove's fourteenth annual karaoke sing-off." A round of cheers rose up. "As always, the winner gets to take home the terrifying and unhygienic Toilet Paper Princess Patty." He reached out and Olivia handed him a doll with an unfortunate haircut. The doll's skirt stretched around a toilet paper roll and it had those unsettling eyes that blinked. "This creepy doll has been in my family's bathrooms for generations and the winner gets to take care of her until next year's competition."

Every year, the doll changed hands based on who won the sing-off. The winner had to kiss the doll on the lips in front of everyone, because it was tradition.

"So, Queen's Cove, I have a question for you," Joe said. "Are you ready?"

Another round of cheers and applause rose up as Joe waved the doll in the air.

The first singer stepped up and belted out a pitchy version of Seal's 'Kiss from a Rose.' The bar didn't care that the grocery store owner couldn't sing. They fed off his enthusiasm, clapping and hollering and cheering him on. They gave the next singer the same warm welcome, and the next. The group of women from the table beside us sang Sister Sledge's 'We Are Family' and got a standing ovation. They returned to their table with bright eyes and flushed cheeks and something sweet and sharp panged in my chest at their happiness.

I thought about Div and his drag show, how fearless and confident he was. How he was afraid but had no regrets.

"I'll be right back," I told Wyatt, slipping out of my seat. He brushed my arm as I passed, a brief gesture that sent sparks up my arm and emboldened me further. I exchanged a few words with Joe and returned to my seat.

Wyatt quirked a curious brow and I bit back a smile.

"You're up to something, bookworm."

I nodded, smiling wider. "I am. It's the dress." I gestured down at it, the sequins catching and reflecting the light. "It makes me bolder."

"It makes you fucking radiant," he bit out, a hungry look passing through his eyes.

Girlfriend, he had said. As sweet as it was, it pinched in my chest. Girlfriend until next week? Girlfriend until he got on a plane?

I shoved the thoughts out of my head. Tonight was my night. I could worry tomorrow.

"Folks, it's time for the last song of the night," Joe's voice boomed, "Hannah Nielsen's singing 'Wannabe' by the Spice Girls!"

"Oh, shiiiiit!" a guy I went to high school with called from the back. "Fuck yes! I love that song!"

Wyatt's eyebrows shot way up with delight. "Yeah?"

I shook my head and took a deep breath. Nerves rattled my ribcage and my hands shook. "Yeah. I don't think I'll ever be ready, but I'm going to go for it."

He winked. "Good girl. I'll be here."

As I passed, he pulled me down and gave me a hard kiss in front of everyone. The table of women beside us lost their minds and I flushed with pride. Wyatt was mine, even if it was just for now.

People clapped and beamed at me as I walked up to the microphone.

My heart thudded in my chest. Joe handed me the mic

and I stepped into place. People could probably see the sequins flickering with light as my chest pounded against them. I swallowed and my throat went tight. Everyone watched. My gaze snagged on Avery, leaning against the bar. She must have just slipped in. She gave me a wide-eyed, beaming grin and thumbs up and I nodded and sucked in another deep breath.

Holy shit. Everyone was staring at me.

Also, I was a terrible singer. Like, awful.

Holy shit.

"Umm..." I said into the mic. "So I'm going to sing a Spice Girls song. Some of you may know that I like them."

The bar burst into laughter and I frowned.

"We are aware," someone said in a dry tone.

Oh. They weren't laughing at me. I played Spice Girls all the time in the store. Of course they knew I liked them. Right. I let out a light laugh.

At our table, Wyatt was watching with an amused, proud expression.

I wanted to be worthy of his pride, and I also wanted to be worthy of my own pride. My mom flickered into my head, so full of life and joy and passion.

Okay. The smile creeped up my face, into my eyes as they crinkled, and I nodded at the bar. At all these people who knew me, and some new faces, like the group of women.

"Yeah, Hannah! Wooooo!" one of them—Shima, I think —screamed and a bunch of new cheers erupted.

"Okay, so, here goes." My voice was shaky.

The opening bars of the song played and a rush of *fuck it* energy whistled through my blood. I had heard this song a thousand times and like every other time, it filled me with excitement, energy, and of course, girl power.

I began singing with the music, not even needing to look at the screen with the lyrics. I knew this song by heart. The lyrics flowed out of my mouth. My head bobbed with the beat. I took a few steps. I made eye contact with people and they cheered me on. I was worthy of wearing this dress up here. I was good enough. I was fun enough. I had a terrible singing voice but people cheered and clapped. Olivia turned up the volume so loud, the roof was going to blow off the place. When I held the mic out for one of the later choruses, half the bar sang with me. My face hurt from smiling.

I was doing it. I was that hot girl, confident and carefree.

My gaze returned to Wyatt, leaning forward, chin on his palm, watching me with a look of pure adoration. My heart somersaulted.

I finished the song and the place exploded. I winced from the noise but couldn't stop laughing and grinning. My heart raced in my chest, my hands shook, and I waited for the embarrassment to set in, but it never showed up.

If my mom were here, she'd be on her feet, laughing with me.

The group of women beside our table screamed their heads off.

Joe took the mic from me and I stepped off the stage, high-fiving people along the way back to my chair.

"Give it up for one of our own, Hannah!"

Another round of cheers rose up.

"Alright, folks, Hannah was the last singer for tonight." His voice boomed across the sound system and everyone fell quiet. I reached the table and Wyatt pulled me into his arms.

"You did it, bookworm," he whispered into my hair.

I nodded and grinned into his chest. He didn't let go, so I shifted to see the stage while leaning against his warmth.

"We judge the karaoke championship against a rigorous set of criteria," Joe continued, "including song choice, dance moves, and overall stage presence." He paused for effect. "The winner of the Queen's Cove karaoke sing-off is... Hannah Nielsen!"

Another explosion of cheers. Over at the bar, Olivia rang

The Wrong Mr. Right

the loud bell and the clanging only revved everyone up more. Wyatt squeezed me and laughed with me before he pressed a hard kiss to my mouth.

"Go on." He tilted his chin to the stage.

"Yeah, Hannah!" The women beside us were chanting, clapping and beaming. "You killed it!"

I walked back up to the stage and accepted the terrifying toilet paper doll from Joe before turning to the crowd and holding it up high in the air to show them.

"You know what to do, Hannah," he said into the mic and everyone laughed. "Toilet Paper Princess Patty awaits."

I made a kissy face and held the doll up to my mouth as Olivia snapped an instant photo. A flash went off the second the doll's plastic mouth touched mine and I blinked.

"She's yours for the year. Don't lose her, please."

I shook my head at him. "I won't. I'll keep her in the bookstore behind a case."

Back at my table, I slipped into my seat as Miri appeared.

"Hannah! Look at you." She wrapped me in a tight hug. "I don't even know who you are anymore."

My throat choked with happiness. I couldn't stop smiling. Wyatt watched me with an amused grin.

"Huddle up," Miri directed, gesturing between Wyatt and me. "I want to get a photo of you two."

Wyatt grabbed my hand and pulled me into his lap. His arms wrapped around me from behind and he pressed another kiss to my temple. Miri took a few shots on her phone before pausing to admire them. She put a hand to her chest with a wistful expression before she returned to her table.

I moved to stand up but Wyatt held me firm.

"Oh my god, you were amazing!" Shima yelled. Empty glasses littered their table and their faces were flushed. They all nodded with enthusiasm.

I beamed back at them. "It was fun."

I didn't know what I was so worried about, singing

karaoke. No one had cared if I couldn't sing. Karaoke was about looking stupid and loving it. I sighed and settled further into Wyatt's chest.

People came up to say hello to us, to congratulate us and chat about my store or Wyatt's surf shop. At one point, I yawned, and Wyatt squeezed my arm.

"You want to go home?"

I nodded. Home. When he said it like that, it hit me right in the heart. Wyatt's house was home and I had been there a week. How could I go back to my place now?

Something passed through our gaze. The green of his shirt made his gray eyes pop, and his gaze turned hungry as it dropped to my mouth. My face was hot. I was hyperaware of where I touched him, where his hands gripped me.

"Wyatt, you're gorgeous," I told him with a small smile.

This should be the part where I normally reminded myself that Wyatt wasn't my type. That he wasn't forever-material. That he didn't want something long-term, that he didn't want something to tie him down to Queen's Cove when he might be leaving in a few weeks.

I couldn't remember any good, concrete reasons why Wyatt wasn't my type.

"You're the only guy who's ever made me feel like this." The words slipped out and my breath caught. A hint of panic hit my bloodstream and I swallowed, watching Wyatt's face carefully.

These past few months, I had grown, but I had also grown around him. Not far from town, there was a forest trail where someone left a bike against a tree decades ago, and the tree had grown around it. They were one now. There was no cutting them apart without destroying the bike or killing the tree.

My heart clutched hard. That was like Wyatt and me. He was part of me now.

Wyatt nodded, watching me with a funny expression on

his face. Sad, almost. "I want to be the right guy for you." His hand rubbed up my back to touch my hair.

"Once we get home," I bit my lip and his gaze flared. Heat pulsed between my legs. "You can give me another lesson."

Hunger passed through his eyes and he nodded slowly. His hand gripped my waist. "Let's go."

26

Hannah

WYATT'S HAND seared my skin the entire way home, resting on my bare leg above the knee across the front seat of the car. My window was down and my hair whipped around. The breeze was welcome against my warm face. Inside my shoes, my toes wiggled with anticipation.

Wyatt and I were totally going to have sex.

I swallowed, bit back my nervous grin, and shot a sidelong glance at him. His fingers drummed against the steering wheel but other than that, he was cool and calm.

Of course he was. He'd had sex tons of times. Probably hundreds.

Me? Three. Three times. Three sub-par, disappointing times with a guy I didn't care about, who didn't care about me.

I blew a breath out.

"How ya doing, bookworm?"

I nodded and met his gaze. Concerned, with hunger in the background, subdued. Like he was holding it back.

I was about to tell him I was fine, but something didn't want me to lie to him. It was Wyatt. He had slowly become something more to me. My stomach flopped and I bit my lip again.

"I'm nervous."

For a second, panic streaked through me at the possibility that we were on different pages. Maybe he had no intention of taking me home and going all the way with me. He glanced between me and the road and his hand moved up to cover mine. He gave me a quick squeeze that made my heart skip.

"Me, too."

"You are? Why?"

A rueful smile passed over his face. "It's you, Hannah. It's different."

His words made my heart beat harder, and a few beats were just for him. He pulled the car onto his street and parked in his driveway. We both stayed seated and he turned to me.

"We don't have to do anything." His Adam's apple bobbed as his throat worked. He watched my expression carefully. "We can go inside and hang out or read or go straight to sleep." He lifted a shoulder. "Or I can take you home if you don't want to stay here again."

I shook my head. "I don't want to go home." I took a deep breath and summoned that bravery thing I had been practicing all night. "And I don't want to go to sleep yet, but I do want to go to bed."

Wyatt's gaze turned hungry and his jaw clenched. "Nice line."

I snorted. "I thought so." I glanced down at his lap. His erection strained against the fabric. The sight of it, the physical proof of his attraction to me, made me ache between my legs for him.

Wyatt wanted me, and I wanted him. When I put it that way, it was so simple.

I leaned over the front seat and kissed him. He kissed me back, pressing gentle kisses to my mouth. Slow kisses. Too slow. Too chaste.

I tasted him and the slow glide of my tongue against his pulled a noise of disbelief and pleasure from his chest. One of his hands came to my hair and the gentle pull against my scalp sent sparks down my spine.

"Let's get this show on the road," I said against his mouth in between kisses and he laughed silently, his breath tickling my face.

"I didn't know you were in such a rush." His voice was so low and teasing, it made my nipples pinch.

I broke our kiss and skimmed my lips down his neck, reveling in the way his breath caught. I gently nipped his earlobe. "I want you."

He lifted me out of my seat and on top of him, straddling his lap. My dress was high on my thighs but I didn't care. I dropped my lips to his and kissed him hard. He wasn't so sweet and slow and chaste anymore. His mouth devoured mine, one big hand wrapped around the back of my neck, anchoring me to him, pulling me down on his lap. I shifted my hips and his hard length made perfect contact with my center. My mouth made a silent O as the sensation made me arch my back. Wyatt's other hand squeezed my ass and he pulled my bottom lip between his teeth.

"Hannah, you make me lose my fucking mind when you say things like that," he rasped.

My hands threaded through his hair and tugged lightly. His hand tensed on my ass and pulled me closer against him. His tongue worked my mouth with urgency, like we were running out of time, and with his grip on my hair, he tilted me whichever way he wanted. Whichever way he needed. I shivered.

"I love it when you use my mouth like you own it," I whispered.

His arousal pulsed between my legs and I moaned into his mouth. He broke our kiss and leaned back to look at me with dark eyes. His chest rose and fell with heavy breaths, like mine.

"I take care of what's mine."

Wetness flooded my underwear at the hot, possessive tone of his words. I wanted to be his, more than anything. He slipped his hand down the front of my dress and rubbed one sensitive peak. I arched and bucked my hips against him and a loud honking noise made both of us jump.

I had pushed against the car horn.

We took one look at each other and burst out laughing. The driveway was dark but a light turned on outside a neighbor's house.

"Come on, bookworm." Wyatt opened the car door and stood, supporting my weight with one hand on my ass and the other around my lower back. My arms looped around his neck. He hip-checked the car door closed, and I set my mouth on his again, tasting him and tugging at his hair, pulling those groans of pleasure and agony out of his throat.

At the front door, instead of opening it, he pressed me against it and ground his hips against mine. My eyes rolled back at the sharp, delicious pressure of his length against my clit.

"Holy shit," I breathed into his mouth. "Wyatt."

"Like that?" He ground his hips again and I jerked a nod. He found a rhythm that made my head fall against his shoulders and my breath thin and shuddery. My dress hitched up around my waist and his jeans brushed my inner thighs. He thrust his erection against my soaking center, scattering my thoughts.

"I'm going to make you come over and over again tonight," he gritted against my ear.

Heat pooled low in my belly and I could barely hold on. My head fell back against the door and I took in his focused frown, the clench of his jaw, the heat in his eyes. He wanted me and it only made me ache more.

"Wyatt," I bit out.

He shook his head but kept thrusting. "I'm going to sink

my cock into your tight little pussy like I've been thinking about for months and I'm going to fuck you like you deserve."

My eyes widened as I realized what the tightening in my center meant. "Wyatt." I nodded.

"Tell me what you need, like we practiced."

"Like that. Just like that." I moaned and leaned my forehead on his shoulder, closing my eyes and holding on to him.

"Look at me while you come for me."

I pulled my head up and met his gaze. I winced as pleasure, heat, pressure, and electricity tightened my body. All I could do was nod. Yes, yes, yes, I said with my nods to him.

He kept rocking a hard rhythm against me and I was so close. Right on the edge. Teetering. "I'm going to taste your pussy again and again until you scream my name and pull my hair, because that's what I need, baby. I need to taste you again."

That did it. My whole body shook against his as I came, paralyzed and screaming silently against his neck as pleasure raced through me, boiled my blood, and scrambled my thoughts. Wave after wave hit me and my hips bucked against his. Far away, he groaned *yes* and *like that* and *fucking beautiful* and *good girl* into my ear.

When he had wrung me out, my head fell back against the door and a slow, satisfied smile crept over his face. He grinned a lazy grin down at me. His eyes were still dark. His throat worked as he set me down carefully, one arm wrapping around me and one hand on my waist.

I slumped against his shoulder. "Wow. We haven't even gotten inside."

His chest shook with laughter as he unlocked the door, squeezing me to his side.

"I have to say, professor," I told him as we stepped inside and kicked our shoes off. My pulse was still beating in my ears and my lungs heaved to get enough air. "You're so dedicated to a well-rounded curriculum."

His head lowered and he brushed his lips against the sensitive skin between my neck and shoulder. "I take my role very seriously."

I tilted his face to mine and kissed him. He straightened up and I had to crane my neck to keep eye contact.

"I love that you tower over me," I whispered against his mouth as he backed me up toward the hallway, en route to his room.

"Yeah? Well, I like how small you are. You fit right under my arm." His arm came around me and he tugged my dress zipper down. My fingers found his shirt buttons and fumbled at them. "You think you'll fit me everywhere?" The teasing, dark tone of his voice made my center clench.

I nodded and it was like the orgasm I just had never happened. I was wet again, ready again, wanting more. Wanting all of him.

We stepped into his room, hands working fast to undress each other. He slipped my dress off my shoulders and it pooled at my feet. I lagged behind, with only a few of his buttons undone. He pulled me against him, slid one bra cup down and slipped a stiff nipple into his mouth. I gasped. The buttons of his shirt were on the opposite side to what I was used to and the tug of his mouth on my nipple made me dizzy.

"Come on, catch up." His finger rolled the other peak and I whimpered.

"I'm trying." A futile laugh escaped me, and my head fell back.

He took mercy on me and undid his buttons, never taking his mouth from my breast. I pushed the shirt off his shoulders and roamed his hard chest, brushing the light chest hair and scraping my nails up his abs. The muscles jumped under my touch, and he shuddered against me before pushing me back onto the bed.

My bra had come off at one point—was that me or Wyatt?—and I lay there in my underwear.

Wyatt loomed over me, placing a hand on either side of me on the bed, hovering and watching like a predator. His gaze traveled over my nearly naked form and desire flashed in his eyes. He wanted me. Something hungry and excited fluttered in my stomach.

"Look at you, lying on my bed like a fucking goddess." He leaned down to suck one pinched peak into his mouth and I arched against his mouth.

"Take your pants off," I gasped.

"Slow down." He kissed up my chest to my neck and his fingers toyed with the edge of my underwear, below my stomach. "I'm not done with you. If I slip my fingers lower, am I going to find you wet?"

I nodded.

He made a noise of satisfaction. "Good girl." He slowly, so painfully slowly, slid his hand into my underwear, and when he touched me, I whimpered.

"Very, very good." He swirled light circles on my clit and I gripped his arms, my nails digging into his muscles as he wound me tighter.

"Look at you, doing so well." His gaze was full of pride, satisfaction, and need. "You know that if you let me do my work, you're going to come. Isn't that right?"

I nodded, chest heaving.

"Mhm. That's what I thought." His fingers worked and my inner walls tightened. It wasn't enough. It was so, so good, so deliriously good, but it wasn't enough. My hips bucked against his hand for more pressure. "What is it, baby?"

"More."

"More what?" His voice was teasing. He knew. He fucking knew it wasn't enough and he toyed with me, but a sick part of me kind of liked that.

I nodded hard. "More. More everything." I reached for his

cock, straining against his jeans, and he groaned as I stroked his hard length. "I want to come on your cock. I want to feel you come while you're inside me."

He laughed a dark laugh against my neck. "Ohhhh, you are in trouble now." His fingers swirled faster. Heat built low in my belly and I arched again. "This is for being brave tonight and going up on stage. Do you know how fucking proud you made me up there, baby?"

Faster, faster, faster his fingers moved and my head fell back. His cock pulsed under my grip and I moaned. He added pressure to my clit and his other hand came to my breast, pulling and rolling and pinching the tight bud.

"Wyatt," I gasped.

"That's for scaring me and hitting your head the other day." His voice was rough and his hand worked faster. He shifted back onto his knees while I writhed on the bed. He studied me with an intense look, focused and watching where his hands touched me. He slipped a finger inside me and I bucked, cried out, and nodded for more.

He raised his eyebrows. "Oh, yeah? That's for being so fucking gorgeous and making me hard all the time." He slid the finger in and out, stretching me. My walls tightened around it. He shook his head in awe. "Holy shit, baby, you are squeezing the life out of my finger." He added a second and I moaned.

The heat coiled around the base of my spine and I was a puppet, strung along by Wyatt as he controlled my body and pushed me toward what I needed.

The second finger added the fullness I needed and I winced with pleasure.

"This?" He curled his fingers and hit that sensitive spot inside. "This is for making me fall head over fucking heels for you." He massaged the spot on the front wall and my mouth fell open. My body bowed, bucked, arched under his touch.

One of my hands clenched the duvet, the other gripped his strong thigh.

"Yeah, Hannah?" His tone was light but his voice rasped like sandpaper. "Is that the spot? Is that the spot that's going to make you come harder than you ever have?"

I nodded. "There. That. Like that."

"Just like that, huh? Fucking hell, bookworm, you make me want to sink into your sweet pussy and fuck the life out of you. Say my name again, just the way I like it."

"Wyatt," I breathed. The combination of his curled fingers and his other hand swirling on my clit was hurtling me towards another orgasm. Any second.

He leaned down and licked my wetness, sucking at my clit and pulling it into his lips, and his groan was what did it. My thighs clenched around his head as I came, my skin hot and cold all over and my body belonging a hundred percent to him as I jerked and chanted *yes* and *Wyatt* and *like that* over and over again. He made encouraging noises in his throat like he loved my taste and couldn't get enough, and his tongue slid over my clit again and again as I squeezed his fingers with my muscles.

I floated back down to earth with a sigh.

"You're such a good girl." His voice was so gentle, so proud, and it slid over me like satin. His hands came to his belt and I watched, fascinated, as he slid it out. He saw me shiver and he smiled. He moved to standing and when his pants and boxers came off, my mouth automatically dropped at the sight of his hard cock. A bead of liquid appeared on the tip and my mouth watered with the memory of him in my mouth, groaning and gripping my hair.

Using me.

I flushed with warmth and bit my lip.

He shook his head. "When you look at me like that, Hannah, you make me fucking crazy." He fisted his cock and my eyes widened as he stroked himself while watching me. "You like watching me do this?"

I nodded.

He grinned and bit his lip, head tilting back. He let go and headed to his nightstand, opening the drawer and pulling out a foil packet.

"No." I said it before I thought about it. "I don't want to use a condom."

His hands froze. "What?"

"I'm on the pill," I breathed.

"I've never gone without a condom before." His eyebrows knitted together and he looked so torn.

"So it's safe then, right?" I nodded at him. "Please, Wyatt, I—" My voice broke off. Brave, I reminded myself. "I don't want anything in between us."

The packet fell to the floor. He looped his hands under my knees and jerked me to the edge of the bed before sliding his length up and down my center, dragging the tip through my wet heat and over my clit. He watched where we connected with fascination. I reached for him, encircling him with my fingers and stroking as he watched, his gaze flicking between my hand and my face. He pulsed in my hand.

He paused and his throat worked. His jaw was tight. "You sure about this, bookworm? We don't have to keep going. We can take a pause."

I shook my head. "I don't want to pause. I want you to come inside me. I want you to make me yours."

His nostrils flared and he pulled one of my legs up so it draped over his shoulder. "You're already mine. Do you need a reminder?"

I nodded eagerly and he shook his head, groaning.

He edged himself inside me. He was so much bigger than his fingers and I whimpered as I stretched around him. He watched my face closely with dark eyes as he slid further, his thickness making my back arch again.

"Fuck, Hannah. You are tight as fuck. So fucking wet for me."

"You keep making me come," I gasped.

"Yeah, I do." A devilish, lazy grin passed his features and he slid further.

"Keep going," I breathed.

"You're fucking ruining me, you know that?" He pulled my other leg up so it draped over his shoulder and sank further into me. My eyes fell halfway closed as he filled me.

He bottomed out and I moaned.

I didn't know sex could be like this, so all-consuming and primal and necessary.

He pressed a soft kiss to my calf while he let my body adjust to his size. "You're clenching me." His throat worked again and he inhaled through his nose.

I rippled around him and he groaned, fingers digging into my waist. He slowly inched out and filled me back up again, making my back bend. He shook his head.

"Not going to last long," he rasped. "Fuck, I love that our first time is like this. I love fucking you bare." He slid out and thrust in a little harder this time and I whimpered.

The noise triggered something in his gaze and he reached for a pillow, hoisting up my hips and slipping the pillow underneath to prop them up.

"What does—" I started but he slid back into me and the way his cock pushed against my inner walls, it turned the dial up to maximum. My vision blurred. "Holy shit."

His dark laugh went straight to my core. My face twisted into an expression of *holyshitwhatthefuckohmygodyesyesyesmorelikethisfuckyes*.

"Are we going to come tonight, Hannah?" Wyatt breathed and I gasped as he kept hitting that spot.

His fingers returned to my clit and he didn't bother teasing me, just moved his fingers fast and hard over the bundle of nerves. Everything inside me tightened, shimmered, and boiled. He hit an angle inside me that made me mindless.

"That's right," he managed. "I'm going to come inside you and it's going to feel so. Fucking. Incredible." He thrust hard with each word and my orgasm barreled through me. I moaned, my hips shook, and he fucked me harder.

"That's my girl, come hard on my cock like I know you can."

I couldn't speak. Hot electricity shot up and down my spine and Wyatt grabbed my hand like I needed. I squeezed him so hard I thought my walls might shove him out.

"Don't stop," I gasped, barely managing the words.

"I won't," he gritted out, increasing the intensity of his thrusts.

"Harder."

He obliged, pounding me into the mattress. My orgasm was still rolling through my blood, paralyzing me, holding me suspended in space, still making me forget to breathe. Still flooding me with this overwhelming pleasure as Wyatt buried himself deep in me.

"Thatta girl, baby. Oh my god." Both hands came to my waist and he gripped me, shuttling into me.

"Use me to come," I gasped, and his gaze flared.

"I'm going to come deep in your pussy and there'll be no question who you belong to." His fingers dug into my skin and the pain was delicious as his hips hammered a fast rhythm against me. "Make me come, Hannah," he gritted out.

He choked out a strangled noise, the muscles on his arms corded and his neck tight. He frowned down at me with parted lips, shuddering. He slowed and his agonized expression eased. He leaned over me and collapsed, pinning me down, breathing hard against my neck, chest heaving against mine.

I wanted to say it. I wanted to tell him that I loved him. Bravery, I reminded myself, but something put a hand up and held me back. I didn't want anything to spoil this moment where Wyatt and I were so connected. I was his, not just because he said it over and over again but because he made me feel like no one else could.

There was too much at stake, and I couldn't risk it.

When he slid out of me, I made an unhappy noise. His hair was messy, eyes heavy like he was drugged. He pressed a kiss to my mouth.

"Be right back. Don't move."

"I can't."

He chuckled as he trudged to the bathroom, returning with a warm, wet towel, brushing it over me in a move that would have made me embarrassed if he wasn't giving me such an affectionate look. When he returned to bed, he pulled me against him and I hummed at the feel of his bare skin against mine.

He blew a breath out. "Holy shit, bookworm. It's never been like that."

My heart lifted.

This is for making me fall head over fucking heels for you. His words played in my mind.

Head over heels. That meant love, right? I'd heard once that people sometimes said 'I love you' during sex when they didn't mean it, but because the sex was intense and it slipped out.

There'll be no question who you belong to.

I swallowed and let Wyatt pull me further into his chest, resting my head against his skin and closing my eyes.

It was too late. It had snuck up on me so quietly and slowly that I didn't realize I had fallen hard for him. There was no pretending anymore, no convincing myself otherwise or distracting myself.

I was in love with Wyatt Rhodes.

27

Wyatt

SUNLIGHT STREAMED in and I brushed my mouth over her nose and cheeks while she slept. Her mouth curved into a soft smile but she didn't wake up. I shifted onto my elbow, careful not to wake her, so I could get a better look at her.

It was a week after we slept together for the first time, and we had spent most of it either in this bed or out on the water. She wanted to skip our morning surf lessons so I could practice but I insisted on going out on the water with her every morning, even just for an hour. I spent the rest of the day surfing, checking in at the surf shop, or hanging out at her bookshop, lounging on a comfy blue chair while she helped customers, packed up orders, or talked with Liya. In the evenings, we cuddled on the couch or in bed while she showed me foreign music videos like the one I was in before I tossed her phone aside and pulled her to me.

Her birthday was in a few days. I had ordered a cake at the bakery—pink champagne, as per my mom's recommendation. I had purchased something cheeky online that I was certain Hannah didn't own, but something was missing. I needed to find a gift that showed her she was loved.

In her sleep, she let out a soft sigh and curled closer against my chest, and I brushed her hair off her face.

Karaoke night had changed both everything and nothing at all. She was still my Hannah, just as she had been before we tangled these sheets up and gave each other everything. She was still the same silly, quick-smiling, brave Hannah she was a week ago.

I was the one who was different.

I was the one who was head over fucking heels for her.

I was in love with her. It was the last thing I ever wanted, and yet it was goddamned heaven.

"We should get up and out there," she mumbled against my chest, eyes still closed.

"It's the first day of Pacific Rim so we won't be able to." The competition had taken over the surfing beaches for the week and they were keeping the water clear of surfers except those competing.

The warmth of her bare skin against mine made my blood hum. My cock stirred the way it always did when she was around.

She made an unhappy noise and I smiled, inhaling. Her hair smelled like tea, sunlight, her bookstore, and her hair products I had insisted she keep in the shower. I didn't mind skipping a couple days out on the water with her. It meant I could keep her in bed longer.

She inhaled sharply and lifted her head, opening one bleary eye. "What time is it?"

"Just after seven. Relax. Liya's opening the shop today, remember? You told her you were packing online orders here."

"Right." Her head came back to my chest. "How are you feeling about today?"

Today was the initial qualifier for the competition. About half of the entrants would be eliminated over the next three days, but I wasn't worried. It was the last two days which would determine my fate.

The pinch of concern I expected in my chest didn't happen when I thought about surfing against the best in the world. I still felt the rush of competition, the surge of energy to do my best and work with the water to ride the waves, but the biting worry that I wouldn't place well never showed up.

"I'm fine," I said simply. "I'm ready."

If I didn't do well at Pacific Rim, if I didn't get that sponsorship deal, I'd be right where I was now, curled up with warm, soft Hannah in bed. My bookworm.

And if I did well? If I placed higher up and scored that sponsorship and was on the next plane out of here? Panic filled my chest at the thought of leaving her. Not Queen's Cove. Queen's Cove would still be here. I could miss it and return. But Hannah, I couldn't leave her.

I almost asked her to come with me at karaoke night, but the music started and I wanted to save it for later, for a quiet moment where I could make it special.

And then I chickened out.

She might say no, but it was more than that. I teetered on the edge of something precarious. Whatever Hannah and I were doing, whatever we were wrapped up in, it was fragile. One wrong move and the entire thing could slip out from beneath us.

If I made plans for the future, they could crumble. If the plans didn't exist, there was nothing I could lose.

So I perched on the edge of the cliff, enjoying what I had with Hannah, terrified to move a muscle.

Her hand tucked between my torso and the sheets. She did that a lot, tucked her hand between my skin and something else. Funny, these little traits you started to notice about someone once you spent all your time with them.

Today. I'd ask her today if she'd come with me. If she could be brave and get up in front of half the town and sing karaoke, or learn to surf when she had never tried before, I could be brave and tell her how I felt.

She made a satisfied humming noise and turned her head, pressing a kiss to my chest. My cock ached and when she shifted and slipped one of her legs over mine, she brushed against it. She opened her eyes with mischief in her gaze.

I knew that look.

"Oh, yeah?" I asked with a lazy grin, raising my eyebrows.

She grinned wider, still sleepy and so fucking adorable. Before she could do anything, I flipped her onto her back. She was giggling and I was dipping my head between her legs.

"Oh," she gasped as I swiped my tongue over her.

Today, I was going to be brave and ask Hannah to come with me, but right now, I had to give her another reason to say yes.

———

"WYATT RHODES, QUEEN'S COVE, CANADA."

I was out in the water on my board, paddling to take my place, but could still hear the cheers rise up on the beach after the announcer spoke. Hannah and my family gathered in the spectator area, seated on blankets. I had told them not to bother coming since today wasn't a big event, but they had insisted.

Each entrant had three waves per round and the judges took the top two scores. The wind was low today and the waves were clean. Despite today being an easier round, my blood hummed with competition. I took a moment to center myself, noticing the way the water lifted and dropped me with my torso draped over my board, listening to the sound of the waves washing against the sand and the spectators talking and laughing, and letting the cold bite of the ocean remind me who was boss.

Hannah took up space in my head as usual. I glanced at

her on the beach again, her light hair catching the sun, and my chest eased a notch. Three waves and I could take her for lunch and ask her to come with me.

She was going to say yes. I knew she would. Why wouldn't she? She'd been stuck in Queen's Cove her entire life like a bug under glass and now that she had broken free, she could see the world at my side.

The store was finally hers, though. Maybe she wouldn't want to leave after all the work she'd put in.

Behind me, the wave approached. I gauged its speed, and when my instincts flashed *now!* in my head, I paddled hard. My arms dipped in and out of the water, propelling me forward, my back muscles burned, and as the water lifted me, I snapped up, used my core to turn, and coasted along the length of the wave. The adrenaline rush I had come to love raced through my veins as my board shot forward.

The spectators cheered but I ignored them, taking another deep breath and paddling back to my spot while another entrant caught a wave. When it was my turn again, I followed the same steps I'd done a thousand times. Gauge wave speed. Listen to instincts. Paddle. Snap up. Engage core. Feel like a fucking king riding on the massive energy of the ocean. Repeat.

When I returned to the beach, I glanced at my scores. Top marks across the board, no surprise. I had been dealt a lucky hand today, with no wind, clean waves, and a clear head.

Hannah and my family surrounded me, and I chatted with them for a few minutes before I pulled Hannah away.

"Let's get some lunch. I just need to stash my board. I want to sit on The Arbutus patio with you and a beer." I leaned down and pressed a kiss to her temple. "I'd put my arm around you but I don't want to get your nice dress all wet." She wore the blue and white striped dress, the same one she had worn to dinner with herself.

She rolled her eyes before tucking herself into my side,

under my arm, with a grin. "I don't care, it's just water. Can we stop at the bookshop on the way? I want to see if that book came in for Randeep, he was asking me about it earlier. I should check in to make sure Liya and Casey are okay." Hannah had hired Casey to help out part-time, now that the store was busier. They had walked into the store and introduced themself as a massive romance fan, charming Hannah immediately.

I left my board and wetsuit at the surf shop, pulled a t-shirt over my head, and took Hannah's hand as we wandered through the streets. The town was busy this weekend for the competition, with surfers wandering around in wetsuits and tourists taking pictures in front of the Queen's Cove sign by the marina. People packed into the alley with the mural, taking photos.

The sun streamed down, the perfect September temperature to sit on a patio with the girl I loved and ask her to come with me.

The bell on the door of Pemberley Books jingled as Hannah opened it and held it for me. The light inside was dim and I had come to love the dusty smell of the books.

"Hey, Liya," Hannah called, waving.

Liya turned with a weird, tight expression on her face. Her eyes were wide. Something flipped in my stomach and my eyebrows knitted. Hannah tilted her head and her mouth fell open as Frank Nielsen walked out of the back room.

28

Hannah

"DAD. I thought you weren't back until October."

Wyatt's hand settled on my shoulder. Blood rushed in my ears while I watched my dad's expression. Liya slipped away to help a customer.

He shifted on his feet, taking in the changes. I couldn't read his expression. Furious? Sad? Confused?

"Your uncle got home early so there was no need for me to stay." He looked around the bookstore, shaking his head at the wallpaper. He reached out and touched a leaf hanging off a nearby vine before he shook his head again. His eyebrows knitted together and his gaze flicked to Wyatt's hand on my shoulder.

Wyatt's hand tightened and he stepped closer so my back was against his chest.

"What is all this?" my dad asked, gesturing around us. His voice was soft, like he couldn't believe it. "Why is everything different?"

"Everything is different because this is a business." My heart was in my throat and unease ripped through me. "I ran the business your way for years and it wasn't working. Now we're doing it my way."

311

Wyatt's hand squeezed me again and I pulled a deep breath into my lungs. Holy shit. Did I actually say that?

My dad's eyes widened, and the way he stared at me was like he didn't recognize me. He blinked. "So your way is to paint over her? To rip out everything she picked out?" He pressed his fist to his mouth and inhaled. "You erased her mural, Hannah. That mural was everything to her."

Something dark and miserable bled into my chest and I swallowed. "No." I shook my head. "I didn't erase her."

Right? I didn't erase her. That was ridiculous.

"You did." His eyes were bright. "We have a duty to remember her, Hannah, and she's slipping away from us." His throat worked. "You lied to me. I had a bad feeling about this, about leaving you all summer, and I was right."

We stood there in silence. The door opened. A tourist took one look at the weird energy in the bookshop and turned right back around.

Wyatt made a noise in his throat and shook his head at my dad. "You're unbelievable."

"Wyatt, no—" I started.

Wyatt gestured around us. "Look at this place from a different perspective, Frank. Hannah turned the store around in a few months. She made it into a tourist attraction. Not only did she do it all by herself, she did it with you dragging her down."

I inhaled sharply and watched as my dad's mouth fell open. "No, Dad—" I shook my head, about to dispute Wyatt's words, but he was right.

My dad was dragging me down.

Pain wrenched my heart.

"You stick me in here," I told him, "and you don't let me change a single thing. You set me up to fail. You say she wouldn't want things to be different, but *you* are the one who wouldn't want things to be different." My voice shook but something surged in me.

Anger.

I crossed my arms over my chest and my nostrils flared. "Do you have any idea how hard it is to run a store from the goddamned nineties? You think Mom would want to keep that ugly carpet for thirty years?" My pulse beat in my ears. "You think Mom wouldn't touch the faded, crumbling mural? You think Mom wouldn't want to throw a few plants in the window?" I paused, waiting for an answer, but he just blinked back at me.

I had never spoken to my dad this way, but finally, I was being honest with him.

"Huh?" My voice was louder than normal. I held a hand to my ear. "Speak up, Dad. What about Mom makes you think she wouldn't want to change a thing? That's you. That's *all* you."

My heart slammed in my chest and I heaved a breath. My eyes stung. "There are flowers on the wall because I like them, and I'm the one working here all the time. You're never here."

That hit the mark. My dad blinked like I'd slapped him. He pressed his mouth into a tight line. "This is all we have left of her," he whispered.

"Maybe it is." I wiped a tear away. "But Mom was fun and silly and wild and bold, and this—" I whirled my finger in the air at the store around us. "—this is for her. The *last* thing she'd want is for us to turn her store into a dusty old tomb." A tear spilled over, running down my cheek before I wiped it away with my sleeve. Wyatt's hand was firm on my shoulder. "She'd love what I did."

My dad glanced at the flowers on the wallpaper like they would bite him. He couldn't get out of this place fast enough. "I don't want to do this but I think I need to take over the store again."

Alarm shot up my spine and my eyes widened. "What? No." I shook my head hard and took a step towards him. "No, you can't. You'll ruin everything I've done."

The bell jingled as the door opened again and we all turned to see Veena from the bakery standing in the doorway. I blinked and turned to wipe the tears away.

"Hi, Veena." I cleared my throat. "You're back."

She stepped into the store with hesitation. Her gaze swept around and the hesitation melted away into something awestruck. She breathed out a laugh of disbelief.

"Hannah." A tentative smile crept onto her face. "Wow. Look at this place."

I cleared my throat. "Um. Is there something you're looking for?"

She turned to my dad and raised her eyebrows. "Well?"

My dad shifted and cleared his throat. "It's not a good time."

Her jaw dropped. "Are you serious? You didn't tell her."

Wyatt and I exchanged a baffled look. I narrowed my eyes at my dad and Veena, shaking my head. "What? What's going on?"

Veena watched my dad with a sad, disappointed expression. "I wish you were as brave as your daughter."

"What is going on?" I repeated, louder. "Dad?"

He looked like he wanted to disappear into the floor. His gaze flicked between Veena and me. He shot her a helpless glance and it hit me.

"I'm visiting a friend for a couple months," she had said in July with a tight, cagey smile.

"Oh my god." I covered my mouth with my hand and blinked.

Veena shook her head at my dad. "I will not be your dirty little secret. I deserve so much more." She turned to me. "The store is beautiful. I hope you know how magnificent you are."

My pulse pounded in my ears. I turned to Wyatt in confusion. His expression was unreadable but his hand rubbed slow circles on my back.

Veena opened the door and walked out. I stared at the door before my gaze swung to my dad.

My stomach lurched and I thought I might be sick, but instead, I burst out laughing. It was one big joke and I was at the center of it. My dad was pressuring me to keep the store the same to honor the memory of my mom but here he was, sneaking around behind my back, moving on from her. My gut twisted hard and my eyes welled up with tears in frustration.

I buried my face in my hands. "Well, I didn't see that one coming."

"Hannah." His voice cracked.

"You're the bad guy." I stabbed a finger in the air. My voice shook. "I lied to you by not telling you about the store but you lied to me, too. And you made Veena feel like crap. She's a really nice lady." I clenched my eyes closed and my hands made fists at my sides. "You're the one acting in a way that would disappoint Mom."

I shouldn't have said it. I clapped a hand over my mouth. It was too far.

"I'm not giving up the store," I added, crossing my arms. "I won't do it."

He clenched his eyes closed in pain. The giant flowers on the walls seemed to grow even bigger. The walls pressed toward me.

"I have to go. I—I need to get out of here." The urge to hide, to disappear, rolled through me. My dad didn't say a word, he just stared at the floor as I backed away toward the door with my hands up, pushed the door open and strode out.

Outside, I leaned against the wall and buried my face in my hands. Tears spilled out and sobs shook in my chest. A second later, Wyatt pulled me into his arms and against his chest. I leaned into his warmth and let myself get tears all over his t-shirt, right there on the street.

"He lied to me," I croaked.

He smoothed my hair down with his hand. "I know." His chin rested on the top of my head and his chest rose and fell as he sighed into me. "I'm so proud of how you handled yourself in there."

A fraction of me was proud, too, but another part knew I could never go back to before, when things were comfortable with my dad. Our relationship had shifted under our feet. I didn't know what it would look like from now on. Maybe it was irreparable.

Wyatt leaned back to study my tear-stained, puffy face. "Do you want to get some lunch or do you want to go home?"

I shook my head, swallowing and wiping my face off. I didn't want to go to my place, and if I went back to Wyatt's, I'd spend the afternoon thinking about everything with my dad.

"Let's go for lunch." I nodded. I was okay. I'd deal with this later.

29

Wyatt

THE WIND LIFTED her hair while she stared out at the water from The Arbutus patio. I reached out and brushed her arm.

"You okay, bookworm?"

She turned to me and nodded. "I think so."

Her tofu bowl sat in front of her, getting cold. "You barely touched your food."

"I'll eat it later."

My heart clenched and I swallowed through a thick throat. Adrenaline still rattled in my veins from what had happened in the bookstore. He didn't see her. He didn't see what she had done, what she had fought against, how brave and strong she was.

But she held her ground. She stood tall and called him out.

"I'm so proud of you," I told her again.

She flicked a quick smile at me. It didn't reach her eyes. She sighed before she put her elbows on the table and rested her face in her hands. "I think I have to move out."

My eyebrows lifted. "Yeah?"

She lifted her head and nodded. "Yeah. It's weird to leave my dad but it's time. I can't live there forever."

It was my opening. I had wanted to ask her all week and here it was, the perfect opportunity. My pulse picked up and I inhaled a deep breath.

"Come with me." I rested my gaze on her pretty face. I let myself get sucked into the brilliant blue-green of her eyes.

She frowned. "What?"

"Come with me," I repeated and reached to take her hand. "Let's travel the world together. You've always wanted to, right? California, Australia, Hawaii, Thailand, there's a whole world out there that you've only read about in books." My heart squeezed. "I want you to come with me. I want you by my side."

I stroked the back of her hand while she blinked at me.

"You can run the store remotely now that you have Liya and Casey," I continued. "You can do the social media from anywhere. Same with ordering and payroll."

Her lips parted at my words and her eyebrows lifted. My heart rattled up into my throat. Fuck, those eyes. I wanted to look into those eyes every day forever.

I swallowed and squeezed her hand. "I'm not ready for this to be over. Think of all the places we'll go. Think of what we'll see. There's so much more than Queen's Cove, bookworm."

The words sat below my vocal cords. Those three words that would change everything. I was always telling her to be brave, and here I was, playing chicken with myself.

I opened my mouth to say it but she pulled her hand from under mine and clasped them in her lap before one of them played with the ends of her hair. A frown grew on her face as she glanced from me to the water to her untouched food, then back up to me. Her throat worked and she shook her head with a wince. "I can't."

My heart stopped. "What?"

She blinked in disbelief and shook her head again, flicking

her hair around. "I can't go with you. After all this? The store is making money again. I can't leave."

"You can run the store remotely." Hadn't she heard me earlier?

"I don't want to." She shook her head, stabbing me in the gut. "Wyatt, are you serious? I have to stay at the store. She would have wanted that. I blew up my entire relationship with my dad over the store. I can't walk away now." She blinked. "I painted over her mural, Wyatt. I can't leave the store like it means nothing to me. My dad wants to take the store over again. If I leave, who knows what'll happen?"

"Are *you* serious?" I leaned forward and she shifted under the weight of my gaze. "After all this, it's still not about what you want? You spent your entire life doing what your dad wanted and now it's time to do what she wanted? She would want you to live your fucking life, Hannah." I softened my tone, swallowing. "Come on, bookworm." I whispered the words, pleading. "Be brave with me."

Her mouth pressed into a line and her nostrils flared. At least she was mad. At least she wasn't fucking hiding like she used to. The people at the next table glanced over at us, listening, but I didn't give a shit.

"Tell me you're ready for this to be over, bookworm."

Fire flashed in her gaze. "Don't call me that."

I jerked my chin at her. I could feel the furious expression on my face. "Go on. Tell me. Tell me you feel nothing."

She wrenched her eyes closed. "It doesn't matter."

"It does fucking matter." My chest strained with pressure. Out of the corner of my eye, I saw Max approach with a pitcher of water and do a U-turn when he saw our table.

Her eyebrows drew down. "You teach me to choose myself and now you want me to choose you?"

"I *do* want you to choose yourself. I want you to choose *us*."

She didn't say a word. She just sat there, petrified. Pain

pulsed in my chest and I rubbed a hand over my face. I had jumped, but the safety net wasn't there, and this was me hitting the ground.

This was it. This was the end, it just didn't happen in a way I expected. I knew it would happen, though, didn't I? Because all things ended and the universe was cruel. It gave you one tiny taste of something spectacular before ripping the spoon away from your mouth.

My chest was going to explode with pressure. I stood and my chair scraped the deck with a screech. Hannah's shoulders hitched. Something flashed behind her eyes.

"You were always going to leave." Her voice shook. "We knew this. You were my practice guy."

The waves I surfed on might be dangerous, but they were nothing in comparison to the words Hannah threw at me. Pain wrapped around my heart and suffocated everything else out.

I leaned down on the table to look into her eyes. "After all this time, you're still afraid."

Her shoulders curled forward and my stomach pitched. My hands itched to pull her into my chest where she belonged, but we couldn't. We couldn't go back, like she said.

"Bye, Hannah. It was fun while it lasted."

I walked out of the restaurant, my heart still at the table with the girl I loved.

30

Hannah

WHEN I RETURNED to the shop that afternoon, Liya was helping another customer in the queer romance section. My dad was nowhere to be found.

Come with me.

The open, vulnerable, trusting look on Wyatt's face appeared in my mind and my stomach lurched.

I want you by my side.

Behind the desk, I rubbed my chest. Something ached.

Tell me you're ready for this to be over.

The keys on the laptop tapped as I logged into our social media. Anything to take my mind off this horrible day. I scrolled past posts, pressing 'like' on images without seeing them.

He was always going to leave. We both knew this. He taught me that everything was temporary and then he acted like it wasn't.

He acted like we were forever.

She would want you to live your fucking life, Hannah.

I swallowed past a knot in my throat. I glanced around the store, at the new flooring and fixed bookshelves and eye-catching wallpaper. It had only been a week but the plants were thriving.

I had put so much work in. Everyone had. My dad was furious, and he wouldn't speak to me for a week, but it was worth it because the store was perfect and special. I had achieved something, changing the store when we had been stuck for so long. Sitting beside Wyatt on the window bench the day we fixed the store up, talking and laughing and eating pizza, it was meant to be.

Like she would want me here.

So why was my chest so hollow right now?

My phone dinged and I unlocked the screen to see notifications on Wyatt's social media accounts. I had posted clips of him surfing this morning during the festival and forgot to check until now.

My heart twisted as I scrolled through the comments and shares. My stomach sank, watching his lean form in his wetsuit coast along the water, and then again as he strode out of the water, flipping his wet hair back.

Tell me you feel nothing.

I pressed a hand to my mouth, wide-eyed and watching the video on a loop. I couldn't do this. I couldn't run his social media now.

My laptop dinged with another notification. Thérèse had posted a photo of a bookstore in Lyon. *Browsing for another true love to add to my collection and thinking of my dear friend Hannah @PemberleyBooks.*

The gold sequinned dress Thérèse had given me popped into my head. How beautiful I had felt wearing it. Its weight, the coarse texture against my thighs and arms, how it sparkled in the light. How great it paired with my plain white sneakers. How I felt like *someone* wearing it, like a main character. That outfit was all me, totally Hannah, and Thérèse had seen it from afar.

The way Wyatt looked at me in that dress.

The way Wyatt looked at me every day.

Realizing what I had lost hit me in the chest and my eyes stung with tears.

"Liya, I'll be in the back for a bit," I called to her, holding my voice normal and steady.

"Okay," she called back through the bookshelves.

In the stockroom, I leaned against the table and cried into my hands, praying Liya wouldn't come back here. How could I possibly explain the situation? I wanted Wyatt, but couldn't have him. He was leaving, but I had to stay, and somehow that last part had slipped past me this whole time. I had never entertained the idea of leaving, but fell for him anyhow.

After all this time, you're still afraid.

Was I doing it right? Was this how she wanted me to run the store and live my life? If Wyatt wasn't the right guy for me, why was this so awful?

I buried my face in my hands. All these thoughts rolled around in my head, warring with each other. I dragged in a deep breath but the smell of the bookstore only reminded me of Wyatt.

Another sob choked out of me. I wasn't afraid. I couldn't leave. This store was her dream, and she would have wanted me to carry on her legacy. This store was where I belonged.

I would just have to get over Wyatt Rhodes.

31

Wyatt

IT WAS *fun while it lasted.*

Three days later, I tipped the rest of my beer back and gestured to Olivia for another. Holden took the bar seat beside me and when she returned, she set both our beers in front of us with a nod.

Tell me you're ready for this to be over, bookworm.

Don't call me that.

Holden shifted in his chair. "Do you want to..." He winced. "...talk about it or something?"

It was the first time he had addressed it. I had been crashing on his couch for the past three nights and he hadn't asked why, hadn't brought up anything to do with her, and hadn't told our parents. Each night he sat here beside me at the bar, commenting on whatever game was on.

You teach me to choose myself and now you want me to choose you?

"Nope."

"Okay."

We took slugs of our beers in unison.

Olivia set two empty shot glasses in front of us and poured tequila. "For the members of the lonely hearts club." She slid the shots toward us.

324

Holden raised an eyebrow. "Where's yours?"

She frowned. "Shut up. I'm heading back to school next week."

Holden nodded. "Like clockwork. Can't risk the two of you being in the same town at the same time."

Olivia was our next-door neighbor growing up. She and Finn were best friends until they were teenagers. They didn't speak anymore.

Her hands stilled as she wiped a glass before she resumed. "I don't know what you're talking about."

Holden made a derisive noise before we reached for the shots and tipped them back. My throat burned and I washed it down with beer. Out of the corner of my eye, a couple took their seats at the table Hannah and I had sat at after her date with Carter, all those months ago. My chest strained at the memory and I frowned into my beer. That night seemed like years ago and yesterday at the same time.

"Thanks." I slid the empty shot glass back across the bar.

"He's doing well," Holden told her. "He's running a crew in the Kootenays but they've got the worst of the fires under control."

She shrugged and held her expression neutral, but her face reddened. "Don't care." She bee-lined to the other end of the bar.

"Leave them alone." I stared at the baseball highlights on the TV above the bar.

"They're being stupid."

"It's not our business." I took another sip of beer.

"It *is* our business. He's our brother. Like you and Hannah being stupid is my business."

I didn't answer. My gut simmered. My jaw clenched and I gripped my beer harder. "Stay out of it." My voice was warning. I drained my beer. "I did everything right. I asked her to come with me and she said no."

He grunted a noise of acknowledgement. I caught Olivia's eye and pointed to my empty glass. She nodded.

Holden glanced at me. "Final round is tomorrow."

"Yep."

Every day this week, I had been competing in heats in the competition. I'd roll off Holden's couch, grab my board from the shop, wait for my name to be called, and let my body take over from there. There was no focus, no thought involved, just instinct and muscle memory. I had been placing well. Not my best, nothing special and nothing memorable, but well enough to advance to the final round.

There was no joy in it, though. No competitive spark.

"You have a sponsorship in the bag, then."

I nodded and thanked Olivia as she dropped off another beer.

"You don't sound too excited."

I shrugged. "Yep. It's good. I'm thrilled. This is what I always wanted." My voice was flat and clipped. I couldn't even muster the enthusiasm to lie to him.

I downed half the beer. What was the point of even going tomorrow? Maybe I didn't want to leave Queen's Cove. Maybe I wanted to stick around. A stupid, hopeful part of my brain said, *she'll come around.* Another part of my brain asked, *what if she moves on and finds someone perfect for her?*

If everything was temporary, then what was even the point of leaving?

Quick flashes of what our life could be played in my head. Hannah and me floating on our boards in South Africa. Hannah and me sitting on the beach on the Gold Coast of Australia. Hannah and me snorkeling in Hawaii.

Hannah and me.

Without her, what was the point? I tried to picture a life without her.

Me sitting alone on my hotel room patio, staring at the water, drinking a beer and thinking about her. Me on a plane, counting clouds out the window, remembering how her hair smelled like tea. Me on my board, watching the sunrise and wondering whether her eyes were more blue or green that day. Wondering whether she missed me like I missed her.

Leaving felt pointless, but staying in Queen's Cove?

I couldn't sit at the bar and watch as she smiled at another guy, as he encouraged her to sing karaoke and draped his arm around her and pressed kisses to her temple. I couldn't watch as she fell in love with someone else. Besides, she'd know. She'd hear if I didn't show up tomorrow or if I bailed again, and she'd know. There was still a spot in my heart that didn't want to disappoint her.

No wonder Finn left.

I stared at my beer. I should have told her how I felt sooner. Then she would have had time to come around.

Holden sighed. "Jesus fucking Christ, this is too depressing for even me."

Olivia and I spoke in unison. "Holden, shut up."

Two hours later, Holden helped me through the door of his house and onto the couch.

"How long are you going to do this?" he asked, setting a glass of water on the coffee table.

Until my bed stopped smelling like her. Until I didn't associate my room with her. Until I stopped picturing her in my living room, reading and staring out the window.

"Don't know."

He shrugged. "Okay. Goodnight."

"'Night."

He headed off to his room and I stared at the ceiling, my head spinning from the booze. I remembered the soft sighs she made as she rested her head on my chest while she was still sleeping in the morning. The way she blushed and smiled when I kissed her neck. The way she brushed her fingers on my arm when she passed by me, a small touch to connect us for a brief moment.

I thought about my aunts, and how the illness had ripped everything from them. How temporary it was despite their best efforts. My chest ached and I rubbed it. Reminding myself that things with Hannah were temporary was supposed to make this part easier, but it still felt like she had pulled my heart out through my throat.

I should have known better the entire time. Or maybe it was right to let it happen. I didn't know anymore.

You're being stupid, Holden had said.

There was one person who had been in this situation before, and I was going to pay her a visit.

32

Hannah

"HANNAH?"

My head snapped up and I straightened from where I stood behind the desk at the store, staring off into space. Liya tilted her head at me, waiting.

"Yes?"

"Where are the new big-bodied heroine romances?"

I tilted my chin to a shelf near the door. "I put them in the new release section."

Liya hustled over and pointed the shelf out to a customer.

It had been three days since the big blowup with both Wyatt and my dad. At home, my dad wasn't speaking to me, but I wasn't speaking to him either, and it was so tense and awkward that I spent most of my waking hours here at the store.

It had been three days of trying to forget about Wyatt Rhodes. I thought it was getting easier. I wasn't crying anymore.

The bench near the window caught my eye, where Wyatt and I had sat after we renovated the bookstore, while everyone ate pizza and listened to Emmett narrate a spicy hockey romance.

The memory stabbed me in the heart.

Maybe it wasn't getting easier.

Be brave with me, bookworm.

I swallowed and searched for something to do. A stack of books sat on the desk. I picked them up and wandered around the store, shelving them.

Liya poked her head around the corner of a shelf. "Do you know where those books on the desk went?"

I turned and her gaze dropped to the last book in my hand. "Uh. Sorry. I thought they were to go back."

She gave me a tight smile. "That's okay." She offered a sympathetic expression that made my blood boil. "Why don't you take the afternoon off? I've got it covered here."

"I don't need to."

She shrugged. "You deserve time off, same as everyone else."

So I could go home and do what? Stare at the walls of a bedroom that hadn't changed since I was a teenager? Make dinner and read my book across from my dad like old times, like nothing had changed?

Everything had changed.

My gaze flicked around my bookstore, so fun and unrecognizable. A book spine stuck out on a shelf so I nudged it in line with its neighbors.

"I'm bringing down the mood, aren't I?" My voice was soft as I ran my fingers over the Alien Romance section.

"No, you're just..." Her words trailed off.

She didn't want to say it, but I knew I was right. "You're okay for the rest of today?"

She nodded quickly. "Yep. Casey will be here in a couple minutes."

WHEN I GOT HOME, I spotted my dad through the kitchen window on the patio with a glass of something bubbly and a book. I poured myself a glass of water and he lifted his head.

"Hannah?"

I drained half the glass before I replied. "Yep."

He appeared at the patio door, watching me with hesitation. "You're home early."

I nodded but didn't offer an explanation. When I moved to leave the kitchen, he gestured over his shoulder to where he was sitting. "Do you want some cider? It's from Salt Spring. I found it here at the liquor store." He cleared his throat. "It's elderberry."

I raised an eyebrow at him. For as long as I remembered, he drank red wine, one glass, if I brought a bottle home or he picked something up at the market, but never cider.

And now he wanted to sit down and have a drink with me. I could see the peace offering in front of me, but without an explanation or apology, I didn't want it. Not like this.

I shook my head. "No, thanks. I'm going to have a nap. I didn't sleep well last night."

He shot me a concerned look. "Okay."

When I stepped into my room, a noise of disgust and disdain scraped out of my throat. I threw myself down on my bed and stared at the lavender walls.

I hated this room. I didn't fit here anymore. I needed to move out, like I said a few days ago to Wyatt.

Instead of napping, I pulled out my laptop and scrolled through rentals in Queen's Cove. Now that summer tourist season was over, there was a lot more selection.

One bedroom, furnished, patio, pets allowed, price a little high but I could make it work now that I was paying myself a salary again.

When I checked the location, my stomach pitched. Down the street from the breakfast food truck.

Which meant it was down the street from Wyatt's place.

"Nope." I closed the window and kept searching.

One bedroom, partially furnished, no patio but lots of windows, only one block from Main Street, including groceries, my work, and the art gallery—

Wyatt's face flashed into my head, listening to me ramble on about how badass Emily Carr's self-portrait was with an amused, affectionate look.

Nope.

One bedroom, unfurnished, pets allowed, with a small backyard with space for a garden. One block from the bar.

Hell no.

My gaze flicked to the figurine of merman-Wyatt, the one I had made before the camping trip. The same one that hung from his rearview mirror.

I stood, picked the figurine up, and dropped it in a desk drawer before sliding it closed.

Everywhere in town reminded me of Wyatt. My bookstore reminded me of him. The bar reminded me of him. The beach reminded me of him. Even my own goddamned bedroom reminded me of him.

I couldn't go, but I couldn't stay. How could I forget him when he was around every corner?

The gold dress sparkled in my closet.

I don't even know who you are anymore, Miri had said at the bar the night I sang karaoke.

I had bleached the old Hannah out of my life and now there was nothing left to show. My birthday was tomorrow, and I had made the store profitable again. I had become the hot girl I always wanted to be. I had fallen for Wyatt. The list was complete, but instead of fixing my life, I had fucked everything up so much worse.

A book sat on my desk, a mafia romance I bought last year and hadn't gotten around to reading. For now, I didn't want to be Hannah or whatever was left of me. I wanted to be someone else, so I lay down on my bed, cracked the book open, and disappeared.

———

"DOES THE SALMON TASTE OKAY?"

I looked up from my book and nodded at my dad across the table. "Yep. It's great." I forked another bite into my mouth and returned to my book.

I had read the same page about eight times. I shifted in my chair and shot a glance around the tiny kitchen. The room felt too small. The walls closed in on me. If I lifted my hand, the ceiling would be right above my head. We were going to run out of air soon.

I couldn't keep going like this. I couldn't slip back into my old life, working in the bookstore for my father, under his thumb, by his rules. I couldn't go back to being shy, quiet Hannah who stared out the window, watched the world go by, and wished she could be a part of it. Now that I had a taste of the gold sequinned dress, I couldn't go back to hiding it under the bed. Or tucking it under the bed and hiding *from* it.

"Wyatt Rhodes was in the store the other day."

My heart lifted along with my head. "He was?" My fork clattered to my plate. He had come looking for me.

I didn't know what the solution would be. I didn't want Wyatt to stay, that would mean giving up on his dream. That didn't sit right with me.

But maybe he had thought of something. Maybe there was a chance.

My dad nodded. "He came in with you."

Right. Before everything went to complete crap.

"Oh." I sank and turned back to my book. "Yeah."

"Are you friends?" His tone was light, and I knew he was curious but holding back from making me uncomfortable.

"Something like that."

"Something more?"

My chest pinched and my mouth drew down into a frown. I shrugged at my book. "I don't know. We used to be. Not anymore."

He made an acknowledging *hmm* noise and nodded at his plate. I read the page for the ninth time.

He put his cutlery down. "I want you to be happy."

A scoff scraped out of my throat and my eyebrows rose. A prickle of bottled-up rage squeaked through. When he shot me a curious glance, I shook my head. "As long as it's on your terms, right?"

"Hmm. The store." He blinked at his empty plate.

"Yeah. The store. I'm not changing it and I'm not leaving." I folded my arms over my chest and set my chin. "I love it, and we're keeping it the way it is. You lied to me."

He crossed his arms, mirroring me.

"You didn't just lie about you and Veena. You told me we couldn't change a single thing about the store because of Mom. You made it seem like I was spitting on her grave by putting up wallpaper. You made that store a tomb for her, and the entire time, you were moving on just fine."

I spat the last words out with fury. My chest was tight and my stomach was in knots. My hands shook with anger. I let out another humorless laugh. "I have been so stupid. God." I sucked in a deep breath. "Why do I have to make up for your guilt? Why can't I move on from Mom too?"

His mouth fell open before he sighed. "I went there today."

I reared back. "You did? When?"

"When you were having a nap." He nodded to himself. "Walked over and took another look. What you did with the store, well, Liya told me everything. She told me how the business was struggling, and she told me you weren't paying yourself."

My eyebrows pinched. "She knew that?"

"She told me you built an online presence from nothing, with no help from anyone. She showed me the pictures you took inside the store." His throat worked. "And of the mural." He exhaled a long breath and pressed his mouth into a line. "It's hard to believe the mural is gone."

We sat in silence for a moment.

"I don't know what else of hers I can cling to," he said, very quietly, wincing. He shook his head. "I don't want to forget her."

"I don't want to forget her, either."

He crossed his arms and stared out the patio door at the backyard. "Deep down, I knew Claire wouldn't agree with what I was doing, keeping the store the same." He shrugged. He looked so helpless. So unlike my dad. "I didn't know what else to do. I still don't."

An idea trickled into my head.

He gave me a side-long glance. "Honey, the store looks really cool. I don't want you to quit."

His use of the word *cool* made me smile. "You think it's cool?"

He nodded. "I do." He winced and put his head in his hands. "That carpet was ugly, wasn't it?"

"The worst. It was disgusting."

"I hope you burned it."

A laugh burst out of my chest. It sounded rusty. "I threw it in the dumpster and gave it the middle finger."

His chest shook and he laughed with me. Our gazes met and something settled in my gut.

"Romance, huh?"

I nodded. "Romance."

"And you really don't want to sell other best sellers? Crime thrillers, lit fic, fantasy, stuff like that?"

"Nope." I crossed my arms over my chest. "I really don't."

He sat back and regarded me. "Okay, then. Pemberley Books is a romance bookstore. You're the boss."

My eyebrows snapped together and I narrowed my eyes at him.

He lifted a shoulder. "I was going to give you the papers tomorrow on your birthday but might as well tell you now."

"You're giving me the store?"

He nodded. "It's been yours for some time now. I should have done this years ago." He rubbed a hand over his face. "I should have done a lot of things differently."

I thought about how I hid away in that store for years, too afraid to do anything for myself. "Me, too."

A bird landed on the fence, and I watched as it perched there. The store was truly mine now, but when I pictured myself there ten years from now, selling books and helping customers, something was still missing.

My dad stood to clear our plates.

"What about Veena?"

His hands stilled as he was rinsing the plates in the sink. "What about her?"

I frowned at him. "Seriously? You hurt her because you were scared. You're being a jerk."

The dishwasher door creaked as he closed it. He flattened his hands on the counter and looked down, thinking. "I don't know, Hannah. I don't know how to do both. I loved your mom so much and Veena—" His voice broke off. "I don't know how to have both."

"Mom wouldn't want you to be unhappy. She'd want you to move on. You don't have to forget her, but it's okay if you date other people and fall in love again. She'd hate it if you were unhappy to honor her or something weird like that."

Unease spiked in my throat. My words made my stomach pitch. My dad hurt Veena because he was scared.

I could have made something work. I could have at least *asked* my dad, I could have thought of other options, we could have tried long-distance, but instead I shut Wyatt down. I *wanted* to go with him, and I said no to both him and myself.

Because I was scared of stepping outside my bookstore, like before.

I'd said some terrible things to him. I told him that he wasn't the right guy for me, that it never would have worked anyway. That he was my practice guy. I put my head in my hands and my heart sank into the floor.

Practice guy. That's what I had said.

My throat tied itself in a knot. *What a way to go, Hannah*, I told myself. *What a way to show him he meant nothing to you*.

I do want you to choose yourself. I want you to choose us.

His words poked holes in my heart.

I pictured my mom across the table from us, crossing her arms with a skeptical expression.

This whole time, I had been so desperate to live exactly like her to make her proud.

"Oh my god." My expression was incredulous. My throat worked. "Oh my god."

"What?"

My head snapped up and our gazes met. She wouldn't want me to follow her step-for-step, like she wouldn't want my dad to be single for the rest of his life. She'd want me to make my own life. That girl singing karaoke in a gold dress? She'd be proud of me for doing the scary thing. For wearing the dress that made me feel pretty, for chopping my hair off even though I wasn't sure if it would look good.

She'd be proud of me for taking risks and being brave.

Be brave with me, bookworm.

"Wyatt Rhodes asked me to come with him," I told my dad. "When he goes pro."

Tell me you feel nothing.

"And you said no."

I nodded again. Shit. Urgency squeezed my stomach. The bright, happy memories with Wyatt pressed on me from all angles. My lungs were tight as I heaved a breath.

I had walked away. I had *it*. Wyatt and I had the thing I always dreamed about and I'd tossed it away like it was trash.

Puzzle pieces clicked into place, one after the other, and I chewed my lip. Wyatt had used *everything is temporary* as a shield but I had used *Wyatt is leaving* and *I have to be exactly like my mom* as my own shields.

When he asked me to come with him, Wyatt had tossed his shield aside.

My heart raced as I pictured quick flashes of our future together. Holding hands on a plane. Floating in the water on our surfboards, enjoying the sunrise.

The nurse at the ER thought you were my pregnant wife.

Sitting on the beach in the sand, keeping a careful eye on our kids.

I had it and I dropped it.

I wanted her to be proud of me. That was what started this whole thing, wanting her to be proud of the person I had turned into, and instead, I had made a huge mess of everything. I was worrying about making the wrong person proud.

I should have been making myself proud the entire time.

Wyatt's lazy, amused grin appeared in my head. The soft affection on his face when I woke up the other day. The way his fingers always found their way to my hair. The way he grinned from ear to ear when I stood up on my surfboard. The look of adoration as I belted out the Spice Girls in my terrible singing voice. His calm, satisfied way of floating on his board after a surf lesson, staring up at the sky.

In my mind, I was back in the bookstore, sitting on the window bench with Wyatt, surrounded by our friends. Surrounded by my beautiful new bookstore. I had thought me being in that bookstore was meant to be, but the *meant to be* part was Wyatt beside me.

I had it all wrong. Everything I thought I knew was simply wrong. I was looking for what was right in front of me, like when I searched for my glasses and they were in my hand the entire time. My mom wanted me to be happy, and I had interpreted that in my own way and taken it way, way too far, like my dad had taken keeping her memory alive too far.

It settled in my gut like a rock.

You were my practice guy.

Asshole, I thought as I put my face in my hands. I wasn't Elizabeth Bennet. I was Wickham, the backstabbing, two-timing liar who hurt and embarrassed Lizzie. I'd dragged Wyatt along, ignored everything that was happening—no, worse, I'd *denied* everything that was happening. I told Wyatt it wasn't real. I was the villain the whole time.

It *was* real, though. I was in love with Wyatt, and because I was too scared of getting hurt, I lied to him and hurt him instead. I chose my own heart over his.

Asshole.

I swallowed thickly. I knew what I had to do. I didn't know if any of it would work, but I couldn't leave everything like this, all broken and misaligned.

Bravery, I reminded myself.

My chair scraped when I stood quickly. "I have to go."

I was going to go get Wyatt Rhodes back.

33

Wyatt

MY TRUCK CRUNCHED up the gravel drive of my aunt's place on Mayne Island just before lunch. Trees loomed over the small rancher. A tiny Yorkie dog ran out to greet me.

"Well, look who it is." Aunt Bea leaned against the doorframe with a cocky smile, salt and pepper hair tied up in a ponytail. She looked like my mom.

I waved. "Sorry I didn't call."

She shrugged me off and stepped forward with her arms out. She wrapped me in a tight hug. "Hi, honey."

"Hey, Auntie Bea."

Half an hour later, we sat in the sunroom at the back of the house with sandwiches while her dog, Cooper, watched for crumbs dropped on the floor. My aunt tilted her chin at me. "Out with it."

My gaze cut to hers and I lifted my eyebrows in question.

"As thrilled as I am to see my favorite nephew, I know you didn't drive three hours and take a ferry to come for lunch." Her mouth quirked.

I nodded and put my sandwich down. Deep breath, in and out. Courage. All that good stuff I tried to teach Hannah. "I wanted to talk to you about Aunt Rebecca."

She smiled. "Mhm."

Another deep breath. I chose my words carefully. "If you had known about her illness…" My words broke off.

"Would I have still married her?"

I nodded.

"I *did* know about it. She told me when we first started dating that there was a history of early-onset Alzheimer's in her family. Her mom had it, her grandfather had it, and she knew she might have it as well."

"And it didn't bother you?"

She scoffed. "Of course it bothered me. I thought about it every day. Every time she forgot something at the grocery store or couldn't remember some celebrity's name, I thought it was starting." She made a noise of regret in her throat. "I let it weigh me down for years."

I didn't say anything, just stared at my sandwich.

Auntie Bea sighed and leaned her chin on her palm. "I thought that by telling myself, here we go, she's starting to forget you, I could manage my own expectations. If I reminded myself constantly about her illness, it wouldn't be a surprise when it happened. It wouldn't hurt so much." Her gaze dimmed and she blinked at her mug, eyebrows pinching together.

"And then it started happening for real. She forgot how to put toothpaste on a toothbrush one morning. She forgot my name for ten minutes and laughed it off while I hid in the bathroom and cried into a hand towel. She forgot her own name. She became someone different and even though I had been preparing myself for it, it ripped my fucking heart out."

I glanced up at her and she shot me a rueful, twisted smile.

"And instead of figuring it out then, I was so deep in fear and confusion that I started preparing myself for the next stage. I held myself back from enjoying things too much with her when she was lucid because I knew it was temporary."

Temporary.

The word pierced my heart like a bullet.

She rubbed her own chest. "Wyatt, when you love someone like I loved Rebecca, it's terrifying, because it's like suddenly your heart is outside your body and you can't protect it. My heart floated beside me in a red balloon and every time it floated too high, every time I got too happy or felt joy with her, I pulled it back down to safety so it wouldn't pop."

She slapped the table and barked a laugh. "And then the damn thing popped anyway."

My chest hurt. I had been telling Hannah that everything was temporary, and I'd been telling *myself* that everything was temporary, but I had been spewing that shit as a way to hold the good things at arm's length. If I didn't expect to keep anything, I couldn't be upset when it was gone.

Except I was upset. How could I move on from someone like Hannah?

Bea gave me a wistful smile. "I should have let it fly, Wy. I should have let myself lean into those good moments because when Rebecca left us, none of those preparations made any difference in how hard it was." She sighed. "Do I regret holding myself back? Yes. Do I regret marrying her, or a single second spent around her? Never."

A vision of Hannah appeared in my head, singing in that sparkling dress, letting her red balloon fly. I thought I was so smart, teaching her how to fail, embarrass herself, and not care, but the whole time, I wasn't even practicing what I preached. I told myself all things came to an end as a way to hold myself back from enjoying time with her, from falling in love with her, and now we were over and none of that helped.

Tomorrow was her birthday. I blew a breath out and raked a hand through my hair.

"What's going on, Wy?" Her hand came to my arm.

I exhaled a sigh through my nose. "I met someone."

She nodded, not surprised at all.

"I think I screwed it up."

"You lay it all out on the line?"

I shook my head. I had held back. The big stuff, the forever stuff, I kept it hidden.

Be brave with me, bookworm.

How could I expect her to be brave when I wasn't?

I should have told her that I loved her. That I wanted her forever. That she never needed to change a single thing about herself to make anyone proud or to find true love because she was perfect as she was. She always had been.

Maybe she didn't want out of the shell she used to hide in. Maybe she wanted to stay in the dusty bookstore under the shadow of her parents. I couldn't make those decisions for her; I could only encourage and support her.

It wasn't too late. My aunt was right. I had to lay it out on the line and pray to the universe that she felt the same way.

My aunt slanted a curious look at me. "Who is it?"

"Hannah Nielsen." Her name felt funny in my mouth. Bittersweet.

She hummed and smiled down at her lap. "I knew her mom, Claire." She tapped her mouth and narrowed her eyes. "You know what, I have some old photos of her."

Ten minutes later, she handed me a photo that made my heart dip in my chest.

This was the missing component of Hannah's birthday gift. My throat was thick as I swallowed, studying the photo. I glanced up at Aunt Bea. "Can I take this?"

She smiled softly at me. "Of course, honey."

34

Wyatt

"IF HE'S NOT HERE in five minutes, he's disqualified," the organizer said to a guy holding a clipboard.

The ocean was calm for this time of day. No wind, clean waves, the kind I sought out at sunrise or sunset. Spectators packed the beach, both tourists and residents of Queen's Cove. Everyone had come out to see some of the best surfers in the world attempt to work with the ocean.

"I'm here." My pulse beat in my ears from the sprint. Ten minutes ago, I had been on the highway, praying no cops were out with their radar guns. The figurine of me as a merman, the one Hannah bought for me, danced and bounced from the rearview mirror while I drove. There was a delay with the ferry so I was cutting it close for time.

I had parked in front of the surf shop, grabbed my board and wetsuit, and gunned it here. I wasn't sure where my car keys were. The truck might still be running.

The organizer shook his head before walking away. The guy with the clipboard signed me in.

My blood buzzed with nerves. This competition had been weighing on me all year, and I was ready. I wanted to make myself proud, and I wanted to make Hannah proud. She had put a lot of work into my social media accounts, and I wanted to follow through. She'd made me so proud these past few months, slaying her own demons, and I wanted to do the same.

It was her birthday today. If things went right later, this was only the first birthday we'd spend together. My gaze swept over the crowd, searching for her before I stepped into the water.

I shifted my board as I waded in. My chest ached every time I thought of her, every time I saw her face in my head. I paddled to my spot behind the break and remembered all the times we had spent out here together.

"Wyatt Rhodes, Queen's Cove, Canada," the announcer said over the speaker system and the spectators cheered loud enough for me to hear all the way out in the water.

Some things never changed. This town took care of its own.

I inhaled a deep breath, centering myself. The ocean lifted me as the waves rolled past. The cold water bit at my toes and fingers. Hannah flashed into my head, lying on her board with her eyes closed, soaking up the morning sun while her hair floated in the water around her head like a halo. I didn't push the image out, and I didn't cling to it. I let it stay where it was, noticed the sharp pang in my chest, and was grateful that I had experienced it at all.

A wave approached and I began to paddle. Everything went silent. Hannah hung around in the back of my head as I paddled harder and snapped up on my board at the right second. I shot forward on the water, balancing on my board and riding the wave, my heart beating out of my chest, the thundering sound of the wave in my ears. The flecks of water on my face. I crouched low on the board, skimming the surface, and my heart soared.

Two more times, I did this, this incredible thing that I never got used to. I left the beach in awe of the ocean, how it granted me the opportunity and interaction. I would soon do this for a living, if the sponsorship went through. Overwhelming gratitude flooded my chest.

And if it didn't work out, a life here, surfing every morning, with Hannah at my side if she'd have me? That wasn't so bad.

It was a fucking dream.

People clapped me on the back, shook my hand, and congratulated me but my head whipped around as I searched for her. Emmett said something to me but I barely heard him.

Hannah. I had to find Hannah.

The crowd thinned as everyone headed to the street festival over on Main Street. That bright blonde hair was nowhere to be seen, and disappointment streaked through my gut.

She might be at her bookstore. I'd stash my stuff and go find her. This wasn't over until I said what I needed to say.

I was storing my board at the shop when the door opened.

"No lessons for today," I called over my shoulder, securing the board in the back of the shop. "Beaches are closed today, but we can book you in for tomorrow."

"That would be great."

My heart shot into my throat at the sound of her voice and I stepped into the doorway. She stood at the front door looking like a fucking dream in the blue and white linen dress.

I stared at her, heart racing.

"I'm sorry," she blurted out, her hands twisting together in front of her. She took a step forward. "I freaked out, and it had nothing to do with you. Actually," she winced, "that's not true, it had everything to do with you. I had this picture of what I wanted." She shook her head. "I was so wrong, Wyatt. I was wrong about everything. I was wrong about you, I was wrong about the stupid birthday goals, I was wrong about trying to make my mom proud." She clenched her eyes closed for a brief moment. "All wrong."

The hope in my chest was like a bubble. It could pop at any second, and it would hurt all over again.

But avoiding it wouldn't prevent that hurt, I reminded myself.

"My dad signed the store over to me." Her voice was a wobbly whisper.

"What?!" I let out a laugh of surprise.

She nodded with her mouth pressed firmly into a line. "Liya is going to be the manager. I spoke to her this morning and promoted her. And we decided to make Casey full-time." Her chest rose and fell with a deep breath and she watched me. "I'm going to run as much of the business as I can remotely."

"Remotely," I repeated.

One corner of my heart lifted but I waited.

"Remotely." She pressed her mouth together in a line and twisted her hands again. "I'm coming with you if the offer still stands. Wherever you go, I want to be there too, because I love you. And I'm in love with you. I lied when I said you were my practice guy." Her face crumpled. "That was a terrible, terrible lie, and I said it because I wanted to make it sound like you didn't mean anything but you do." Her gaze lifted to me, pained and full of affection. "You mean everything to me. I want to be brave with you."

"You mean everything to *me*, bookworm." My words were soft but immediate. Instinctive. "The offer still stands."

She nodded and a tiny smile appeared on her mouth. "It does?"

This feeling in my chest? This consuming, expanding, squeezing pressure outwards like I was about to explode like a supernova? This was what it was all about. This made it all worth it.

Lay it all out on the line, I told myself. I drew myself up and took a deep breath.

"Yep." I took a step forward. "Before I tell you how much

347

I love you, before I tell you that you are the love of my fucking life and that you're a part of me, I want to tell you that I realized something."

"Okay." Her voice was quiet and tentative. "Go on."

"I said I knew everything was temporary, and I used that to keep myself back from all the good things. You said everything you knew was wrong? Well, me too, bookworm."

I walked over to her and put my hands on her upper arms. The warmth of her skin was heaven. I could smell her shampoo and it made my chest ache again.

"When things were too good, when I was too happy, I reminded myself it wouldn't last so it wouldn't hurt when it was gone." I gazed down into her eyes and nearly laughed at how I could ever think this was temporary. Her name was tattooed on the inner walls of my heart. "But it didn't help one bit. It was the worst thing that ever happened to me."

"I'm sorry," she whispered.

"I'm sorry, too."

I took another step into her space, studying the amber flecks in her eyes while my hands brushed her arms. "I love you. I should have said it instead of 'come with me.' I love you and I want you forever."

She nodded with a watery smile. Her hands came to my waist. "I love you, too."

I pulled her to me and kissed the love of my life.

35

Hannah

"MAKE A WISH."

We sat on Wyatt's front porch that evening, watching the sunset splash breathtaking colors across the sky. He held a cake, tiny flames dancing on the candles. His loving grin and the warmth in his eyes made my heart flip in my chest.

"I don't have anything left to wish for," I told him, biting my lip. I let out a little laugh. "I don't know why I was so worried about turning thirty."

Instead of making a wish when I blew the candles out, I thanked the universe for giving me everything I wanted. All the flames went out except one, and Wyatt's eyes flared with mischief.

"One boyfriend who loves you." He winked.

"One boyfriend who loves me," I whispered, matching his smile.

He set the cake down and cut each of us a piece. I took a bite and hummed with satisfaction.

"What kind of cake is this?"

"Champagne."

We exchanged a grin, and I knew he was thinking of the

beer bong night at the bar with Carter, too. He reached behind him and pulled a gift bag forward.

"Ready for your gift?"

I nodded eagerly, clasping my hands together. He set the bag on the porch between us and I reached in.

My hand closed around a box, and when I pulled it out and saw what it was, my eyes were saucers. "Wyatt!" My voice was a high squeak and he laughed.

His gaze raked me with roguish amusement and my face heated. "You like it?"

"You got me a *sex toy*?" I whispered the word and he laughed harder. It was small enough to fit in the palm of my hand and hot pink. *Seven stimulating suction settings!* the package boasted. It explained how the toy would apply suction pressure to my clit. I swallowed and a wave of heat hit me between my legs.

"Come on, bookworm." His voice was low and teasing and his eyes were full of something hot. "Be brave with me."

I bit back a smile. We'd put his gift to use later. I reached back into the bag and pulled out something flat and rectangular, wrapped in tissue paper. When I tore the paper away, my heart shot into my throat.

It was her and me in front of the bookstore. Her brilliant smile shone through the photo as she smiled at me, propped on her hip. I was a baby. I had a fistful of her hair, trying to eat it, and she was laughing.

My hand came to my heart. The way she looked at me in this picture, how could I *ever* think she'd be disappointed in me?

I met Wyatt's warm gaze and sighed. "Thank you."

He nodded and reached for my hand. It was the little touches like that, wasn't it? Wyatt noticing I liked champagne and having a cake made in that flavor. Wyatt buying me something sexy because he knew it would make me feel good. Wyatt finding the perfect present that showed me he saw me.

How could I ever have thought Wyatt wasn't the right guy for me? He was the *perfect* guy for me.

"Professor?"

"Yeah, bookworm?"

"Kiss me."

Epilogue - Hannah

Elizabeth sat on our front step when we pulled into the driveway. She lit up at the sight of Wyatt's truck and waved.

"Sorry we're a bit later than expected," I called over, climbing out of the passenger seat. "I hope you haven't been waiting long."

She shook her head, standing and walking over. "I've got my coffee, I've got a beautiful view, and I was happy to wait to see you two." She wrapped me in a tight hug and my heart squeezed.

We were home.

Wyatt and I had been on the Gold Coast of Australia for a month. Wyatt had placed well in the Surfers' Paradise competition and had been doing promo shoots for next year's ads. When we could, we still went out on the ocean first thing in the morning, wherever we were.

I tried not to think about the sharks.

"Did you sleep on the plane?" Elizabeth asked, reaching for one of our bags.

I shook my head. "Wyatt did but I just read my book."

Wyatt gave her a hug. "Hey, Mom."

"Hi, honey. Good to have you two home, even if it's just for a bit."

Elizabeth came inside with us and made us tea while we settled in. I smiled at how she made herself comfortable here, taking care of us when she knew we were tired from traveling. Wyatt dropped our bags in our bedroom and returned to the living room, where he settled on the couch and gestured for me to join him. I tucked myself into his side.

"How's the shop doing?" he asked Elizabeth.

Wyatt had sold the surf shop before we left to an Australian who had moved here last year.

The tap ran while she filled the kettle. "Doing well. He fits right in with everyone."

Wyatt closed his eyes, sinking into the couch. "Good."

I watched his handsome face for a moment before Elizabeth reentered the room.

She set my tea down on the coffee table. Her eyes sparkled. "Ready for tomorrow?"

I nodded and swallowed. "Can I tell you something?"

"Of course."

"It doesn't seem like a big deal. Is that…" I chewed my lip. "Bad?"

She laughed. "No, honey. It's not bad. It means you're already there."

I glanced at Wyatt again, already asleep, breathing softly, and my heart panged. A couple months ago, I almost blew everything up because I was scared.

I loved this guy so much. More than anything. I was so glad I made the right decision.

Elizabeth and I chatted for a few minutes, catching up on town events and our trip before she stood.

"Well, I'm going to get going." She walked her mug over to the dishwasher. "I'll see you bright and early tomorrow."

"See you tomorrow."

While Wyatt was napping, I dropped into the bookshop to say hello to Liya and Casey.

"Yes, that one is very popular." My dad was studying the titles on a shelf, tilting his head to read them before he pulled another down and handed it to the customer. "This one has the 'only one bed' trope as well." He noticed me standing at the door and his face lit up. "Honey, you're back."

"You're home!" Liya rushed over and wrapped me in a big hug. My dad was next. Casey rang the customer through behind them.

"Only one bed?" I asked my dad, a smile still glued to my face.

He nodded. "Liya and Casey have been educating me." He leaned on the front desk and adjusted his glasses. "There's a lot to learn about the romance world. Veena and I have been reading through the store."

After sufficient groveling, my dad had convinced Veena to move in with him. I spoke with them both on FaceTime once a week, discussing books, the trips they took around the island, the veggies they grew in the backyard, the changes they were making to the house.

They were good together, my dad and Veena, and they were happy.

The bell on the door rang and two teenage girls entered the store.

"This is so cool!" one of them said before heading to the hanging chair.

"Do you have any rom-coms with two girls?" the other asked my dad.

"Yes, that would be in our queer romance section." He hustled off and she followed. "Do you want enemies to lovers, friends to lovers, or grumpy sunshine?" His voice traveled through the shelves. "This one is popular. Very funny."

From the blue squashy chair, I watched with a smile as my dad hustled around the store, helping people find stories. The photo of my mom and me that Wyatt had given me for my birthday hung on the wall behind the desk. Pride shone from her eyes as she beamed at me. My heart tugged and I knew somewhere in the universe, she was looking at me with the same expression now.

———

"Hannah, I love you, but I need to know something," Avery called the next morning from my kitchen. I was in the bedroom, changing. Through the windows, the sun was beginning to rise, and golds, pinks, and oranges painted the sky like something in an art gallery. I stared out at the ocean and thought about all the times Wyatt and I floated out there, talking and staring at the sky, falling in love.

"What's that?" I called back, zipping up my dress.

"Do you fucking hate me or something?"

I laughed and walked out, down the hall, and into the kitchen. Avery rested her forehead on the bar counter. Working in a restaurant, she got home late and didn't handle sunrise wake-ups very well. She wore a maroon dress that cinched at the waist with embroidered flowers on it.

"I appreciate you being here."

Her head whipped up and her breath caught at the sight of me. "Oh, Hannah." Her throat worked and she gave me a watery smile. "You look so beautiful."

I glanced down at the floor-length white dress. The sleeves flared and the fabric draped perfectly over my body. I skimmed my palm over the delicate lace.

"I'm so glad you chose the boho style," Avery breathed, shaking her head. "It's not what I would have expected for you but it turned out to be perfect."

I smiled. "Like Wyatt."

She nodded. "Yeah, Han. Like Wyatt." She reached for my bouquet on the table, a small collection of soft pinks and deep reds and greens from the Queen's Cove area the florist had put together yesterday. "Ready?"

I took the bouquet from her, running my fingers along the pearl pins on the handle. "Ready."

We made our way to the beach and left our shoes at the edge of the sand. Everyone waited for us closer to the water— Elizabeth, Sam, Holden, Finn, Emmett, my dad, Veena, and in the center of them all, Wyatt.

I nearly laughed in surprise at the sight of him in a suit. My Wyatt in a gray suit. It fit his tall, slim form perfectly, and the bright white of the shirt made his tan even deeper. The gray fabric made his hair blonder. He watched me approach, gaze never leaving mine, and I had the sensation he was trying very hard to memorize this moment, like I was.

When I got close enough to the group, they quieted down and he stepped out and wrapped me in a hug.

"Good morning, bookworm." His voice was soft in my hair.

"Good morning," I whispered back, aware that everyone was listening to us.

He pulled back to look down into my eyes. "You're beautiful, you know that?" He tucked a strand of hair behind my ear.

"With you, I do." I raised an eyebrow at him. "I'm surprised you're in a suit. Don't get me wrong, you look incredible." I gave him a quick, heated smile that told him how much I was looking forward to getting him out of it later, and that familiar roguish grin crossed his face. "I half expected you to wear a wetsuit."

He laughed, and my heart squeezed at the sound.

Wyatt kept his arm firm around my shoulder and turned to the group. "Let's do this before my girl changes her mind."

Everyone laughed, myself included.

I shook my head, smiling from ear to ear. "Not a chance."

Emmett performed the ceremony there on the beach to

the sounds of the waves rolling in and to Avery and Veena and someone, who I was pretty sure was Holden, sniffling. The sun slowly rose, the sky changed colors and Wyatt held my hand. He rubbed his thumb over my skin while watching me with all the love and adoration and euphoria that I felt for him.

Emmett said the words that bound us together and Wyatt placed a simple band with a pale blue stone onto my finger.

Blue like the dress you wore at Emmett's wedding, he had said when we saw it in the jewelry store a few weeks ago in Australia. *The first time I realized how beautiful you were.*

I slipped a silver band onto his finger, and he leaned down to kiss me, pulling me into his chest and reminding me that we belonged to each other.

I had so much to lose with him, but I was going to be brave and love him with my whole heart.

My dad watched with a proud smile on his face, and my heart panged, thinking about my mom, missing her and wishing she could see me now, but grateful that I knew her. Grateful that she lived on in my bookstore and in my memories.

Later, after the families had brunch at our house and had gone home, Wyatt dragged me into our bedroom.

"Let's have a nap." He kissed my neck as he backed me toward the bed.

"A nap, huh?" I grinned and then gasped as his teeth scored the sensitive skin beneath my ear. His hand was already working at my zipper and I pushed his jacket off.

"Mhm." The low, hungry cadence of his voice sent a zing of desire through me and I made quick work of the buttons on his shirt.

I turned my head to meet his mouth and he groaned deep in his chest when he coaxed my lips apart. The slow glide of our mouths drugged me and made my head float.

"Hey, bookworm?" He pushed the dress off my shoulders and it pooled at my feet. His hands found the top of my strapless bra and he slid the cups down and pinched me, pulling a light moan from my mouth.

"Mmm?" I nipped his bottom lip.

"Remember that conversation we had the other day?" His breath tickled my mouth.

"Which one?" My bra lay discarded on the floor somewhere next to his pants, and I leaned into his warm hand on my chest, loving the way he knew exactly how to touch me. One of my hands rested on his hard chest and the other palmed his stiff erection. I thrummed between my legs with every brush of his fingers on me.

"Oh, shit," he breathed against my mouth, clenching his eyes closed as I stroked. "The conversation about having a baby."

My hand stilled on his cock and I opened my eyes. Wyatt had casually brought up the idea of having children a couple weeks ago and asked how I felt about it. I liked the idea of having a baby with him, but I was scared of the whole pregnancy, childbirth, and baby-shooting-out-of-my-ladyparts situation.

But I loved him and he'd be an amazing father. We had so much love for each other. I wanted to love someone the way my mom and dad loved me.

"I remember."

His hands came to my hair and he tucked a strand behind my ear. "I think we should start."

I inhaled a deep breath with wide eyes, gaze locked with him. "You want to have a baby now."

He smiled and nodded. "I love you. And seeing everyone today, all together," his throat worked and he blinked, "it made me want that but with our own family. We love each other so much."

I nodded and gave him a soft smile. "Yeah, we do." I pulled in another shaky breath. "A baby." I nodded to myself. "A real baby."

He laughed and pressed a kiss to my temple.

"I'm scared," I admitted. "Not just of babies. What if we screw it up?"

He nodded. "Yeah, we might. But I don't think we will. We should be brave."

"Brave," I repeated, nodding. I thought about my mom, and how much she loved me, and all the memories I had with her. My heart ached in the best way. I nodded again at him and gave him a bigger smile. "Okay."

"Okay?" His face lit up. "Are you sure? We can table it."

I shook my head hard. "Nope. You're right. We'll never be ready, but I want to try. Whatever comes our way, we'll figure it out together."

Wyatt kissed me hard and his love filled me all the way to my toes. "I love you, bookworm."

———

She's helping Holden find a wife... but she's the only one he wants. Read *In Your Dreams, Holden Rhodes*, a friends with benefits, grumpy-sunshine, boy-obsessed rom-com with Holden and Sadie! Read on for an excerpt.

———

Want a bonus spicy scene with Wyatt and Hannah? They're on their honeymoon in Bali, and Wyatt wants to put that toy to good use…

Go to www.stephaniearcherauthor.com/wyatt or scan the QR code below.

Excerpt from In Your Dreams, Holden Rhodes (Holden and Sadie)

Sadie's phone buzzed and she glanced at the screen before showing me.

It was a candid photo of her chatting with Wyatt and Hannah under the streetlight on Main Street, posted on the Queen's Cove Instagram account, and she was fucking gorgeous.

She wore a red dress that showed off her incredible tits. Her hair was loose and wavy around her shoulders. She was mid-laugh, her eyes bright and sparkling.

I turned to her. "You looked like *this* to go out on a date with *me*?"

A wash of pink grew on her face and she shrugged, taking her phone back. Our fingers brushed and the sensation of her soft skin against mine stole my attention.

Warmth pulsed in my chest at the idea that she dressed up to go out with me.

If we had gone out and she had worn *that dress*, I definitely would have kissed her.

My gaze dropped to her plush mouth. Her teeth pinned her bottom lip as she watched me. Blood pounded in my ears as my gaze alternated between her eyes and her mouth. She glanced at my mouth, and my cock stirred.

I wanted to kiss her, and I think she wanted to kiss me, too. Energy crackled around us.

"Holden," she breathed. I could see her pulse going in her neck.

My hand came to her jaw, tracing the line until my thumb brushed over her bottom lip. Her shaky breath tickled as she exhaled, watching me with heavy eyes.

I wasn't supposed to kiss her, but I couldn't remember why.

"You shouldn't be looking at me like that." Her voice was soft.

Fuck it.

I tilted my head and ran my lips up the side of her neck, barely touching her. She shuddered under my touch. My cock ached, straining against my zipper. Fuck, she smelled good. Light, warm, and sweet. I pressed a line of kisses down her neck to her shoulder.

"Close your eyes and you won't see me looking at you like this."

My hand was in her hair, tilting her head back.

Jesus, she was so fucking pretty. An angel.

"I mean—" She broke off with a gasp as I sucked the spot between her neck and shoulder. "Hard to think when you're doing that."

"So don't think," I murmured before tilting her head back.

I paused an inch from her mouth and searched her eyes for any sign of hesitation. She closed the distance and pressed her soft lips to mine.

Read *In Your Dreams, Holden Rhodes* or listen in duet audio!

Author's Note

Hello again, you beautiful romance reader, you. Thank you from the bottom of my heart for reading this book. I would love if you could rate or review it online.

Hannah hit close to home for me because in my twenties, I didn't know what the hell I was doing in terms of sex. Neither did my partners! We were all fumbling around based off public school education and awkward discussions with parents. They didn't explain the good stuff, you know? (And yeah, that would be kind of awkward if they did, but that's also my sex-negative conditioning talking there). In sex ed, did they mention the clit once? No! So Hannah is kind of like me in my twenties. Confused about sex.

Then, I started reading romance. The sex in romance books isn't always realistic, but it prioritizes women's pleasure. I'm so confused when women don't read romance. I'm like, how do you know how to have an orgasm?

This is a good part to mention that in my mid-twenties, a new boyfriend realized I had a tough time getting to the finish line, and bought me my first vibrator. What a champ. The relationship didn't last but I will always remember and appreciate him for that. The world needs more men like that. A vibrator isn't a competitor, it's a team mate.

Shoutout to Dr. Brené Brown and Oprah for their podcast episode about vulnerability, which made me sob in my car and helped uncover Wyatt. The terror of losing something you love. I feel it every time I look at my partner, a guy I've talked to almost every day since I was twenty years old (we were friends long before we were together). I feel it when I hug my dog. When I'm laughing with my brothers or parents. Memento mori, right? Death is inevitable, so we need to lean in to those moments of joy while they're here.

Thank you to friends Maggie North and Helen Camisa for reading an early draft and providing encouragement and insightful feedback. Both of you say all the smart things and I'm just over here furiously taking notes on how to be like you.

Thank you to Sandy for your surfing knowledge. You're a rad feminist dude and I promise Carter is not based on you.

Thank you to editor Jeni Chappelle, for leading me in the right direction with your clever notes.

Thank you to spectacular people Brett Bird and Alanna Goobie for proofreading. The enthusiasm you two have for romance books makes my heart happy.

Shoutouts to my soulmates, many of whom listened to me fret over this book and told me that, like always, it was going to be okay. If it were up to Bryan Hansen, this book would be about Hannah Nielsen, Queen's Cove's first dominatrix. We'll save that for her forties.

Thank you to Tim, who knows me far better than I know myself, and still loves the hell out of me. I feel lucky every day to have you.

Lastly, shoutout to you, dear reader, because I wrote this for myself, but I wrote it for you, too. Read what you love, wear whatever makes you feel gorgeous, and be brave with me.

Turn the page to discover more spicy,
laugh-out-loud romances from Stephanie Archer.

THE VANCOUVER STORM SERIES
STEPHANIE ARCHER

**He's the hot, grumpy goalie I had a crush on in high school . . .
and now I'm his live-in assistant.**

After my ex crushed my dreams in the music industry, I'm done
with getting my heart broken. Working as an assistant for an
NHL player was supposed to be a breeze, but nothing about
Jamie Streicher is easy. He's intimidatingly hot, grumpy, and can't
stand me. Keeping things professional will be no problem, even
when he demands I move in with him.

**Beneath his surliness, though, Jamie's surprisingly sweet and
protective.**

When he finds out my ex was terrible in bed, his competitive
nature flares, and he encourages and spoils me in every way. The
creative spark I used to feel about music? It's back, and I'm writing songs again. Between wearing his jersey at games, fun, rowdy
parties with the team, and being brave on stage again, I'm falling
for him.

**He could break my heart, but maybe I'm willing to take that
chance.**

Behind the Net *is a grumpy-sunshine, pro hockey romance with
lots of spice and an HEA. It's the first book in the Vancouver Storm
series and can be read as a standalone.*

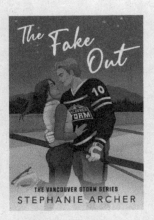

The best way to get back at my horrible ex? Fake date his rival.

Being the team physiotherapist for a bunch of pro hockey players is challenging enough without my ex joining the team. He's the reason I don't date hockey players.

Vancouver Storm's new captain and the top scorer in pro hockey, Rory Miller, is the arrogant, flirtatious hockey player I tutored in high school. And he's just agreed to be my fake boyfriend. I get sweet revenge. Rory gets to clean up his image. It's the perfect deal.

Faking with him is fun and addictive, though, and beneath the bad boy swagger, Rory's sweet, funny, and protective.

He teaches me to skate. He sleeps in my bed. He kisses me like it's real.

But is there anything fake about our feelings?

The Fake Out is a pro hockey fake dating romance. It's the second book in the Vancouver Storm series but can be read as a standalone.

My arrogant fake fiancé? I can't stand him.

Cocky and charismatic Emmett Rhodes isn't a relationship kind of guy, but now that he's running for mayor of our small town, his bachelor past is hurting the campaign.

Thankfully, I'm the last woman who would *ever* fall for him.

We're total opposites—he's a golden retriever and I'm sharp and snarky, but he'll co-sign on my restaurant loan if I play his devoted fiancée. Between romantic dates, a prom night re-do, and visits to a secret beach, things heat up, and the line between real and ruse is lit on fire. I'm starting to see another side of Mr Popular, and now I wonder if I was all wrong.

We can't keep our hands off each other, but it's all for show . . . right?

A hilarious, enemies-to-lovers, fake dating romantic comedy with lots of spice and an HEA. This is the first book in the Queen's Cove series and can be read as a standalone.

The deal is simple: the grumpy guy will pay off my debt if I find him a wife.

Holden Rhodes is grouchy, unfairly hot, and has hated me for years. He's the last person I'd choose to inherit an inn with. As we renovate the inn and put his dating skills to practice, though, I see a different side of him.

What if I was all wrong about Holden?

When we add 'friends with benefits' to the deal, our chemistry is so hot the sparks could burn down the inn. Holden's a secret romantic, and I'm secretly falling for him.
I'm terrible at bartending, a video of a bear stealing my *toy* went viral, and everyone in this small town knows my business, but Holden Rhodes is so much more than I expected.

I don't want him to find love with anyone but me.

A grumpy-sunshine, friends-with-benefits, small town romantic comedy with lots of spice and an HEA. This is the third book in the Queen's Cove series but can be read as a standalone.

The guy who broke my heart is now an arrogant, too-hot fire-fighter . . . who's hell-bent on getting me back.

This summer, I have one goal: field work. I need it to finish my PhD. I never expected Finn Rhodes to offer help. He broke my heart twelve years ago, and now that he's back in town, I want nothing to do with him. The only problem? He insists we're meant to be together.

I'll pretend to date him, but actually? I'm trying to get him to dump *me*.

Between hiking the back country and cringe-worthy dates designed to turn him off, I begin to remember why we were best friends. Despite how hard I try, Finn isn't interested in dumping me… and now I'm not sure I want him to.

Finn's always been trouble. The kind that might break my heart. Again.

Finn Rhodes Forever *is a spicy, second chance romantic comedy. This is the fourth book in the Queen's Cove series but can be read as a standalone.*